Working with Bacchus

Working with Bacchus

Adventures of an impassioned Scot in an Italian vineyard

COLIN FRASER

MITCHELL BEAZLEY

For Sonia

In gratitude for her constant interest and encouragement during the writing of this book, for her skilled work with the photographs, and for her innumerable and always invaluable comments.

Working with Bacchus
by Colin Fraser

First published in Great Britain in 2005 by Mitchell Beazley, an imprint of Octopus Publishing Group Limited, 2–4 Heron Quays, London E14 4JP.

A CIP catalogue record for this book is available from the British Library.

ISBN: 1 84533 092 7

The author and publishers will be grateful for any information which will assist them in keeping future editions up-to-date. Although all reasonable care has been taken in the preparation of this book, neither the publishers nor the author can accept any liability for any consequences arising from the use thereof, or the information contained therein.

Commissioning Editor: Hilary Lumsden
Executive Art Editor: Yasia Williams
Managing Editor: Juanne Branquinho
Editor: Emma Rice
Production: Julie Young

Phototypeset in Simoncini Garamond by Intype Libra Ltd
Printed and bound in the UK by Mackays, Chatham

Contents

Author's Note

Working with Bacchus is a very personal account of an experience that I lived intensely for twenty years in the Sabine Hills to the north-east of Rome. It is not a treatise on viticulture and wine-making, for I am most certainly not qualified to write such a thing. Any skills I developed were self-taught and gained through osmosis from helpful specialists, not to mention through trial and error. As the Italians say, "Experience is the sum total of all the mistakes you've made".

My hope is that after reading the book, persons drawing the cork of an elegant bottle of good wine will be better aware of the sorts of decisions, risks, setbacks, problems, regulations, and sheer hard work – but fun and satisfaction too – that lie behind the nectar they are about to enjoy. Nectar indeed, the drink of the gods in Greek mythology, but how earthly the challenges of making it!

There was also the challenge of coming face to face with peasant culture and values and their effect on day-to-day activities in the vineyard. Some of the traditional practices were very positive, but others often hindered achieving the results that only more modern techniques make possible. It was a constant process of give and take as I tried to understand and accept some ingrained attitudes and practices, while using reasoned argument to push for change in others. It was ironical for me to come face to face with the issue of communicating with rural people to help them improve the way they do things, for it was precisely my field of professional work to advise governments of developing countries about such matters. I often found that it was easier to give such semi-abstract advice than to succeed in practice in my own bailiwick.

I hope that readers will also gain some insights into the beautiful and complicated country that is Italy. It is often disorganized and bureaucratic, but it is also magical. The human values of its people, including the simple rural folk I came to know and love, more than make up for the difficulties one can encounter with its legislation and procedures. Like so many other northerners who have settled in Italy, even in moments of the deepest frustration about some of its ways, the enchantment is so deep-rooted that I know I can never leave it for long.

Italy is rather strict about applying the 'privacy law' that limits the use of people's real names, unless it is 'in the public interest' to do so. I have therefore changed the names of most of the people who figure in the book; and nor will readers find Castel Sabino on a map. Nonetheless, the people and the places described are real, and the events and incidents recounted most certainly took place.

Finally, I would like to thank those friends who took the trouble to read the typescript of this book and provide me with many useful comments. In particular, I am grateful to Ellen Aune, Silvia Balit, Rose Marie Clarke, Kay Killingsworth, Paul Maguire, Giovanni Padroni, and Michèle and Vikram Shah.

Italy, May 2004

1

Buying a Mighty Oak

The voice over the telephone was deep and measured: it took me a moment to put a face to the name it announced. Then I remembered Roberto Paoli. He was the tall, self-assured man in his late thirties I had met about four months earlier in a village called Castel Sabino in the hills northeast of Rome.

"I may have found the sort of property you're looking for," he said over the 'phone. "It's ten hectares. There's an old house that hasn't been lived in for the last eighteen years, and a barn. And there's an oak tree near the house that's worth more than the rest of the property put together."

Roberto Paoli is a *geometra* (surveyor). Surveyors in the United Kingdom used to have a much larger role in designing buildings and supervising their construction than they do today, and a *geometra* in Italy still has some of the combined functions of an architect and a civil engineer. In rural areas, a *geometra* will mark out property boundaries, draw up building plans, deal with the local authorities for building permissions, and supervise the works. He can also put vendors of property in contact with potential purchasers, and earn a commission if a deal is completed. It is all part of his day's work.

I had met Roberto Paoli because I was hunting for a property within ninety minutes drive from Rome. It had to be an existing vineyard or a property where I could plant one. I had spent numerous weekends driving around in Umbria, Lazio, and southern Tuscany, leaving cards with anyone who seemed to have good contacts in the community. I had visited property after property but none of them measured up to what I was looking for.

Wine has held a fascination for me since the age of ten, when I was living with my parents in a wine-producing area of Switzerland near Lake Geneva. We had the top two floors of a large house surrounded by vineyards. The owner of the house in which we lived, and of the vineyards, had built another house for himself, and used the ground floor of our house as his winery. A bent old man called Louis, invariably wearing a blue smock, lived in a small room off the winery. He always gave off a strong smell, which, in my ten-year-old innocence, I did not realize was the stale wine reek of the two-litre-a-day man. I came to recognize that smell easily in later years.

The winery on the ground floor of the house we lived in was fascinating to a child. Barrels, presses, pumps, and pipes – I knew nothing of their workings but it was a whole world of musty smells and dark wood, presided over by Louis. His craggy old face softened as he took me on regular tours and tried to explain to me how wine was made and what each piece of equipment was for. Modern wineries are nothing like as romantic as that one, but at least today's hygienic conditions and superior technology produce quality wines that would have been produced more by luck than judgement half a century ago.

The house in Switzerland was in the outskirts of a small village. Shortly after arriving, my parents threw me into the local school for six months, to learn French. I certainly learned it, for it was, in effect, a total immersion course, even if that term had not yet been invented in that far off year of 1946. In those days, it was quite normal for school children to help with farming operations during peak periods and, to my delight, the village school was closed down for ten days to free the children to help with grape picking. It was my first experience of a vintage. I remember asking the owner of the vineyard, a debonair gentleman with the double-barrelled name of Panchaud de Bottens, whether I could eat any grapes. I could hardly believe my luck when he said, smiling, that I was allowed to eat as many as I liked. He, of course, knew full well that after the first few bunches one's appetite for grapes wanes to nothing when you have been picking for several days.

The vines in that part of Switzerland are pruned so that their bunches are close to the ground, maximizing the reflection of heat from the stony soil. Picking grapes that low was hard work, but the atmosphere during the vintage was one of chatter and fun. At the end of the vintage, Monsieur Panchaud de Bottens thanked me for my efforts and gave me sixty Swiss francs. I bought my first watch with the money, but more significant was my initiation into the world of grapes and winemaking, a world that has fascinated me ever since.

At the time of my quest for a property in central Italy, I was working for the United Nations Food and Agriculture Organization (FAO) in Rome where, over a period of almost seven years, I was on a series of contracts that ranged in length from three months to one year. This was because of funding vagaries in the UN system. And my situation was doubly inconsistent because I was in charge of a group of people, who were mostly on continuing contracts. In this somewhat precarious situation, I felt the need for a second activity as an escape hatch should my FAO work terminate. As an agriculturist, what could be better than a return to my roots, combining that background with my fascination for wine? I therefore wanted to buy an existing vineyard, or establish one.

Roberto Paoli was answering my questions about the property that was for sale. Where was it exactly? Was it flat or steep land? Which way did it face? How much were the owners asking? And so on. The answers to my questions all seemed rather promising, so I took leave from my job in Rome the next afternoon to go to see the property. My car was in a workshop for routine maintenance, but a friend and colleague lent me her Fiat 500, that genius of engineering that put millions of Italians on four wheels for the first time. It also gave rise to the joke that many Italians were small because they were conceived in them.

I headed out of Rome on the Via Salaria, so named because the ancient Romans transported their salt along it from the Adriatic coast. It was a fine September afternoon in 1974. As I trundled along in the Fiat 500, the flat lands of the Tiber Valley gave way to the Sabine Hills: the rolling foothills of the Apennines (the range of mountains that runs down Italy like its backbone). The road gradually climbed with vistas of sunlit valleys, olive groves, and hilltop villages, quintessential Italy. This area northeast of Rome is still in the region of Lazio – less famous and less frequented by tourists than Tuscany or Umbria.

As I got closer to Castel Sabino, the road climbed even more steeply and into a wilder and harsher landscape, with higher and higher ranges of hills marching into the distance. Roberto Paoli was not available to show me the property that afternoon, but he had told me how to reach it. He had also advised me not to make myself too evident as I walked around it. I reflected that a Fiat 500 was the ideal means of transport when one wanted to be inconspicuous in Italy.

Castel Sabino sits on a promontory overlooking a deep valley that rises as a steep and forbidding mountainside opposite the village. And on the end of that promontory sits an enormous castle. It was built by a cardinal in the seventeenth century. Around its huge base are clustered the small houses that make up the rest of the village. These humble homes were where the serfs, retainers, and other dependants lived, looking after their master's interests, while he luxuriated in the 350-room palace towering above them.

The property I had come to look at was situated above the village, in the opposite direction from the promontory. I took a steep, unsurfaced, and tree-lined road up towards the cemetery, the little Fiat bouncing around on the loose stones. Then, as the road levelled off, I came out of the trees and found myself on an open, sunny plateau. I was on the property that I had come to see. To the north and west it was bounded by the road, which led to the walled village cemetery with its surrounding cypresses.

I parked the car in the entrance to a field gate and walked onto the land. It was pasture with a few scrawny olive trees in one part, while various sorts of smallish trees, mainly elms, punctuated the rest of the area. At the base of each elm was a grape vine that climbed high into its branches.

This was the sort of agriculture that in Italian is called *promiscuo* (promiscuous). I had always smiled inwardly at the term because of its connotation in English when applied to people. But, when applied to Italian farming, it is in its meaning of "mixed or disorderly". In fact, even though it may appear disorderly, there was a sound basis for it in subsistence agriculture. Pasture or grain crops were grown between the trees, which acted as living supports for vines to climb on, at the same time taking the vines' vegetation and grapes high out of the reach of grazing animals. Similarly with olives, which are naturally low and bushy if left un-pruned, man's intervention has been to prune them in such a way that they are forced to assume the form of a tree, thereby raising their leaves and fruit too high for animals to damage. Thus, the farming system was pasture, grain, tree crops, and livestock production all on the same piece of land . . . a delight of promiscuity.

I walked across the sunlit plateau near the road and the cemetery and found that on the other side, facing south, the land tilted quite steeply down into a small vale with a line of trees at the bottom. On the highest point of the land there was an open-sided stone barn with a tiled roof and, below it, nestling behind the small hillock on which the barn was situated, was the derelict and abandoned house. It was also of stone and quite small. Between the barn and the house was the oak tree that Roberto Paoli had praised. It was indeed magnificent, a towering green presence with broad-stretched branches that seemed to be reaching out to protect the house set lower on the slope. I was to hear later that in bygone years its branches had also stretched over many bucolic parties, with music, and wine.

The land faced south and southeast and to my inexperienced eye it looked suitable for a vineyard. My agricultural studies in England had given me a good general understanding of farming, but viticulture was an area of specialization about which I knew next to nothing. However, regardless of its suitability for a vineyard, which I would have to explore in greater depth, the property was enormously appealing. From the high point next to the barn, I could see for miles in all directions, range after range of hills and valleys waning into the distant blue haze. And to the south, the view from the house was over a verdant vale dominated by the mountainside opposite the promontory with its castle.

My main concern after that first lurking visit was the altitude of the property. The village of Castel Sabino was at about 550 metres (1,800 feet) above sea level, and I estimated that the property was at least 50 metres (165 feet) higher. My first step on returning to Rome was to buy a detailed military map of the area. Sure enough, I found that the cemetery, which was at the same height as the plateau area of the property, was at 609 metres (2,000 feet) above sea level.

I knew enough about vineyards to be aware that, in central Italy, the usual altitude range for quality wines was from about 350 to 500 metres (1,150 to 1,640 feet). Much below that, the heat would cause a short ripening season, and wines from such hot areas often lack subtlety and finesse. But at too great an altitude, there could well be the problem of the grapes not ripening properly. This would result in acidic wines of low alcohol content.

I began to get myself into a nervous state as I worried about whether or not to go ahead with the purchase of the property. I was very taken by it, but what if the investment in the purchase and the planting of a vineyard were to be brought to nothing by the effects of the altitude? How much difference would those extra 100 or 150 metres (330 or 490 feet) above the usual range for vineyards in central Italy make? I obviously needed expert advice, and urgently.

My first plea for help went to an Italian friend, the late Giuliano Cesarini who was working for the Italian government but frequently came into FAO. He was organizing farming cooperatives for the Government's development programme in the south, and many FAO people used to go on weekend tours to visit them. Giuliano Cesarini was totally committed to what he was doing, was getting excellent results and, in addition, was a warm and helpful person. He responded to my plea for help by arranging for a tree-crop specialist from Florence to come down to Rome the very next week so that I could take him up to Castel Sabino to see the property.

I collected the specialist from the Roma Termini train station and we drove up to Castel Sabino, in my own car by then, rather than the Fiat 500. I told him of my concerns about the altitude of the property. He was non-committal but was watching the countryside with great intensity as we drove.

We reached the property and walked over it together. He seemed almost to be sniffing around like a hunting dog and remarkably taciturn for a Tuscan. I was watching him anxiously, until he finally made his pronouncement:

"Buy it! Buy it immediately! You'll produce good grapes and wines here. Look at those cypresses by the cemetery. They need a Mediterranean climate and look how well they have grown." I can still hear his Tuscan accent as he said, "*Compri!*" (Buy!) because he aspirated the letter "c" like all true Tuscans, so that the word became "*Hompri*". It was endearing and comical at the same time.

He explained to me that the south and east orientation of the property was ideal. It was important for a vineyard to have the morning sun to drive off the cool night air, and the midday sun for general heat. That heat would linger for the rest of the day, so a westward orientation to catch the afternoon and evening sun was not important.

That same evening, happy and relieved because of the Tuscan's verdict, but still wondering what I was embarking on, I called Roberto Paoli and told him that I wanted to buy the property. We arranged to meet a couple of nights later in a bar in Castel Sabino, from where we would go to negotiate with the owners.

Roberto Paoli was waiting for me at the appointed time and we had an *aperitivo* together. He told me that he had checked over the paperwork of the property and found that it was not ten hectares as the owners had said, but only seven. By then I was already in love with the property and I said that it did not matter. Even that area planted to vines would call for considerable investment and effort. But of course, it would affect the price I was willing to pay.

The owners of the land were one of the village butchers, Lorenzo, and his parents; they lived in the countryside about ten minutes drive from the village. In the car, Roberto Paoli and I agreed on a figure we would offer, which was a lot less than the asking price.

We arrived outside a small stone house and Lorenzo ushered us into the kitchen where his parents were waiting. The atmosphere was very tense in that simple and bare room as we settled down at the kitchen table. On one side an elderly couple of peasant farmers and their butcher son, while on the other sat this bearded, fair-haired stranger who drove a car with CD plates and must have seemed as foreign as a Martian to them.

Roberto Paoli, sitting at the head of the table, took control of the situation. In his commanding manner he told the owners that he had checked the papers of the property and that, contrary to what they had said, it was seven hectares, not the ten they claimed. This pronouncement was followed by a long silence as the owners grappled with its implications, but they did not try to dispute Roberto's findings. Then Roberto, after leaving the silence to develop for just the right amount of time, said that in the circumstances my offer had to be much less than their asking price, and he named the figure we had agreed upon. If the owners had had any difficulty in grasping the implications of the smaller size of the property prior to that moment, the translation of the fact into Italian lire brought them face to face with the reality. Consternation spread across their wrinkled features, but they quickly pulled themselves together and began protesting loudly that the offer was far too low.

The discussion ranged back and forth for some time, until Roberto asked if I would mind going outside for a few minutes. It was a relief to escape. I went outside and leant against the wall of the house. It was a beautiful autumn night of clear starlight that just illuminated the shape of the surrounding hills. I could feel the warmth of the day's sun that had been absorbed by the wall I was leaning against. It was an old house, built in the traditional material of the area, as was the one I was trying to buy. The area around Castel Sabino, despite its present elevation, was under the sea in pre-history, and so the land is full of pebbles and quite large stones rounded by the action of water. These round stones, held together with mortar, and probably cow dung, too, were the historic building material of the area. It was known locally as *budingo*, perhaps something akin to "pudding", I thought, as I waited against the wall and let its warmth soak into my back.

I could hear the voices of the owners still raised in protest in the kitchen, and Roberto's calming resonance. Gradually the volume of the voices diminished until finally Roberto came out. He told me that if I increased my offer a little, he thought the owners would accept. So we agreed on a higher offer, but still well short of the original asking price, and Roberto went back into the kitchen. While I waited, a great wave of doubt flooded over me, for the altitude question was still worrying me. But before I could change my mind, Roberto came out and said that the sale was agreed.

We went back into the kitchen together and were invited to have a glass of wine while Roberto wrote out the preliminary sale and purchase agreement, the so-called *compromesso*. It was the first local wine I had tasted, and it was terrible beyond words. It was turbid, very acidic, and obviously very low in alcohol. As with home-made peasant wine that I have drunk on thousands of occasions, and in hundreds of locations in many countries, its producers were very proud of it and asked me for my comments. I have spent much of my life working with peasant farmers, and to tell them the truth would be simply unacceptable. One is forced to make some comment of muted praise and then quickly deflect any detailed discussion by asking a question about the wine, for example, what grapes was it made from?

I sipped Lorenzo's wine while he rambled on about how *genuino* it was, *fatto d'uva* (made from grapes). The wine was so bad that I thought seriously of asking Roberto to tear up the *compromesso* that he was writing out, but once I have made a decision I hate going back on it. The concept of wine being good simply because it is "genuine", which in peasant terms means it is made in the most traditional of ways without any technology or additives, has dogged me ever since. Add to it the peasant belief that all bottled wines are rubbish because they are made "artificially", and you are faced with a cultural divide. These beliefs are widespread in almost all rural communities that produce wine at the household level for their own consumption. It is the very devil to debunk them, though I still try. Even Italians who have spent much of their lives in a city will praise to the skies some murky, amber liquid from their native village that passes for white wine. For them, its "genuineness" makes it, by implication, far superior to a clean, crisp, and well-made white wine in a bottle.

In trying to reason with people who praise the "genuineness" of bad wines, I even try to marshal arguments about what the word means in today's world where so much is modified or created by human intervention. Among dictionaries' definitions of *genuine* are "real, true, natural" and "not counterfeit". So one must ask whether a white wine that has become a deep yellow colour and lost its freshness because it has been oxidized by too much contact with air is any more real, true, and natural than the wine that has been protected from oxidation by proper winery techniques? And as for "natural" and "non-counterfeit", an unnatural and counterfeiting process begins when the grapes are crushed to make wine, for the must would not be exposed to air and oxidation if it were left inside the natural protective skin of the berry. So what is the justification for demonizing techniques that improve the vinification process and produce better wines? In any case, there are very strict regulations about what can be added, and in what quantities, to wine in the making, so consumers are protected. But none of these arguments appear to change people's minds about the merits of what they call genuine wine.

Driving back in the car to the village with Roberto, I commented on the wine we had drunk. He told me that most of the wines produced by families in the area were similar, and he thought there were several reasons for it. One, he said, was that the traditional way of growing vines up trees took the fruit so far from the root of the vine that it could not ripen properly, and another was that the people simply did not know enough about winemaking.

"You know," he went on, "grapes not ripening properly is an old problem here. My father and my grandfather and their friends used to get a big copper cauldron, put it over a fire and boil about five or ten per cent of the grape must. They'd let it bubble away for ages until its sugar and colour were concentrated. Then they added this concentrate to the rest of the must. It gave a sort of cooked taste to the wine. Some people around here still do it, but local grape production has declined a lot in recent years because so many people have gone to live and work in Rome. So now, the families that want to make wine for their own use buy a lot of grapes off lorries that come round the villages in October".

So who was right? Had the Tuscan expert in whom I had put so much faith given me a correct judgement, or were there inherent difficulties in producing ripe grapes in the Castel Sabino area? But the die was cast. I had signed the *compromesso* and paid the normal ten per cent deposit pending the completion of the sale. To withdraw from the sale would cost me that deposit. I was in a nervous state. Was this a wine producing area or not? I could not think that the Tuscan might have been wrong, and Roberto mentioned that in quite recent times a new owner of the castle had removed and burnt many gigantic old barrels from the cellar. So there was certainly a tradition of winemaking in the area. But if the wine they produced was all like that of Lorenzo's parents, my venture would be doomed to failure from the start.

The grape harvest in the Castel Sabino area is usually in the second half of October, and this was only a few weeks away when I signed that fateful *compromesso*. I decided that when the vintage began, I would go around and measure the sugar content of the grapes being harvested. In the meantime, I found a number of books on Italian viticulture and looked urgently for information on altitude. I did not find very much, except that the highest vineyards in Europe are near a village called Morgex, in the Aosta Valley just south of the Mount Blanc tunnel. The area lies at 1,300 metres (4,265 feet) above sea level, and in the previous twenty years or so, the village priest had helped to revive the traditional white wine, Blanc de Morgex. According to the information I read, it was a delicious and delicate wine with a fine bouquet and taste, and it had about 8.5 per cent alcohol by volume.[1]

The report finished with the fanciful idea that sunlight radiating off the glaciers of Mont Blanc helped the grapes to ripen. I say "fanciful" because the notion seemed odd when I read it, but within a couple of months I had actually gone to Morgex to examine the situation for myself. One could not see Mont Blanc at all, at least not from the vineyards I visited. The wines were indeed fresh and fragrant, but I wanted to make more robust wines with the usual twelve or more per cent of alcohol.

As the vintage around Castel Sabino drew close, I bought a densimeter, known in Italian as a *mostimetro*. It is a small glass tube, weighted at one end so that it will float upright. The higher it floats in a liquid, the greater the density. When floated in grape must, the scale on it measures the sugar, expressed in grams per

---

[1] The alcohol content of wine is expressed as per cent by volume, but I will not burden the rest of the book by adding "by volume" each time I mention an alcohol percentage.

one hundred grams of must. An Austrian professor called Babo invented it: hence the reading on the scale when it is floating is called the Babo degree.

So, with the grape harvest under way, I spent a Saturday driving around the Castel Sabino area and stopping whenever I saw anyone picking them. I received some strange looks as I got out of my car and approached the grape pickers carrying my *mostimetro* in its plastic tube, a small kitchen sieve, and a jug. I would introduce myself, tell them that I was buying the property by the cemetery with the idea of planting a vineyard, and would they please give me a bunch of grapes so that I could test its sugar content? They always obliged and gathered round, looking somewhat perplexed, as I began the messy job of squeezing the bunch over the sieve with my hands, poured the must from the jug into the little grey plastic tube, and floated the densimeter in it.

The results were catastrophic. Most of the readings were in the range of fifteen to sixteen Babo, and some were even lower than fourteen. The rule of thumb I had learned was that each full Babo point of sugar per cent would give about 0.65 per cent of alcohol after fermentation, so even in the best cases of a Babo reading of about sixteen, the resulting wine would have less than 10.5 per cent alcohol. And as for the worst cases of fourteen Babo and below, the wine would only have a maximum of about nine per cent alcohol.

The pickers always wanted to know the result of the test. When I told them, and mentioned the approximate alcohol level of the wine they would produce, they would shrug and make some comment that it was about normal for the area. Of course, it was a totally different situation to the one that I had been imagining for myself. If I was going to grow wine grapes, they had to be good. By then, I had tasted many of the local wines, and they were almost all as bad as that first one I had tasted in the home of Lorenzo's parents. My ambitions went far beyond that. The local people, on the other hand, had been brought up in this area of very poor subsistence agriculture, on smallholdings where they barely eked out a living. They looked for quantity, rather than quality, in everything they produced. The poor quality of their wine was of no particular concern as long as they had enough of it. Traditionally, in the poorer rural areas, wine was also a nutrient for people, a part of their diet.

I was tortured by doubts as to whether the poor grapes and wines of the area were an intrinsic and insoluble problem, or whether using modern viticultural and winemaking practices would produce the results I wanted. So I went to discuss the matter with the people in the offices of the Inspectorate of Agriculture in Rieti, the provincial capital.

Italy was the first country in the world to have an agricultural advisory service. As long ago as 1839, and even before Italy was united as a single country, there was a meeting of agriculturalists in Pisa to discuss the need for non-formal education and technical assistance for farmers. This meeting and others ultimately led to the creation – region by region and beginning later in the century – to groups of agricultural specialists and advisers financed by banks, landowners, and the like. They went into the countryside to make on-farm visits and run training courses in the evenings. The teams were called *Cattedre Ambulanti d'Agricoltura* (Itinerant Chairs of Agriculture). They were so successful that the United States Extension Service, launched in 1914, is said to have drawn heavily on the Italian experience.

Then the Italian State laid its bureaucratic hand on the *Cattedre Ambulanti,* and in 1907 they were institutionalized, given legal status, and coordinated by the Government. Nevertheless, they continued to function well until the 1930s when Mussolini finally institutionalized them to death: he changed their name to Provincial Agricultural Inspectorates, and the new title alone gives an accurate idea of how their functions changed under the Fascist regime. Still today, they have remained almost unable to cope with anything except administrative matters, made more complex by the European Union, which has added a plethora of paperwork to that already abundant under the Italian Government.

So I was not too hopeful of getting much technical assistance as I walked up the steps of the House of Agriculture in Rieti that Saturday morning. Even so, I felt that I should make contact with Alberto Beccari, the head of the Provincial Agricultural Inspectorate. I told him that I had signed the agreement to purchase a property of seven hectares at Castel Sabino and that I was going to plant a vineyard on it. Beccari was in his late fifties, an avuncular figure, and as my explanation of my intentions proceeded, a frown of concern deepened on his forehead.

"Are you quite sure you want to plant a vineyard?" he finally asked. "You know grapes don't ripen properly up there at Castel Sabino. It's too high."

He obviously saw the shock on my face. I explained that the property was well exposed to the south and east and told him what the Tuscan had said. Beccari was obviously intrigued: he said that he would like to come up and look at the place the following Sunday morning. He duly came, giving up his free time, the first of innumerable helpful gestures I was to receive from Italians. After we had wandered around it for a while, he said, somewhat grudgingly it seemed: "Well, you might be all right. The property is certainly placed well and faces in the right direction. I suggest you get an analysis of the soil done as soon as possible. Let me know how it turns out. This area is generally calcareous and vineyards do well in alkaline soils like this".

A couple of weeks later, under a November sky of scudding cloud with rain pelting horizontally, I was digging out samples of soil from many different places on the property. Even on a bleak day like that, with the tops of the nearby mountains lost in the gloom, the place had a special appeal. It was wild and elemental. I loved the contrast with that halcyon afternoon of warm sun and luminous countryside of only a few weeks earlier, when I had made my first visit in the Fiat 500.

I found that the soil in the highest part near the old barn mainly consisted of the round, water-washed pebbles and stones characteristic of the area, some of them up to about than twenty centimetres (eight inches) in diameter. The land lower down was a rich, reddish clay. I decided to group the samples from each area separately and have two lots of soil for analysis.

At least the results of the analyses were positive. The pH of both samples was around eight, an appropriate level of alkalinity for vines. The land was rich in potassium, which my readings had informed me was a vital element in the ripening process of fruit; there was quite a high level of nitrogen, probably because of the droppings from the sheep that had grazed on the property for years, and only phosphorous and magnesium were in short supply. All of this information was essential for deciding on initial fertilizer treatments, as well as for the choice of rootstock for the vines, but more of that later.

By now, the whole business of planting a vineyard at Castel Sabino had become a challenge and, at the same time, also something of a wager. I often wished that the property were in a recognized wine producing area. In talking to many, many people, I found that most of them considered the Sabine Hills to be good olive country, but when I mentioned wine, they said they had never heard of a decent one produced there.

Some people from Rome, who had a small weekend home very close to my property, came to see me one day to introduce themselves. It turned out that we had common friends. They asked me what I intended to do with the land I had bought, so I told them about my plans to plant a vineyard. They looked somewhat surprised, but made no comment. A few weeks later, I heard from our common friends what they had said about me and my plan: they had said that I seemed pleasant and congenial, and intelligent, too, but that I must be out of my mind to want to plant a vineyard at Castel Sabino.

These people, however, were in no way linked to agriculture, and I did not take the remark seriously. I was later to find out that most of the local people were saying that *l'inglese* – as I was referred to behind my back – must be off his head to invest so much money in planting a vineyard; I would "soon finish my money" and leave.

Had I known what the local people were saying at the time, I might have taken the matter more seriously, for their comments were at least based on centuries of farming experience in the area. And one should never brush off lightly the experience of peasant farmers, as I knew all too well from my work with them in developing countries.

I did not know what they were saying about me in Castel Sabino, however, and the main point in my mind was to wonder why the wines of the Sabine Hills had such a poor reputation. Was it because no one had ever seriously tried to produce decent wines? And what about all those barrels in the castle? Perhaps in the last half century the people of the area had preferred to leave the relative poverty of rural life to seek their fortune in Rome, rather than trying to make a decent livelihood by modernizing their farming? Or perhaps they did not have the resources of knowledge or of finance to be able to do so? All of these thoughts churned in my mind as I went ahead with my plans, driven no doubt by some stubborn Celtic streak.

All of my wakeful hours not spent at work in FAO were absorbed by the venture I had started. My bedside table was piled high with books on viticulture and oenology. I was looking for general information on these subjects, but the question of altitude and the varying opinions I had received were always tugging at the back of my mind.

2

The Arcane Arts of Water Divining and Cheese-making

There was no mains water supply on the property. The people who had lived there until eighteen years before had carted water up the steep hill from a fountain in the village, hundreds of metres away. Indeed, for several years after I bought the property, there were neighbours laboriously trundling wheelbarrows loaded with water in plastic containers to their homes. Personal washing was perhaps low on their list of priorities, but carrying water to boil their pasta and wash their dishes, as well as for their animals, was a horrendous task. And my property was even further from the fountain than most.

I was going to need water in considerable quantities. Quite apart from domestic use – and water for rebuilding the house, of course – I would need it for spraying against plant pests and diseases in the vineyard. There was talk about the local authorities expanding the network of piped water supply, but that could take years. In fact, it was eight years before the property and the area around it were finally connected to a piped supply, so bringing centuries of carting water in wheelbarrows to an end.

I needed to drill a borehole on the land. Roberto Paoli told me about the

Gaspardo brothers. They were drillers and water diviners; they were so certain of their divining skills, Roberto said, that they only charged half of the agreed price per metre (three feet) drilled if they did not find water. I had heard about water diviners, but I had never imagined that they would wager on their accuracy in this way. The Gaspardo brothers, each with a son who worked with them, lived about forty kilometres (twenty-five miles) away. I telephoned and one of them, Renato, said he would come to Castel Sabino the following Saturday morning.

He arrived as promised and, after a very brief exchange of greetings, he walked straight to a nearby bush and cut himself a Y-shaped twig. I had not intended to accompany him on his divining mission, for I was concerned that my presence might upset his mystic powers. He assured me, however, that I was welcome to go with him. We set out from the house and went up to the old barn. Renato Gaspardo, a small, weather-beaten man in his fifties, was holding his Y-shaped twig in two fists. He gripped it with the bottom end of the Y pointing away from him, exerting pressure with his thumbs and rolling his wrists inwards to twist the two prongs of the Y against the natural springiness of the twig. This tilted the single point, the base of the Y, upwards so that it became a sort of spring-loaded antenna.

As we strolled along I asked him whether the divining twig had to be from any particular type of tree or bush, but he said it made no difference provided it was flexible enough to be held in the necessary twisted position. Then, up behind the old barn, the point of the Y dipped suddenly downwards. Gaspardo stopped.

"There's water here," he said, "but the signal's not very strong'".

He walked away a few metres at right angles from the direction we had been walking and came back towards me with the point of the twig cocked upwards again. As he came level with the point where the twig had twitched downwards before, it dipped again. Gaspardo stopped and scratched his head thoughtfully. Then he shook it and indicated that we should go on.

As we ambled along he explained to me that this was a limestone area and that the problem in such areas was that ground water was often lying in what were called perched water tables. The limestone itself was permeable, allowing the water to percolate downwards. But if it encountered a layer of impermeable rock, it would be forced to flow along it. A borehole could find it there, but if the drillers inadvertently broke through the layer of rock, the water would escape downwards into the limestone below. All the drilling would have been in vain. There were some other boreholes in the general area of Castel Sabino, so there was a good chance of finding ground water – if one knew where to drill.

We made our way towards the cemetery and were quite close to it when the twig dipped suddenly downwards again. Gaspardo repeated his walk off to one side and came back towards me, and again the twig dipped at the same point as before.

"There's much more water here," he pronounced.

Thinking as a good Scot should, remembering that the charge for the bore-hole was by the metre (three feet), I asked him how deep the water was. He pulled a folded measuring rule from his pocket and asked me to open it, place the zero end on the ground, and hold it vertically. He knelt on one knee, put the point of his divining twig on the ground against the rule, and then slowly began to raise the point up it. Opposite the seventy-centimetre (twenty-eight inch) mark the twig pitched downwards.

"For me," Gaspardo said, "the water is seventy metres (230 feet) deep. But my son, Alvaro, is much better at estimating depth than I am. I'll have him come up next weekend".

Alvaro came alone. We walked around the land again and he found water at the identical spots his father had. At the second one, I asked him about the quantity of water, and he confirmed that there was plenty. In response to my next question about its depth, he pulled a small transparent plastic ball on a string from his pocket. The ball was partly filled with water. He held the end of the string, and the ball began to oscillate like a pendulum. I was quietly counting the oscillations. When they reached a hundred or so the movements of the ball changed from left/right to circular.

Alvaro Gaspardo neatly coiled the string and put the ball back in his pocket.

"The water is between a hundred and a 105 metres (330 to 345 feet) deep," he said. His tone was one of certainty and finality.

"But your father said it was at seventy metres," I said, shaken by the cost implications of the greater depth.

"Well, there may be some water at seventy metres, but the vein where there's a good quantity is between 100 and 105 metres down."

Again thinking of my pocket, I asked whether he could follow the vein of water down into the dip, to the lowest point on the land. That point was at least twenty metres (sixty-six feet) lower than where we were standing, implying a considerable potential saving in drilling costs.

"If we drill down there, we'll have to make an all-weather road," Alvaro said. "We need to have water all the time we're drilling. With winter coming on, this field will be so muddy that we wouldn't be able to get a truck up and down there without a gravel road. Making that road wouldn't be much cheaper than drilling the extra metres at this higher point. And at least you'll have a well-head that's more accessible up here."

His logic was faultless, so I signed a contract, but with the Gaspardos' usual proviso that if they did not find water, I would pay only half the price per metre drilled.

The Gaspardos used a percussion drilling rig, a primitive looking contraption, but one that proved surprisingly effective. The part that actually did the work of digging was a large and heavy steel tube over two metres (six feet) long. Let into its lower end was a hinged steel flap that opened inwards into the tube. The tube was attached to a steel cable that ran over a pulley on a gantry and down to the drum of a motor-driven winch. This winch repeatedly pulled the tube several metres up and then allowed it to drop vertically into the bottom of the hole. Water was regularly poured down the hole so that the rock and soil being pulverized by the repeated blows from the tube turned to mud. This mud forced its way past the flap in the bottom of the tube, slowly filling it. From time to time the tube was winched to the surface and emptied of its load of mud.

The rhythmic thump of the drilling went on for weeks. By now it was well into winter, and winter at Castel Sabino could be bitingly cold. The drillers had little to do except make sure their rig was working all right and pour water down the hole from time to time. There is a northeasterly wind in Italy, the *tramontana*, which brings freezing air at high velocity from central Europe. Despite the brilliant clear skies and sunshine that the *tramontana* also brings, the drillers had to wrap up like Eskimos during their long hours by the rig.

When the depth was approaching seventy metres, I began hoping again that Renato Gaspardo had been right about the depth of the water. But no water was found.

"Aren't you worried that you won't find water?" I asked Alvaro Gaspardo, who was working the drilling rig.

"No," he replied. "At least not until we get to a 105 metres."

On a Saturday about six weeks after they had begun the borehole, they had reached a depth of roughly ninety metres (295 feet). There was still no sign of water. I asked when they thought they would reach 100 metres (330 feet) and they said that, if all went well, it would probably be about Wednesday. I said I would come up to see them towards the end of their working day.

Dusk was gathering as I arrived. I got out of the car and walked towards them. I was very concerned that they would not have found water, for without it, how could one run a vineyard, let alone rebuild a house and live in it? Alvaro Gaspardo's face and that of his helper were expressionless as I walked towards them. The drilling rig was still thumping away, but it seemed that they were not letting the tube drop from as high as usual.

"Did you find water?" I asked anxiously. Alvaro and his assistant looked at me impassively, without replying. Then they began to grin broadly.

17

"We found gravel at a 100 metres," Alvaro said. "That was a hopeful sign, but not a certain one. At a 101 metres, we hit water. We're now at a 104 and going gently. We expect to find hard rock and we have to be careful not to break it."

They did find the rock layer that was supporting the perched water table, and they finished the borehole at 105 metres, exactly as predicted by Alvaro. The borehole proved able to provide at least fifteen litres of water a minute, year in year out. A submerged pump raised the water to a storage tank built on the highest point of the land, near the old barn.

I was still in awe of the Gaspardo family's occult talent a few days after the borehole had been completed when I chanced to meet up with a very competent and renowned Anglo-French hydrologist in FAO. I knew him quite well, so I told him about my experience with the Gaspardos. He nodded from time to time until, at the end of my tale, he said, "Oh yes, I know water divining works, but I don't believe in it!"

"Why ever not?" I asked.

"There is no scientific basis for it," he replied, and we both burst into laughter.

One Saturday, not long after the drilling of the borehole had begun, a small car drove on to the property and stopped. I still knew very few people in the area and I thought that someone had come to talk to the drillers. But the neat man with a trilby-style hat and jacket who got out of the car walked towards me. He was about sixty, slight in build, and with a neatly trimmed moustache. He came up to me, held out his hand, and introduced himself gravely, with a small bow of his head.

"Piero Coppi. Shepherd. A pleasure to meet you. I believe you're the person who has bought this land."

Piero Coppi told me that for more than fifteen years the previous owners had allowed him to graze his sheep on the land in winter. He asked me whether I would be willing to grant him the same favour – in exchange for the occasional cheese, of course.

I agreed willingly. I would certainly not be planting any vines for many, many months, and I am also very fond of sheep's cheese, or Pecorino. When fresh, Pecorino is still soft and white with a tangy and slightly acid flavour. As it ages, its flavour becomes stronger and its consistency harder. After several months it can be grated and added to classic pasta sauces, such as *alla matriciana*. This sauce and its name derive from Amatrice, a village high in the Apennines and not very far from Castel Sabino. Sheep and pigs are the basis of the agricultural economy in the Amatrice area, and not surprisingly, their pasta sauce reflects this. Some years after first meeting Piero Coppi, I was invited for lunch in the

Amatrice home of an oenologist friend. He summoned me to the kitchen to watch his every move as he prepared the pasta sauce. In its original and classic form, it uses olive oil, garlic, tomatoes, some hot red pepper, salt-cured pig's cheek, and grated Pecorino.

My friend had been born and brought up in Amatrice before going to live and work in Rome, and he was fiercely proud of the traditions and the pasta sauce of his native village. He knew that I also love to cook, and as he stirred, he delivered a lecture to me on the subject of the sauce.

"Colin," he said quite sternly, "make no mistake. This sauce should never, ever, have onion in it. Garlic, yes, and plenty. But onion, no. All those restaurants that serve *pasta alla matriciana* with onion in it don't know what they are doing. Many use salted bacon, and not pig's cheek. I can accept that because it may be difficult to find salted pig's cheek, but it really should be cheek. We've used that here for centuries because it is an excellent way of eating a part of the pig for which there is little other use".

One now finds *pasta alla matriciana* all over the world. My friend from Amatrice would blow a fuse at some of the versions offered under that name, and I have eaten none as good as the one I watched him cook in its place of origin.

So, I was happy to get the occasional whole Pecorino from Piero Coppi in return for having his sheep graze on my property. In addition to the cheese, I was getting the benefit of the sheep droppings to add to the land's fertility. But the biggest advantage of all was that I came to know Piero well over the ensuing months. He was a man of great dignity and with a deep knowledge of rural life in the area. Chatting with him was an educational experience.

Piero Coppi's home was in a tiny village that lay in a valley called Valchiusa high above Castel Sabino. Its altitude, at more than 1,200 metres (3,940 feet), made its winters very cold with frequent snowfalls. But in the summer it was a green paradise with excellent grazing. Piero told me about the traditional patterns of transhumance in the area. For countless centuries, shepherds from the high hills brought their flocks lower by stages as the decreasing temperatures of approaching winter stunted the growth of the pasture. Areas like Castel Sabino, at about 600 metres (2,000 feet), were a first staging post, and as the winter began to bite there, too, they moved on down through the Sabine Hills. By the depths of winter, they and their flocks had reached the meadows of the Tiber Valley close to Rome. Frosts are quite rare near Rome, and the flocks overwintered on rich pastures. Then in early spring, the long trek back toward the hills and mountains began, again by stages as the warmer temperatures began to stimulate the grass to grow.

There were numerous tracks used by the shepherds to move their flocks. The tracks still exist today, and are occasionally used by walkers, but for the most part, people speeding through the idyllic countryside of the Sabine Hills in their cars are not even aware of their existence.

Piero remarked that there had been no road to his village of Valchiusa until after World War II, and that the gravel road built then had only been asphalted quite recently.

"They thought," Piero said, "that building a road to make the village accessible would help it to develop, but in fact all that happened was that it made it easier for people to leave. We're only four cats living up there now," he said, using the common Italian expression that signifies almost nobody.

Piero had made the journey of some 100 kilometres (sixty-two miles) on foot with his sheep from Valchiusa to rich lowland pastures, and back again in the spring, more times than he could remember. He had first made that journey when he was a boy, but by the time we met, he had given up going anywhere lower than Castel Sabino for the winter. He said he had become too old and lazy for long treks. But laziness was certainly not one of Piero's features. He was up at five in the morning every day to milk his sheep, come rain or sunshine. I did not envy him this task: anyone who has ever worked with sheep will know how disgusting they are when it has rained and when the wool on their back legs is caked with shit, as it always seems to be. To sit in the open on a stool behind a wet ewe before dawn on a wet, blustery and cold morning, and to reach between its legs to find its udder and milk it, is not my idea of dignified work. But Piero, with waterproof leggings to protect himself from the worst of the sheep's filth, seemed inured to the task.

Then he and his wife, who was always with him, would spend the morning making their excellent cheeses. They used simple equipment that was kept beautifully clean. In the afternoon, Piero would make his rounds of the local shops to sell his produce. People came from afar to buy it.

But all that is now finished, at least legally. In the last few years, a combination of European Union and Italian regulations now requires shepherds to take their milk to authorized cheese-making plants. Certainly, this may result in greater hygiene and safety for consumers, but the individuality of local produce has suffered, and that is a sad loss. And as for hygiene, that of Piero and his wife, a plump, matriarchal figure, was faultless. They once invited me to lunch in my still-to-be-rebuilt house. They were camping out in it during the day to look after their flock and make their cheeses. They had a plain table on which they put their cheeses to begin hardening in their round, wooden moulds. The tabletop was scrubbed white wood. For our lunch, they covered it with a spotless, starched white cloth, and they served home-made *fettucine* followed by grilled lamb on brilliant white plates and with sparkling cutlery. Fortunately, whatever the European Union and the Government may say about all milk being taken to authorized cheese-making plants, in many parts of rural Italy today, you can still persuade shepherds to sell you a cheese they have made themselves.

Piero explained to me one day that sheep's milk, wool, and meat had been the origin of the great family fortunes of Rome. Today, palaces, streets and squares bear their names, and the families are subjects for gossip columns. But the creators of their original wealth hundreds of years ago were shepherds or wool merchants. Of course, during that period, wool was by far the most common material for clothing, and it was a source of great wealth for those with a commercial flair.

It was a revelation for me to think that such famous noble families as the Orsini, Colonna, and Odescalchi, had probably once been shepherds or wool merchants. Sheep had founded the fortunes that enabled them to buy up large tracts of land and build the castles and palaces in Lazio from which they dominated the villages spread below them. And they dominated them in every sense, for apart from owning most of the land in the area, they were often cardinals as well. They used their combination of terrestrial and ecclesiastical power to exploit the subservient peasants mercilessly, promising them a better life in paradise and, at the same time, terrorizing them into doing their bidding on earth on pain of eternal damnation if they did not.

3

The Hunt for Knowledge

I was thirsting for knowledge about vines and grapes during the months after I had signed to buy the property, and I was reading everything I could get my hands on. However, I was also going to need direct advice from specialists in viticulture. I have always found that little pleases a genuine expert more than giving advice to someone who is truly interested in learning and needs help. So I had no compunction about calling people I vaguely knew, or people whose names were given to me by mutual friends, to ask for advice.

Of course, there were some people in FAO who knew about viticulture and were helpful. One had even been the vineyard manager for Archbishop Makarios in Cyprus for twenty years, but in FAO he was supervising agricultural projects in West Africa, a region certainly unsuitable for viticulture. Another, an Italo-American, had been a researcher in vine diseases and a teacher at a university in California before coming to FAO. He, too, had no further involvement in viticulture. I found it rather sad that such technical people had to move out of their field of expertise and into management and administration in order to get promoted in FAO.

The most important lead given to me by one of these people was to an Italian institution I had never even heard of – the Experimental Institute of Fruit Culture near Rome's second airport, Ciampino. It was just south of the city and only a short drive from where I lived. The name of the person they said I should contact was Doctor Pellegrino Manzo, the second in command at the Institute. This lead was to prove of central importance to the whole of my venture, for above all I needed expertise that was specific to Italy, and in particular to the central part of the country. I called Doctor Manzo and made an appointment to see him.

The Via Appia that leads out of Rome towards Ciampino Airport is a four-lane road of bustling cut-and-thrust traffic, but when I turned off it, almost directly opposite the airport entrance, I found myself on a rural road that meanders through a pastoral Italy of open fields and umbrella pines. The entrance to the Institute for Fruit Culture leads up a drive lined with cypresses, beyond which I could just see orchards and small plots of vines. The buildings of the Institute were quite modern.

I was to learn later the history of the place and of one of its famous directors, Alberto Pirovano. He was the son of a nursery owner and had limited formal education. Working with his father, he developed a passion for plant breeding. He was so adept at it that today there are numerous varieties of fruit he developed being grown in many countries around the world. Perhaps he is best remembered for his creation of a white table grape variety called Italia, a slightly oval, crunchy, and quite delicious grape.

The story of the creation of Italia is another of those classic examples of serendipity. In 1912, Pirovano crossed an Asian grape variety called Bicane with Hamburg Muscat. It was one of a series of crosses he made and he numbered it P 64. Over the following years, he checked the progeny of all his crosses, discarding the ones that were not performing well. In 1915, while carrying out his check of the progeny, he decided that P 64 was not showing any useful results and should be discarded. He told a nursery worker who was with him to dig it out and throw it away.

However, the workman did not do as he had been ordered because, the very next day, he was called up to fight in the war that had just broken out that year in Italy. But the following year, Pirovano's cross P 64 did magnificently and continued to do so. He named his new variety Italia. Today, it is famous worldwide. It is planted on tens of thousands of hectares, in as far-flung places as Colombia. And Italia grapes are exported from their native country to many parts of northern Europe.

In the 1930s, Pirovano was not much in favour because he never joined the Fascist party, and he did not take much trouble to hide his distaste for the regime. Meanwhile, varieties of fruit he had created were being adopted in many countries with a Mediterranean climate, such as Argentina and Chile. However, with the end of the Fascist regime in Italy, Pirovano came back into the fold. He was honoured with a professorship for his great contribution to fruit culture, and he was nominated director of the Experimental Institute for Fruit Culture at Ciampino. He had died before my first visit there, but Doctor Manzo, whom I went to see, was Alberto Pirovano's assistant for many years.

I was feeling a little uneasy as I knocked on the door of Doctor Manzo's office. It was true that working for FAO had given me the lead to him, and he had been very pleasant on the telephone when I asked for an appointment, but even so, I was still just a foreigner seeking advice for a personal project. However, Doctor Manzo ushered me into his simple office with great courtesy and friendliness. He did not seem in the least surprised or put out by the fact that a foreigner should come along and importune him for advice in this way. And I am sure he would have behaved in just the same way without my FAO connection, for I came to know him very well over the following years, and he was by nature the most warm, kindly, and helpful person imaginable.

Doctor Manzo was in his mid-fifties, a small, dapper man with greying hair brushed back from his forehead. He was sprightly and active, as I found out on the many occasions we were in vineyards together – both mine and other people's – over the following years. He came originally from Avellino, to the east of Naples, and he had maintained a strong southern accent. He was a talented plant-breeder himself. He developed a table grape variety named after his wife, Matilde. It is widely grown in the Puglia region of southeastern Italy and has been so economically important to that region that as recently as 2003 – when he was over eighty years old and long since retired – he was presented with a special award by the regional government of Puglia for his achievement.

Pellegrino Manzo, or Pino as everyone called him, became fully involved in my venture at Castel Sabino, and he also became a dear friend. He came to the property countless times and we would also meet socially in Rome, but of course the subject of grapes and wine invariably dominated the conversation.

During one of our early meetings, Pino Manzo said, "Don't forget that the *scasso* is a fairly expensive operation when you're planting a vineyard. You'll have to take that into account in your cost calculations."

I well knew that the verb *scassare* in Italian meant "to break" and that a person who said he was *scassato* usually did so after some punishing exercise that had left him exhausted, with all his muscles aching, or that a car described as *scassata* was a wreck on four wheels, but I could not imagine what *scasso* had to do with planting a vineyard. Pino Manzo explained that the usual practice in Italy to prepare the land for planting a vineyard and other tree crops was to bring in a powerful crawler tractor with a single furrow plough, and plough the whole area to be planted to a depth of at least a metre (three feet)– a true "breaking" or *scasso* of the land.

In the UK, where I had ploughed a great deal in my younger years, and as an instructor in farm machinery even taught people how to plough, the depth of ploughing normally ranged from twenty to twenty-five centimetres (eight to ten inches). I knew that in the Mediterranean area they often plough deeper than that with the idea that the more loosened soil there is the more water it will retain, but my mind boggled at the idea of doing a *scasso* to a metre deep.

Pino Manzo explained that the idea was to loosen the soil to help the roots of the young vines penetrate. Ploughing would also turn the soil upside down so that the rich topsoil would be deeply buried. As the roots of the vines reached downwards, they would find that topsoil, and its nutrients would make the vines flourish.

"Why don't I just have the land criss-crossed with a ripper or sub-soiler?" I asked. A ripper or sub-soiler is a giant steel tooth mounted behind a powerful tractor. The tooth can easily penetrate to a metre or more to loosen and break open the soil. "It would surely be cheaper than ploughing," I added. "A really big crawler tractor, pulling two, and even three, ripper teeth, could criss-cross the whole property in two or three days, whereas ploughing with a single-furrow plough will probably take a week or more."

"Well, I suppose you could use a ripper but the *scasso* is the traditional way of preparing the land for vines and tree crops. We know it works well," Pino Manzo replied.

I did not insist. It was the early days of knowing Pino Manzo and I did not want to upset him by going against his advice. Nor did I want to take the risk that the vines would not establish themselves well. However, it was my first encounter with the "traditional way" of doing things in vineyards and, as the years passed, one of the major challenges in mine turned out to be persuading the people who worked in it to change some of those traditional ways. In fact, that turned out to be a key factor in improving the quality of the wines.

The next thing I learned from Pino Manzo was that the choice of rootstock for a vineyard is as important as the choice of the grape varieties. Grape vines, known as *Vitis vinifera*, are grafted onto American rootstocks following the lethal attack on European vineyards by the aphid-like phylloxera bug. This bug is thought to have originated in the southeast regions of the USA, where the local vines were resistant. By 1854 it was attacking the leaves of European vines planted in California. An entomologist called Asa Fitch was the first person to describe it. He thought that it only attacked the leaves of vines, but in fact phylloxera has two distinct life forms. Eggs laid in the roots hatch and, while some "crawlers" move to other roots and the roots of neighbouring vines, others climb above ground and attack the foliage of the vines. In certain humid conditions these crawlers can also develop a winged version of themselves, capable of flying further afield.

The first symptom of a phylloxera attack in a vineyard was that a few vines in a small area would quite suddenly start to go yellow and die. Then the attack would spread out like an oil stain from that first afflicted area until the whole vineyard was stricken. This was first noticed in Europe in 1863, but no one knew the cause. When the dead or dying vines were dug out, it was found that their root systems had been destroyed, but it took some time before it was recognized that the phylloxera bug had a life stage in the soil and was responsible for the terrible damage. The Latin name it was given, *Phylloxera vastatrix* (the devastator), eloquently describes its destructiveness.

Phylloxera seems to have reached Europe with the vines that were being imported from America in the late 1850s. They were being imported because there was another vine problem that had originated in America called powdery mildew. Some American grape vines seemed to be resistant to it, and there was therefore an interest in trying them in Europe.

Vineyard owners in the last half of the nineteenth century were desperate for a solution to phylloxera, for the whole viticulture industry was being destroyed. Indeed, by the end of that century, it had killed off no less than two-thirds of all of the vineyards in Europe. The Gilbey family of England, of Gilbey gin fame, had a vineyard near Bordeaux. Their vineyard manager was sending them reports every few days of the progressive damage in the vineyard, and their alarm showed in their letters to the manager. Surprisingly, in those years some century and a half ago, no letter between Bordeaux and London or vice versa took more than four or five days to reach its destination, despite the slow speed of the available transport.

Finally, the solution to phylloxera came from the same place as the problem – North America. The bug lives only off plants of the *Vitis* family, but there were members of that family in America that had developed a resistance to it. Most of these resistant types are American wild vines producing fruit that is practically useless for making wine or anything else. However, grafting *Vitis vinifera* onto the roots of these resistant vines might solve the problem. This solution was proposed at a conference on viticulture held in Beaune in 1869, and it proved to be the solution.

Today, the only major wine region in the world where vines are not grafted onto American rootstocks is Chile. This is because the bug has never managed to cross the massive barrier of the Andes from Argentina to the east. So in Chile, the *Vitis vinifera* vine still grows on its own roots, as it did in Europe before phylloxera arrived. Some people claim that *Vitis vinifera* growing on its own roots produces grapes of better quality than when it is grafted onto different roots. Certainly, many Chilean wines are excellent, but it is difficult to attribute that quality to any one particular cause, for grape and wine production is influenced by a multitude of factors.

During the European fight against phylloxera, the selection and development of the American wild vines to provide the best rootstocks became a highly specialized field. Most of the early work was done in France, and many of the rootstocks developed in the 1880s are still being used today, even if many newer ones have also been developed. In Italy there are more than forty different ones in use. Pino Manzo explained that some produced more vigorous growth than others, that some were especially resistant to drought or wet conditions, that some were more tolerant of high lime content in the soil, and so on.

The main problem, Pino Manzo explained, was that many nurseries selling grafted vines for planting used a rootstock called Kober 5BB. This was because it was the easiest, and so the cheapest, for them to propagate. They were able to play on many purchasers' ignorance about rootstocks, and indeed, many small farmers bought only on the basis of the variety of *Vitis vinifera* they wanted, without even bothering to ask what rootstock it was grafted on. While Kober 5BB was an excellent, vigorous rootstock for deep and moist soil conditions, it was not very resistant to drought or highly alkaline soils. So many people ended up with vines that did not perform well. In effect, their own lack of knowledge, and the less than professional behaviour of the nurseries, doomed the vineyard to substandard performance from the very beginning.

However, the rootstock's suitability according to the type of soil and the climate in which it is to be planted is not the end of the story. Some rootstocks are more compatible than others with the variety of *Vitis vinifera* that are grafted onto them. So the question of which grape varieties I would plant soon became an issue for discussion with Pino Manzo.

I was initially thinking I would sell grapes to local people to make wine for their own consumption, rather than producing wine seriously myself, for setting up a winery would be costly and would have to go into a second phase. One of the advantages of starting an agricultural enterprise as intensive as a vineyard was that the initial capital outlay to buy the quite small area of land was relatively limited: the rest of the investment could be spread over time. This would be quite different from buying a large farm, for example for growing cereals.

There appeared to be a good market for grapes in Castel Sabino. Most of the active population had migrated to Rome to live and work. However, they had kept their houses in the village and their plots of land, but they hardly had the time or inclination to look after their vines. So, with many of the vines in the area abandoned – and without pruning and care a vine runs riot and degrades in only a few seasons – their only option if they wanted to continue with their domestic wine-making was to buy grapes from the trucks that arrived in Castel Sabino in October every year. Most of the trucks brought grapes from an area near Viterbo called Vignanello or from the Abruzzo region to the east of Castel Sabino, well known in the wine world for its robust red Montepulciano d'Abruzzo.

Most people living in and around Castel Sabino had a storeroom to keep their jars of home-preserved tomatoes for making pasta sauce and their hams and salamis, but which also served as their *cantina,* or winery. Thus, people bought grapes off the trucks that came into the village and hauled them off to their simple, and often dirty, *cantina* to make wine for family consumption. According to estimates I got from local people, between 1,000 and 1,500 quintals[2] (100–150 metric tons) of grapes were being sold off trucks that came to the village. I reasoned that I should be able to corner a good part of that market. I hoped that people would prefer locally grown grapes to grapes brought in from other areas.

This strategy would to some extent influence the choice of varieties to grow, but there was also the altitude factor. Different varieties of grapes need different numbers of "degree days" – the average daytime temperatures in the growing season multiplied by the number of days – to ripen. The varieties grown in, say, Germany or northern France need fewer degree days to ripen than the varieties generally grown in warmer climates further south. For Castel Sabino, relatively cool at 600 metres (2,000 feet) altitude, it would have been ideal to plant some of the early ripening varieties used further north in Europe. According to Pino Manzo's estimate, they would almost certainly be ready for harvest by about mid-September in most years. And in a very unfavourable year, they would still ripen by mid-October.

However, grapes that ripened in mid-September would present a serious problem for my initial strategy of selling grapes to the villagers, for all of the grapes grown locally were varieties that ripened – if they did – in the traditional harvest period beginning around mid-October. That was also the period in which the trucks arrived bringing grapes from other areas. Thus the local people made their wine in the second half of October. If I were to offer them perfect grapes from early ripening varieties in mid-September, I would be unlikely sell a single bunch, for they would not have their *cantine* ready.

Pino Manzo summed it up. "They've been winemaking in the second half of October for centuries. Preparing a *cantina* is a quite lot of work for them. They have to wash all the equipment and fill their barrels with water so that their staves

[2] A quintal is 100 kilograms (220 pounds). In Italy, it is the unit of weight always used for grapes.

swell again and do not leak. From what we've heard them say, it seems that their winemaking is a weekend activity, so they're short of time. I think we'll have to go for varieties that ripen in the traditional period around mid-October."

The prevailing legislation was another factor that could not be ignored in my choice of grape varieties. Italy is a land of laws and regulations. Italians will tell you that there are 80,000 of them compared to only 5,000 in Germany. I cannot vouch for these figures, but I do know one astonishing fact about Italian legislation that is most certainly true. In 2003, the Central State Archive published the minutes of the proceedings of the Government that Mussolini set up at Salò on Lake Garda, in Northern Italy, after those who had taken power in Rome had signed an armistice with the Allies. The Salò regime lasted just 600 days in the period 1943–55, while the Allies were fighting their way up the Italian boot. The recently published minutes of that Fascist administration in Salò show that in those 600 days no less than a thousand laws were passed. They included such things as the creation of the Employment Book that is issued to workers today, and some educational reforms that also found their way into postwar Italy. There, they joined a multitude of other laws that were promulgated by Mussolini during his years in power before World War II.

No law in Italy is ever cancelled from the national legislation. Frequently, a new law is passed to modify an older one, and then another law is passed to modify the most recent one, each step adding another layer of complexity until many of the laws become subject to different interpretations. Some Italians say that all existing legislation should be thrown out and a new beginning made. They also ask how it is possible for a democratic country, and a member of the European Union, to have thousands of its prevailing laws signed by Benito Mussolini, the inventor of a thoroughly undemocratic system like Fascism. However, the majority of Italians treat much of the legislation as a joke. The problem is that if the authorities do catch up with you and decide to throw their complex book of rules at you, you can find yourself in very deep trouble and menaced by Draconian penalties.

The Italian Government has legislated for what grape varieties are "recommended" or "authorized" for each of the country's provinces. For the province of Rieti, in which Castel Sabino is located, there were seventeen recommended and seven authorized varieties. The purpose of the legislation was to try to create or preserve the typical characteristics of wines produced in different parts of the country. However, it is difficult for legislation to take into account the climatic differences in a province like Rieti, for its altitude above sea level ranges between 150 and 2,200 metres (500 and 7,200 feet), producing wide variations in the summer temperatures. Strangely, given the large areas of hills at quite high altitude, there were virtually no high-quality, early-ripening varieties in the approved list for the province.

The Government restrictions on grape varieties that could be grown in the various provinces of the country were also linked to the subsidies for planting vineyards. These were available for many years, especially in the 1960s, and the funding came mainly from the European Union. The choice of grape variety to be planted was among the criteria for becoming eligible for a subsidy. As is well known, the subsidies for planting vineyards led to the great European "wine lake" in the 1970–80s, which in turn led to further subsidies to pull out poor quality vineyards in the 1990s.

Fortunately, after subsidies for planting vines disappeared, the stipulations about varieties were no longer applied in practice, even if they still existed on paper. And so, many Italian grape growers ignored the regulations about varieties on the basis that if they were using only their own money, they would plant whatever type of grape they wanted. This has led, in recent years, to new ranges of wines, many of which include classic varieties used in other countries such as Chardonnay, Cabernet Sauvignon, Syrah, and Malbec. These were not even mentioned in the lists of approved or recommended varieties when I was planning my vineyard in the 1970s. The Government then had to run to catch up, changing its regulations about approved varieties to reflect what grape growers had already done successfully.

If I were to meet the needs of local buyers it would be simplest be for me to grow varieties already common and appreciated in the area. So I began chatting to the locals about what varieties were traditionally grown around Castel Sabino. It did not prove very helpful. The usual answer was that there had been – and there still were – a few vines producing grapes that they called *uva nostrana*. This is virtually impossible to translate, except very loosely as "home-grown" or "local grapes". All the people I talked to said that a characteristic of *uva nostrana* was that the clusters had red stalks. Some people said they thought it was a type of Cesanese with a red stalk. Cesanese is a recognized and quality grape variety grown mainly in the hills south of Rome, but none of my research into Cesanese came up with a type with a red stalk. I saw many samples of *uva nostrana* from vines growing up trees in the traditional way. It certainly did have a red stalk, and the grape berries were so few in number and spread so sparsely that the stalk was visible for most of its length. The grapes looked very poor, and readings of their sugar level did not show that they ripened any better than other grapes in the area.

After many discussions with Pino Manzo, we ultimately decided that the vineyard would be planted over a three-year period. This would spread the work and capital costs in a more convenient way than trying to plant the whole property in one operation. We also decided to begin with two hectares of the red Sangiovese variety. Sangiovese was on the recommended list for the province of Rieti and is widely grown in Central Italy, especially in Tuscany and Umbria. It is the principal variety used in Chianti wines as well as in many of the recent and very high quality wines often known as "Super Tuscans".

A problem I was to discover later, however, was that there was considerable confusion surrounding the Sangiovese variety. Although almost certainly native to Tuscany, where it seems also to have been called San Gioveto in earlier times, there are in fact several different clones of Sangiovese. One clone, which goes by the name of Prugnolo, is grown in the area around the town of Montepulciano and produces the famous Vino Nobile di Montepulciano. Another clone known as Sangiovese Grosso, Prunello, or Brunello was noted and selected around 1840 near Montalcino and gave rise to Brunello di Montalcino, one of Italy's finest red wines. Another clone goes under the name of Morellino and produces a good, sometimes excellent, wine called Morellino di Scansano in the hills to the east of Grosseto, in southwest Tuscany. And yet another clone of Sangiovese is grown in the Romagna area not far from Bologna.

Nurseries were not offering clonal selections when I planted my Sangiovese. Had they been, I would have chosen one of the clones used to make some of today's outstanding Sangiovese varietal wines, but when Pino Manzo and I were discussing the matter, we had no choice. Our only possibility was to choose a high quality nursery and trust to luck. Pino told me he knew of one near Pisa that he deemed professional and that he would approach them when the time came.

4

Of Cemeteries, Builders, and Beams

In parallel with planning the vineyard, I had to renovate and enlarge the dilapidated house. Such an operation, anywhere, is invariably fraught with problems, delays, and frustrations, and Italy is no exception. But before I could even begin work on the house, I ran into a serious obstacle. There is an old Italian law, still in force in many communities, that prohibits building within 200 metres (660 feet) of a cemetery. The house was 180 metres (590 feet) from the cemetery. The regulation distance had not been reduced in Castel Sabino, as it had in many other places. I was blocked until I could find a way round this regulation. I would have to negotiate with the mayor of Castel Sabino. Roberto Paoli asked him to come up to the property one Saturday morning, and he agreed.

I had already submitted my request to the *comune* (municipality) for building approval to restore the original small house and enlarge it. The building committee, which by law was to meet on a regular basis to adjudicate on applications, had not actually met for more than three months. The mayor was therefore at some disadvantage when we met on my land to discuss the problem. Like my friend Piero Coppi, the mayor of Castel Sabino was a shepherd from Valchiusa. During World War II he had helped the anti-Fascist partisans who were based in the wild hills above Valchiusa. As a result, he had earned some political credits with the Christian Democratic party that governed Italy in the postwar years. These credits had helped him to be elected mayor of Castel Sabino.

The mayor was in his sixties, a serious and taciturn man with a heavy limp and a built-up boot. He looked about as cheerful as the grey clouds scudding low across the sky on that morning of our first meeting. I had prepared my little speech in my mind and I delivered it politely. I was going to plant a vineyard on the property; I could hardly look after it if I had no house to live in, and I had put in the request for building permission more than three months ago. I went on to tell him that the vineyard would provide some work for local people, and that I needed that planning permission rapidly.

His reaction to my statement was not favourable.

"Your house is less than 200 metres from the cemetery and the regulations don't allow building so close. You could build a new house, and a better one, further away. You've got enough land.'"

"Look, it's only twenty metres short of the 200," I said. "Building a completely new house would be more expensive, and with all the other investment I'm going to make for the vineyard, I can't afford additional costs."

It was probably not true that building a new house would have been more expensive, and certainly not if I had built a modern box. But I preferred a rebuilt and enlarged old house with stonewalls, wooden beams, and old roof tiles. The mayor would not have understood my preference for such a house, even if I had told him, because in most rural areas of Italy old houses are still equated in people's minds with the poverty and discomforts of the past.

The mayor looked at me in silence for some time. It was a nervous moment. I began to think I should start expanding on why he and his building committee should approve my request, and I was marshalling my thoughts to open my mouth, when he tipped his head very slightly. The move was almost imperceptible. He stuck out his hand to shake mine, said *"Buongiorno,"* turned, and limped away. Two weeks later Roberto Paoli called me to say that the *comune* had approved my building plans.

During the actual renovation and building, I ran into all of the problems that one comes to expect. Roberto Paoli was supervising the work, which was being done by a small local builder called Enzo Francone. He was a very good builder, and one of the few in the area willing to work in stone, while most of the others would only build in concrete blocks or *tufo*, blocks cut from soft sandstone.

A major problem was that both Roberto and Enzo were highly competent, of about the same age, and each had a sense of his own importance. The result was frequent confrontations between them about how to handle the numerous problems of the renovation of the house and its extension. But despite the occasional shouting matches and the inevitable delays, the work progressed as well as could be expected. However, it did involve much time spent looking for old roof tiles, seasoned chestnut beams, and the like, so that the house could be restored in the original style of the area, and the new part built to match it.

The supplier of beams and roof timbers was a delightful old rascal called Mario Ricci who was based in Rieti. I frequently went to see him to discuss my needs, to place my orders, and even more, to find out why he had not delivered as promised. In fact, I ended up spending many hours in his company, often over several glasses of wine to help wash down some salami or ham while we talked about many things. He had been a fervent Fascist during the Mussolini era and had strong feelings of nostalgia for that period of his life. This was not unusual in that part of Italy: indeed, there was a mountainside not far from Rieti where the word DUX, the Latin for *Duce* (leader) by which Mussolini was known, was cut into the vegetation. It could be seen for miles, and well into the 1970s, persons unknown regularly cleared any new vegetation obscuring the letters.

Mario Ricci had a wonderful sense of humour and fully saw the contradictions of the Mussolini era. He talked about the grand shows of Italy's military might on successive weekends in the 1930s when warplanes would fly over cities in formation to impress the Italians on the ground of the country's readiness for war. The only problem was that they were always the same squadron of aircraft that moved around the country for their weekend demonstrations. He also talked of how Italian soldiers were sent to fight in Russia with the same uniforms and footgear they had used in Abyssinia. Of course, they died like flies in the Russian winter.

Mario Ricci's party piece, once he had drunk enough wine, was suddenly to appear serious, assume a glowering expression, thrust his chin forward belligerently, then throw his head back and shout loudly, "*Italianiiiiii!!!*" He drew out the last syllable so that it lingered like an echo. The facial expressions, the head movements, and the shout of "*Italianiiiiii!!!!*" were a perfect imitation of how Mussolini opened his harangues from the balcony in Rome's Piazza Venezia when he was urging his fellow countrymen on to war and greatness.

After his shout, Mario Ricci would burst out laughing and almost fall off his chair in merriment, tears of laughter streaming down his cheeks. In all of my many years in Italy, it was the funniest takeoff of Mussolini that I ever witnessed.

Years after my sessions in Rieti with Mario Ricci, I came across another and even more hilarious take off of Mussolini in a long passage of Louis de Bernières magnificent novel *Captain Corelli's Mandolin.* As I read it, with tears of laughter in my eyes, I suddenly remembered dear old Mario Ricci, long since dead, helpless with laughter at his own imitation of *Il Duce.*

Despite his own Fascist past, Mario Ricci delighted in ridiculing *Il Duce* and his attempts to turn Italians into a fearsome war machine. During World War I, the Italians fought like lions and showed enormous bravery when fighting the Austrian invaders in northern Italy. However, in Mussolini's time, the average Italian was much too realistic to be stirred to similar military sacrifices by an egocentric and bombastic leader who promised them national greatness through colonial conquest and, later, by throwing in his lot with Hitler. After centuries of exploitation and injustice exercised by potentates, including those of the Catholic Church, most Italians are understandably sceptical of the motives behind any form of authority. This perhaps explains the Italian disregard for rules and regulations. When wearing seatbelts in cars was made compulsory, it was very soon possible to buy a tee-shirt with a belt printed on it so that the police would be fooled into thinking that its wearer had buckled up. And many drivers, still today, do not do up their belts.

There has been a similar reaction to a much more recent law requiring people to wear helmets on all types of powered two-wheeled transport. After a couple of months of quite strict enforcement, many youths are now again belting around bareheaded on their scooters, and without provoking much action by law enforcement officers to stop them. The only explanation seems to be that history and culture have worked against the creation of a true civil society in Italy. Thus, the average Italian inherently believes that the powerful are always trying to take advantage of him, and laws are only made in the interest of others. The same thinking applies to laws concerning such things as seat belts and helmets, despite their obvious safety benefits to their users. There is a well-known Italian saying that goes, "Invented the law . . . invented the trick to get around it!"

I did not have to use any trickery to get around the problem of building permission, only some persuasion. Fortunately, meeting the rest of the legal building requirements was even easier. For example, because Castel Sabino was in an earthquake area, like most of Italy, all of the outside walls of the house had to have a reinforced concrete ring built into them at intervals of 120 centimetres (forty-eight inches) in height. And the roof had to be completely removed from the old part and a similar reinforcing ring built on to the top of the walls before replacing the roof. Anyway, I had no desire to get around that legislation; I had experienced an earthquake once in Latin America and knew how frightening they were, so the stronger my house was, the better.

I wanted the windows and shutters, and the kitchen cupboards, to be made of chestnut, a local and rather hard wood. Most of the carpenters were reluctant to use it, preferring to work with softwoods. After talking to several in Castel Sabino, I finally went to see Rocco, a carpenter in a neighbouring village. He had a reputation for working with chestnut and was a personality in the area.

Rocco was a bald, smiling man with a fascinating wartime experience. He had been with the Italian army in Albania and then Yugoslavia, where Tito's partisans captured him and a number of comrades. The partisans decided to execute the Italians, and began to shoot them one by one. Rocco was only seconds away from his turn to be shot when one of the partisans suggested that they stop and find out whether any of the Italians who were still alive could be of any use to them.

Rocco stutteringly told them that he was a carpenter and that if they needed any doors or window frames, he could make them. He could even build wooden huts, if they wanted. They decided not to kill him, but they did not use his carpenter's skills. Instead they wanted to see whether he would be any use to them in combat. They tried his willingness and strength by giving him a heavy mortar barrel to carry on an all night march through forests, and up and down steep slopes. Luckily, Rocco was strong and very fit: he was still a compact and sprightly man when I knew him many years later.

The partisans were impressed, and so he spent the rest of the war fighting with them, ambushing German occupying troops, sabotaging bridges, and raining mortar bombs from the hills on to German positions. When the war finally finished, Rocco walked all the way back to the Sabine Hills and took up where he had left off as a carpenter.

Sitting over the inevitable glass of wine with him one day, I said, "Rocco, I have met a number of carpenters over the years, but you're the only one who still has all his fingers and thumbs. How's that?"

"Well, I'm also the only carpenter I know with all his fingers," he said with his infectious grin. "All the young apprentices who've worked with me and gone on to become carpenters have chopped off fingers. One of them has lost four fingers. The last one was only a year ago. He should know better at his age. I'm very careful and I always pay attention to what I'm doing when I'm using power equipment in the workshop. And I'm very quick to move my hands out of danger if I need to." He laughed and added, "People round here say I'm a *polverone* (cloud of dust)".

I could not imagine what he meant when he said he was described as "a cloud of dust". Rocco had to explain to me that it was a local expression applied to people who were so quick-moving and active that they raised a cloud of dust. He may have been that, but he was also a highly accomplished artisan. The doors, windows, and kitchen cupboards he turned out, from a batch of seasoned chestnut he had put aside for me, were beautiful. They were admired by all who saw them.

There were many frustrations and delays with the work on the house, but after about eighteen months, I was able to sleep in it for the first time. My two teenage sons from my first marriage, Stuart and Iain, were on holiday from their school in England at Easter 1977 and were there to share the event. I have always believed that children should be allowed to drink small quantities of alcohol in the home. I was brought up that way, drinking tiny amounts of wine at dinner with my parents from the age of ten. As a result, I think, I did not go berserk when I reached the legal age to drink. I hoped that Stuart and Iain would be the same, and so, like most Mediterranean children, they could have a little wine with a meal if they wanted it.

However, that Easter, when they were about seventeen and fifteen, and when as usual I offered them some wine, they both shocked me.

"I'd prefer some beer, Dad," Stuart said. "I don't like wine much."

"So would I," piped up Iain, the younger one.

I could hardly believe it. Here I was, planting a vineyard, a process that my sons were following with some interest during their visits, and yet they preferred beer to wine. It was hard to accept.

At least my sons liked the house. It nestled on the slope, and its outstretched, covered porches, stone walls, old tiles on three different roof levels, and chimney stacks gave it a timeless air. Inside, it had terracotta floors made from handmade tiles, complete with the marks of finger strokes, like those used in ancient Rome. Indeed, the brickyard where I found them dated from Roman times and was operated, in the summer only, by five old men paddling around barefoot. Once the tiles had been laid and I had buffed the rougher edges off them with a sanding disc, treated them with oil and wax repeatedly, and polished them, they looked magnificent. The ceilings had the open chestnut timbers I had bought from Mario Ricci, and there were quite large areas of stonework left showing on the inside of the house, too.

The house had turned out elegantly rustic and traditional. For me, it had something of an old English country house about it, especially because of the exposed beams. The local people were not so enthusiastic, it seemed. When they came inside for the first time, they would look questioningly at the areas of visible stonework in some of the walls. One person asked me if I had run out of money and needed to save on plastering. Another, looking at the outside of the house, asked me why I had not cement rendered the stone walls. And why ever had I planted a Virginia creeper on the house? It would only be a way for animals and insects to get in through the windows. But I was very happy with the way the house had turned out, and I felt that all the love and care taken on its rebuilding were fully justified. As far as most of the locals were concerned, it merely confirmed my eccentricity.

5

The Mad Ploughman

The *scasso*, **the metre-deep ploughing of the land prior to planting vines,** was best done in June, Pino Manzo explained. The reason was that the hot summer sun and the thunderstorms of August would help to weather and break down the clods left by the ploughing. Pino managed to find a contractor with the appropriate equipment and one day in early June of 1976, an articulated truck pulling a low-loading trailer struggled up the hill to my land. On the trailer were an enormous Caterpillar tractor and a man-high, single-furrow plough.

The owner of this outsize rig was a rakish young man called Angelo Giacomelli. He made his living from doing the *scasso* on properties all over central Italy when the owners wanted to plant vineyards or fruit orchards. Within minutes of unloading his rig from the truck, the Caterpillar was roaring and grunting across my land, while the plough behind it was bursting open a furrow that seemed as deep as a grave. Mounds of soil, stones, and rocks that had never seen the light of day, and upended tree stumps, formed an apocalyptic landscape. It looked as though an atom bomb had been dropped on my land.

The scene fascinated passing locals. As Giacomelli reached the headland and hauled on the rope that tripped the mechanism to raise the plough, the great implement reared out of the ground and exposed its working parts, polished to brilliance by the soil. The rig clanked around on the headland and when

Giacomelli pulled the rope again to lower it, the plough seemed to collapse like a shot giraffe.

"*Madonna!*" said one onlooker. "The whole thing seems to fall apart." (The word he actually used for fall apart was *sbragare*, which literally means to "de-trouser". In rural areas of central Italy the word is often used to describe a collapse or something falling to pieces.)

Angelo Giacomelli was on the property for some ten days. His stay was prolonged by several breakdowns. When something went wrong he would fly into the most impressive rage. He would stand beside the rig ranting and shouting an uninterrupted string of curses and obscenities. On one occasion, he was so incensed by some breakdown that he was literally jumping up and down with rage. He then tore off his fancy peaked cap, flung it on the ground, and jumped up and down on that too.

I gazed at the chaos left behind after he had gone and wondered how I would ever get it cleaned up. There were tree stumps and rocks to be removed and the whole area of lumps and bumps would have to be levelled and smoothed out.

I needed a tractor and implements to remedy the mess and to prepare the land for planting the first vines in the following spring. At least in matters of farm machinery, I felt myself on firm ground, a quite different situation from my abysmal initial ignorance about viticulture. For my first job after qualifying in agriculture had been as a technical instructor in a large training centre near Coventry, England, operated by Massey-Ferguson, one of the world's major farm machinery manufacturers. The company's tractors incorporated the inventions of Harry Ferguson, the Ulsterman who can justifiably be called the father of the modern farm tractor. He pioneered the Ferguson System, a means of linking an implement to the tractor, of raising and lowering it, and of controlling its depth of work through a sophisticated hydraulic system.

The steepness of some of the slopes where I planned to plant vines would call for a four-wheel drive tractor or a crawler, but a crawler could not be used to transport grapes on the asphalted roads of the area. So it would have to be a four-wheel drive tractor, but Massey-Ferguson was not producing such models in those days. So I went to the farm machinery fair held every November in Bologna to see what Italian manufacturers had to offer. As an employee of Massey-Ferguson, I had often been sent to machinery fairs myself to be on the company's stand and answer questions from actual or potential customers. Now the boot was on the other foot as I approached each manufacturer's stand. After a general question about the tractor models available, I started getting down to details about the hydraulic system and other technical features. The salesman would usually go glassy-eyed for a very brief moment before pulling himself together and delivering an articulate stream of generalized piffle about how marvellous his company's products were, but without answering my questions.

Then, finally, I ended up on the stand of SAME, one of Italy's major tractor manufacturers. The representative that I approached with my questions was also quick-witted, but without the tendency to bluff his way along. As soon as I asked my first technical question about SAME's hydraulic system, he looked at me sharply.

"You seem to know about tractors," he said.

I told him about my five years as an instructor with Massey-Ferguson. He chuckled.

"Well, let me tell you," he said. "When SAME wanted to build its first tractor with a hydraulic lift, we went and bought a Ferguson engineer to design it for us."

This won me over completely, of course, and I was even more convinced when he called over a stocky, smiling man and introduced him to me. He was Bruno Fabri, the main sales agent for SAME tractors in the province of Rieti. We agreed to meet in his office not very far from Castel Sabino the following weekend to discuss my needs. At that first meeting I ordered a fifty-horsepower, four-wheel drive SAME Falcon, a tractor that served me well for twenty years.

Bruno Fabri was an exuberant character and that first meeting became one of many. He had a wonderful sense of humour and loved to eat, drink, joke, and laugh. Together, on Saturdays, we visited several manufacturers of other equipment such as vineyard ploughs, disc harrows, and the like. Some of these manufacturers invited us to those long and rambling Italian lunches that begin around 1pm and only wind up at about 5pm. One of these lunches was in a tiny village in Tuscany called Monteriggioni, close to the implement factory we were visiting and not far from Siena.

Monteriggioni perches on a low hill and is completely enclosed behind medieval walls and watchtowers. It was originally built in 1213 as a fortress to protect the Republic of Siena. In those days Italy was made up of numerous small States that were usually at war with one another. Once you have driven up the cypress-lined road and passed through the gate in the massive wall of Monteriggioni, you find yourself in a small open square. Apart from a few cars, nothing about the square and its surrounding houses seems to have changed since the fortified village was first built.

There is a well in the square, and next to it a restaurant appropriately called *Il Pozzo* (The Well). On the autumnal day that Bruno Fabri and I were invited to *Il Pozzo* for lunch, we were happy to go into the warmth of the brick-vaulted restaurant. The food was superb Siena fare, starting with local salamis with *crostini* (pieces of toasted bread with various things including game pâté), followed by two different pastas and grilled wild boar, salad, and fruit. And the wine was even better, its adundance helping the conversation to flow.

When you have finished the actual eating at such meals, the restaurant owner will often plonk down three or four bottles of different *digestivi* (liqueurs) on your table from which to help yourself liberally. When you finally get up to leave, you are on excellent terms with your lunch companions, even if you only met them a few hours before. On this occasion in Monteriggioni I had to think hard to remember what implement or implements I had agreed to buy from our host before the lunch.

One day Bruni Fabri called me in my office in Rome. "Do you like lamb brains?'" he asked. I told him I was very fond of brains fried with artichokes, a typical Roman dish, and asked him why he wanted to know.

"I've just sold a tractor to a farmer in a village between Rome and Rieti and he wants to celebrate the event. He's invited me to dinner tomorrow night to eat lamb brains. I told him I would like to bring a friend. Do you want to come?"

I quickly accepted because an evening in a farming family's home with Bruno Fabri was much more attractive to me than an evening in Rome.

In those days of subsidized loans for agricultural machinery in Italy, many very small farmers, some with only two or three hectares of land, were buying new tractors and implements that could hardly be justified by any rational economic criteria. Frequently, therefore, small farmers often ended up with debts they could ill afford to pay. So in effect, the subsidized loans were probably of more benefit in helping the manufacturers sell machinery than they were in helping small farmers like the one who invited us to his home to eat lamb brains.

We settled into the simple kitchen where there was the most delicious smell coming from the oven. After some *prosciutto* and olives as a starter, the farmer's wife arrived at the table with a big platter. On it were arranged several lambs' heads cut in half, resplendent with teeth and eye sockets and with the baked brain showing. It was the first time I had ever eaten brain from its original container. It took me a moment to overcome my initial shock. But Bruno Fabri was attacking his brains with gusto, so I soon overcame any squeamishness that might have held me back. The brains were delicious.

Driving back to Rome afterwards, more than replete with food and wine, I came around a bend and found myself behind a military troop carrier. Italy is one of those relatively rare civilized countries that spend more on education than it does on arms and, in general, the military presence is barely noticeable. The vehicle in front of me was tracked like a tank and it was travelling at an astonishing speed. To find a tracked troop carrier storming down a narrow country road in the middle of the night had me wondering whether the lamb brains had some hallucinatory ingredients.

In the first years after I first met Bruno Fabri he was selling over 120 tractors a year, no mean feat for a one-man band, and his business was providing him with an excellent living in a large and recently built home. He was an outstanding salesman who knew instinctively how to get on with his potential customers, most of whom were relatively simple, small farmers. His sense of humour and fun was infectious, and we spent quite a lot of time together socially over the ensuing years.

Sadly, however, Bruno's bookkeeping and financial records were not up to the level of his gifts as a salesman. His relations with the SAME company deteriorated, and they alleged that there were irregularities in his payments and commissions. They cancelled his agency agreement. Bruno protested that any errors were on the part of SAME, but he did not have the detailed paperwork to prove it.

With his means of livelihood taken from him and forced to rely on his wife's salary as a teacher, Bruno lost his sparkle. He aged before my eyes. His previously serene face took on the grim lines of his struggle to prove that he was right and SAME wrong. Finally, SAME launched a lawsuit against him and he had to declare bankruptcy. It was a sad way for such a gifted salesman and delightful character to go. He had advised me well on what makes and types of equipment to buy to use with the tractor, particularly at the beginning when I needed to clean up the mess left by that mad ploughman, Angelo Giacomelli.

6

Ferruccio

Ferruccio was about forty when we first met, almost exactly a year younger than
I was. He was short and rotund and invariably wore, even indoors, the Italian
version of an English pork pie hat. It was of tweedy cloth for the winter and straw
for the summer. Below it he had a round and weathered face out of which two
bright blue eyes twinkled. When he was preparing to deliver some funny
comment, which was frequently, he had a unique way of pushing his hat back
with one finger, exposing a snow-white forehead and a few straggly hairs on his
balding pate above the ruddy complexion of his lower face. At the same time his
eyes would crinkle and take on an increased sparkle.

Ferruccio, and his family too, are central to this story of vines and wines. They
lived in a simple pink house surrounded by oak trees at the far side of my
property, about 300 metres (330 yards) away and slightly higher than my house.
We could see each other's homes clearly, and on a still day voices could also be
heard from one to the other. They were a family of peasant farmers who were
barely able to eke out an existence from their "promiscuous" farming on a
relatively small-holding. It was therefore natural that Ferruccio, and other
members of the family too, would come to work on my land.

Over the coming years, Ferruccio became my right-hand man. He looked after
the vineyard with a small group of other workers and helped me in the winery at
weekends. I have always appreciated and enjoyed rural people, probably because

44

I was brought up in a rural area, and also because I have spent much of my adult life working with them. I find their inherent dignity, practical nature, and earthy humour very appealing, and these same traits seem to be common to peasants all over the world. Ferruccio and his family became close friends over the years.

Ferrucio drank wine in navigable quantities, mostly that which he produced himself. It was similar to the other wines produced by the locals, ranging from disgusting – because the barrel it was kept in was mouldy on the inside – to just drinkable. But he drank even the worst of it regardless, for peasants throw nothing away. And I learned to drink it too, because it is impossible to turn down a generous offer from rural people without appearing rude and superior.

Ferruccio would go out to work in the fields in the morning with nothing but a cup of coffee in his stomach. But then, at 10am sharp, it was *colazione* time. This is the peasant and farm worker breakfast that seems to be common all over the world. Ferruccio's consisted of ham, salami, or cheese, all produced in the home, with bread and his first swill of wine for the day. He then went back to work, but never without his faithful companion, a large bottle of wine with a screw cap. He carried it in a khaki canvas bag slung over his shoulder. He would set this down carefully on the ground, or against a tree, near where he was working, and he would return to it at regular intervals throughout the day for an abundant swig.

One summer afternoon, after I had known him for some years, I needed to talk to Ferruccio, or Ferru, as I always knew him. This was in keeping with the laconic habit of curtailing friends' names in the rural areas of central Italy, a habit that often had friends calling me simply "Co". In fact, such abbreviations are a sign of friendship and intimacy, and I was always pleased to be called "Co"; it made me feel that I had been accepted as part of the local scene, despite being a foreigner who spoke Italian complete with mistakes and an accent.

When I was looking for Ferruccio that summer afternoon, he was using his walk-behind hay mower to cut the grass on a neighbour's land. The machine was so noisy that I had no trouble finding him. It was exceedingly hot and humid even at 600 metres (2,000 feet) above sea level. When I came up to him, the sweat was running down his face and falling from his chin in large drops, and his shirt was stuck to his body. The mower was in fact heavy to manoeuvre, and the land was irregular and very sloping.

We sat under a tree. He reached for his companion in its khaki canvas bag and unscrewed the cap. As always, he then wiped the neck of the bottle with his hand and passed it to me for a first swig.

"Good God, Ferru," I said, "it's much too hot to drink wine. Didn't you bring any water with you today?"

"No, you know I only put that stuff in my mouth to brush my teeth," he replied, before gulping thirstily at his bottle of wine.

"Seriously, Ferru, how much wine do you drink in a day?" I asked. After some discussion we worked out that it was at least two litres a day.

"Mind you, Signor Colin," he added, "it's more than two litres a day when you come to dinner with us. You don't set a very good example."

I happened to have a calculator in my shirt pocket. I pulled it out and did some quick calculations.

"Ferru, do you realize that if you started drinking wine seriously at sixteen as you once told me you did, I've just worked out that in the thirty years or so since then, you've drunk almost twenty-two thousand litres of wine. That's more than a big petrol tanker truck full."

Ferruccio pushed his hat back off his forehead. "Really?" he replied. "Well, it's my fuel. And thank God I don't have to pay Government tax it on like you do on petrol!"

Everyone in the rural areas of central Italy has a nickname, and usually a very apt one. It is hardly surprising, therefore, that Ferruccio was known as "The Funnel".

Ferruccio's wife was called Giuliana. She was a large, saturnine woman with hunched shoulders that had earned her the local nickname of "The Mule". Despite her somewhat daunting appearance, she was, in fact, very kind. Nevertheless, in my early days of knowing her we had a disagreement about my working with the tractor on Sunday. After the deep ploughing of the land in June, I had to wait for the autumn rains before I could begin trying to level it and prepare it for planting vines in the following spring. By then my tractor and most of the implements had been delivered by Bruno Fabri, so at weekends I spent hours on the tractor, even after dark using its lights, as I tried to make some order out of the chaos. I pulled out large stumps with a chain and levelled the worst irregularities with a blade on the back of the tractor and with a cultivator. Weekends were the only time I had available, and I had not yet found a tractor driver. Anyway, I was happy to be using again the skills I had acquired as an instructor in farm machinery so many years before.

Then Giuliana said one day, "You shouldn't be working the tractor on Sunday afternoons". I expected her to continue and explain why, either because Sunday was a day of rest or that the noise of the tractor was a disturbance. But Giuliana was always Delphic and she refused to elaborate. Nevertheless, she went on insisting on her point despite my pressing her to explain.

She did not have an easy time with Ferruccio because, in contrast to his general bonhomie with others, he was an intractable male chauvinist with her and his two daughters. He invented many epithets to throw at Giuliana. They were usually abusive, profane, or both and for the most part they were only meant in jest. But that was not always the case. Quite frequently, after Giuliana had listened to him quietly while continuing about her business in the kitchen, she would grab the very long and sharp knife used for cutting ham and, holding it out in front of her, move towards him as if she were going to attack him with it. Ferruccio would then tip his hat back off his forehead, his face alight with the pleasure of having riled her. And he would catch my eye and start to laugh.

There was one phrase he used frequently to Giuliana that took me several years to fathom. After they had had some discussion, he would shout, in the local dialect, *"Che ti pozzi guastar . . . sciapa!!"* In loose translation, this means, "May you go rotten . . . you saltless thing!" In Italian, the word *sciapa* is used to describe food that lacks salt, but the same word is also used to describe someone who is stupid and dull-witted. I finally understood that Ferruccio was using the word in its double sense in his insult to Giuliana; he was calling her stupid, and also hoping she would go rotten like a ham that has not been cured with enough salt. It was an epithet grounded in the local peasant culture, for in those days, all small farmers in the area made *prosciutto* from their own pigs.

I never found out whether Giuliana's criticism of my working the tractor on Sunday afternoons was serious or just her sardonic humour at play. Whenever I asked her later she just smiled enigmatically. However, I doubt that she was being serious because no one in the family was particularly religious, and Ferruccio was always telling scurrilous tales about the various local priests. One of the funnier ones concerned a priest who was afraid to walk after dark along the road that passed by the cemetery. I heard the story many times, and it always ended with Ferruccio saying:

"What sort of a priest is it who's frightened of the dead? *Porca Madonna,* they're supposed to believe that spirits go to Heaven or Hell, not hang around in cemeteries." (*Porca Madonna* is generally considered to be among the most blasphemous of oaths and Ferruccio used it quite regularly.)

Another butt for his humour was a priest who, probably for no good reason, had acquired the reputation of being something of a Don Giovanni. He had therefore come by the nickname of *"Don Pistola"* (Don Pistol). This nickname was almost certainly invented by Ferruccio, but he only laughed whenever I asked him if he was responsible for it.

Of course, no one used this nickname to the priest's face, but Ferruccio recounted with delight that the priest had gone to visit a farmer in his home one afternoon and found the farmer's son up a plum tree in the front garden picking the fruit. When the priest asked the boy where his father was, the lad shouted loudly towards the house, "Papa! Papa! Come out here. Don Pistola wants to talk to you".

The story went on that while the priest was waiting for the farmer to appear, his son said, "Father, would you like some plums? We've got so many that even the pigs refuse to eat any more".

7

Squaring off

The layout for the vineyard was to be based on the accepted practice of the time in central Italy. The rows were to be three metres apart, which gives plenty of room for a normal tractor and implement to work between them. The traditional, older vineyards, and those further north in Europe, generally have much narrower rows. These require a special, narrow vineyard tractor or manual labour. Within the rows, according to custom in central Italy, the vines were usually 1.25 metres (four feet) apart, which gives a vine population of 2,650 per hectare. Yields of about twelve to fourteen tonnes of grapes to the hectare were usually aimed for in wine-producing areas in the hills, which implied 4.5–5 kilograms (ten to eleven pounds) of grapes per vine.

Such grape yields were far higher than those obtained for producing quality wines in other parts of Europe. And many grape-growers in Italy obtained yields that were very much higher – as many as thirty tonnes or even more to the hectare – by using different training systems. The reasoning went that much of Italy had near perfect climatic and soil conditions for wine-growing, far better endowed by Nature for wine production than areas such as Burgundy or the Loire Valley. It was, therefore, unnecessary to limit yields to the piffling four or five tonnes per hectare common in less favoured areas. Furthermore, in those years, the European Union was buying up excess wine and distilling it into alcohol for industrial use, and this certainly favoured high yields.

However, a crucial fact was being ignored: high grape yields do not produce high-quality wines. In the years after I planted my vineyard at Castel Sabino, Italian thinking about planting density and yields changed dramatically. Planting at least 4,000 vines per hectare, short winter pruning, and thinning of bunches in summer to keep yields in the four to eight tonnes per hectare range are now practised widely among quality producers. This has also been favoured by a fundamental change in wine-drinking habits in Italy where modern lifestyles, increased urbanization, and sedentary work have caused people to drink much less wine than in the past. However, they want the wine they do drink to be of good quality, and they are usually prepared to pay for that quality. Hence the vast improvement of Italian wines in the last two decades, and the much higher prices they now command.

The strategy of lower grape yields to obtain higher quality wine is increasingly applied in Italy, even in the most favourable conditions. At the 600-metre (2,000-feet) altitude of Castel Sabino, it would have been ideal to have a denser than usual planting and a policy of hard pruning to keep yields far lower than those projected by Pino Manzo. Unfortunately, however, my initiation into grape and wine production began too early to be able to take into account what is now becoming the accepted wisdom about density of planting and about grape yields as they relate to wine quality.

So, after discussions with Pino Manzo on the subject, we decided to follow the normal criteria of the time. But there was one change because I had bought a special vineyard plough. It ploughed three furrows, but the last plough body had a sensing rod in front of it. When this rod touched the base of a vine, it activated a small hydraulic piston, which moved that last body around the vine without damaging it, and then let it go back into the row. The aim was to leave only a very small area of soil unturned at the base of each vine while at the same time ploughing the rest of the space between the plants in the row.

Pino Manzo and I considered that this special plough would work best if it had more space between the plants in the row, so we decided to plant the vines in pairs 2.5 metres (eight feet) apart instead of the more usual single vines at 1.25 metres (four feet). One vine of the pair would be trained to the left and the other to the right.

Once we had decided on the general layout, we had to do the *squadro,* or squaring off of the land. We were going to plant an initial two hectares of Sangiovese in the central part of the property. This included the relatively flat area at the top of about 1.25 hectares and the slope below it of about 0.75 hectares.

I had no idea of how to do the *squadro,* but Pino Manzo told me over the telephone that he would help us and bring the required instrument. So we fixed a Saturday a couple of weeks ahead for the operation.

"Meanwhile," Pino said, "get Ferruccio to cut that large clump of bamboo you've got at the bottom of your land. Then have him chop the canes into lengths of about thirty or forty centimetres (twelve or sixteen inches). He should cut them diagonally so that they have a point. And he should also leave some full-length canes".

The appointed Saturday in early February was a day of *tramontana*, that northeasterly wind from central Europe that whisks away all haze and humidity, burnishes the cobalt sky, and puts a sheen of brilliance on all the colours in the landscape. By now, after many hours of work on the tractor, I had tidied up and levelled the first two hectares we were going to plant. The wind had dried the surface and it was a perfect day for working on the land.

Pino Manzo had brought two instruments with him for the *squadro*. The first was a device that looked like a simple theodolite (surveyor's instrument). When you looked through it you saw a vertical hairline in the lens. This optical part was set above a round, horizontal plate that was marked off in degrees. The idea was to start by placing this instrument in one corner of the area to be planted and to set up a baseline in one direction. This meant looking through the instrument and precisely aligning several tall bamboo canes pushed into the ground. Then, the optical part was turned through ninety degrees to set up another baseline of canes perpendicular to the first. The rest of the squaring off was simply a matter of stretching a cord along the baselines and then measuring off the three-metre (ten-feet) spacing of the rows along one baseline and the 2.5-metre (eight-feet) spacing between pairs of vines along the others. Each point had to be marked with one of the short bamboo canes driven into the soil.

On the face of it, the operation appeared to be relatively easy, but it turned into a pantomime, at least at the beginning. We were going to leave a track between the upper flat area and the lower sloping area of the land in order to reduce the length of the rows, and also to allow the tractor and people to traverse the vineyard. But even so the rows were going to be more than 150 metres (166 yards) long above the gap for the track. To add to the complications, that large flatter area had a hump in it that made it impossible to see from one end to the other.

Setting up the bamboo canes in the lines established by the instrument was easy enough: we merely planted the canes closer together near the hump so that we could line them up visually over the top of it. The fun began when we tried to lay out the very long length of cord to mark the line for measuring off the spaces, for the wind kept bellying it into a curve. When there was a lull in the wind and the cord appeared straight, we would lower it quickly to the ground, where inevitably some clod of soil would divert it to one side. And of course, because it was lying on the ground we could not follow its line by eye when it disappeared over the hump. Getting the cord straight for each row called for a lot of tramping around. We cursed the wind in Italian and English, but in the end we succeeded in getting part of the two hectares marked out. It bristled with the short pieces of bamboo that marked each place where a pair of vines would be planted. It was very satisfying to see that all of the bamboo canes lined up perfectly when looking along the lines or diagonally.

Ferruccio's father, Armando, as restrained as his son was outgoing, helped with the *squadro*. He was in his seventies, very tall for an Italian but bent with arthritis. He struggled up and down the field bringing bundles of bamboo canes and generally helping out. He was stick-thin with a bony face and pale-blue watery eyes, like those of an old hunting dog. His feet were so large that Ferruccio used to say his father bought his shoes by the metre rather than by size.

Armando had for many years been the president of the local association of small farmers affiliated to the Christian Democrat party. His nickname simply remained *Presidente* for the rest of his life, and his dignity and poise were worthy of that name. Everyone in the area sensed its fitness and called him by it.

Although he had had less formal schooling than his son – about three years in all – Armando nevertheless had clear and well-formed handwriting, and he also had a good knowledge of geography. He listened assiduously to the radio news every evening at seven, sitting with his ear close to his old valve-type receiver and studiously ignoring Ferruccio's fun-making about why papa didn't watch television like everybody else. But Armando didn't have much good to say about television, and I never did see him watching it. I was once on an FAO mission in El Salvador during its civil war. Shortly after some Americans had been assassinated in the street outside their hotel, I telephoned from San Salvador to speak to Ferruccio about progress in the vineyard, but Armando answered. He was very concerned that I was safe and well, for he had been following events on the radio. He had more idea of where El Salvador was and what was going on there than did Ferruccio.

We worked on the *squadro* for two more Saturdays after that first one when Pino Manzo had helped get us started. On the last day, Ferruccio and I were sticking the short bamboo canes into the ground when he suddenly stood up and looked towards his house. I also straightened to follow his gaze and saw a tiny, dumpy figure come shuffling unsteadily along the side of the house. The figure turned along its rear wall, which was facing us. It then disappeared into the door of the *cantina* where Ferruccio's family made and stored their wine. Ferruccio looked at his watch.

"I thought so," he said. "It's ten-thirty, and that's mamma going for her morning glass or two in the *cantina*. You can set your watch by her. Ten-thirty every morning and four-thirty every afternoon. Just watch her when she comes out: none of that shuffling. She'll stride out like a trooper." And sure enough, when she did emerge, wiping her mouth with the back of her hand, her tread was more vigorous and certain as she made her way back to the front of the house.

Mariolina, Ferruccio's mother, was in direct contrast to Armando, her somewhat austere husband. She was tiny, less than 1.5 metres (five feet) tall, and almost as broad. She was several years older than Armando, and she could neither read nor write. It was a mystery how she knew when it was ten-thirty and four-thirty for her visits to the *cantina*. She seemed to think that no one knew about these, although, of course, everybody did.

Mariolina suffered from diabetes, which was probably a factor in her obesity. Her doctor had put her on a diet and prohibited her from drinking wine. Armando was very strict with her, and it was mineral water only for her at meals. But he also knew about her twice-daily sallies to the *cantina*, even if he pretended not to.

Mariolina had passed on her round face and rotund form to Ferruccio. And she had also passed on her sense of humour. Most Wednesday evenings in the late spring and summer, I used to go from Rome to their house on my motorbike, have dinner with the family and discuss the work in the vineyard. After one of those occasions, and as I was leaving, Ferruccio said teasingly, "Why don't you take mamma for a ride on the motorbike?"

"Don't be silly, Ferru," I said, "Mariolina's feet wouldn't even reach the foot rests".

"Well in that case," Mariolina chipped in, "I'll start growing tomorrow and you can take me on the bike next month".

When the family first had a telephone installed, Mariolina had some trouble with it. It took her a long time to discover which end of the receiver was the earpiece and which the mouthpiece. I would hear her faintly as she was shouting into the earpiece: "*Pronti! Pronti!! Pronti!!* Ah, this thing's useless. I can't hear anything".

At the same time I was shouting even more loudly: "Mariolina, Mariolina! Turn the thing around. Listen in the other end".

In Italy the usual way of answering the telephone is to say *pronto,* which basically means "ready". Mariolina ultimately worked out which were the speaking and listening ends of the receiver, but she never gave up her quaint *pronti,* the plural version of the word *pronto.* No one ever found out why she insisted on the plural form, but she would never give it up, despite urgings from her family to use the normal *pronto.*

8

The Moon and Chestnut Poles

The layout for the trellising wires and the types of supporting poles to use in the vineyard took up many discussions with Pino Manzo. Many vineyards use concrete poles to support the wires, but Pino rightly pointed out that they were likely to break if knocked by the tractor or an implement. Furthermore, there were many chestnut forests in the area, and they were regularly coppiced for poles and beams. We therefore decided to use concrete poles at the head of the rows and chestnut poles for the intermediate ones.

Ferruccio knew where some coppicing was in progress down the valley below Castel Sabino, so one Saturday morning we set out in my car to go and negotiate for chestnut poles. It was a cold and windless day. The road followed the long, winding lake that filled the valley bottom. The hills and villages that surrounded the lake were reflected in its glass-like surface. It was a morning of such breathtaking beauty that it seemed almost a sacrilege to be going to negotiate for something as mundane as chestnut poles.

Even Ferruccio, not normally much impressed by the beauties of nature, seemed to be awed by the scenery as we drove along in silence. But then he suddenly said, "We have to make sure the poles have been cut with the waning moon".

I looked across at him sharply. I wondered whether he was teasing me, but his face was totally serious.

"What's the moon got to do with it?"

"It's simple. If they're not cut with the waning moon they'll be full of sap and they'll rot almost immediately."

During my technical training in agriculture had I never heard such a theory and it seemed totally ridiculous. I did not laugh, however, for Ferruccio seemed so serious that I didn't want to offend him.

"Well, I'll tell you what, Ferru," I said, "you can ask the woodcutters that question about the moon when we're negotiating for poles because I don't really believe it can make any difference. I've been looking at various textbooks about how to treat poles so that the part in the soil doesn't rot too quickly".

"What's in books is one thing," Ferruccio replied, "but practical experience is another".

We finally came across a truck loaded with poles parked on the roadside with several men, and even more mules, standing nearby. The broad hillside above was littered with chestnut poles. They were lying between the few chestnut saplings left standing at regular intervals to renew the forest before it would be coppiced again, after about twenty years.

Ferruccio and I had agreed that he would do the negotiating as if he were buying for himself. I was just a friend who had brought him there. We went over to the men and greeted them. As is common among rural people when business is to be done, nothing was said about why we were there, and no one asked. Ferruccio ambled over to the truck and pulled down a pole to examine it. It was about fifteen centimetres (six inches) in cross section at its thickest part and well over two metres (seven feet) long. He turned it slowly around to look at it from all sides, and then pulled down a second pole and did the same. The men watched him in silence.

Finally he put the poles back on the truck, and went back to the men. "How much?" he asked the man who appeared to be the leader of the woodcutters.

"750 lire." (At the time, that was about thirty-five UK pence.)

"That's too much!"

The man gave a take-it-or-leave-it shrug.

"And were they cut with the waning moon?" Ferruccio asked.

"Of course!" said the leader of the loggers, in an aggrieved tone of voice that implied that he was offended by the question.

I looked up at the very large expanse of hillside above us. It was obvious that the logging team must have been working the site for several months, and I wondered how one could ever know which trees had been cut with a waning moon by the time they brought them down from the hillside on mule back. And I could hardly imagine a commercial operation that would be halted while awaiting a change of moon phase.

A long silence followed while Ferruccio went back to the truck again and examined another pole. I began to get impatient. This could go on all day, and I felt rushed because weekends were the only time I had for tending to the development of the property.

"Listen," I said, "we'll need several thousand of those poles over the next two or three years, so let's go to the bar down the road, have a coffee or a drink, and discuss the matter seriously".

An hour later, we had agreed a price of 600 lire each, delivered to the property.

How we were going to protect the poles from rotting in the ground for as long as possible was a challenge. The books said that the best way was to stand the poles bottom end down in drums filled with a five per cent copper sulphate solution for several days. (Copper sulphate is, of course, that pretty blue and crystalline substance that is also used in swimming pools to stop algae from growing.) As the sap evaporates from the tops of the poles, they suck up copper sulphate solution from the bottom. However, for this to work properly, the poles have to be recently cut. Having just seen the pole-cutting operation with my own eyes, I could not imagine how it would be possible to insist that the poles had to be cut shortly before they were delivered.

The local practice was simply to drive chestnut poles into the ground without any protection and to change them when they rotted. This could be all right for a tiny vineyard with a small number of poles, but with several thousand poles involved, I had to take measures to make them last as long as possible. I decided in the end that the only practical solution would be to use the simple method of charring the end that was to go into the ground over an open fire and then coating it with tar. I found that in practice this protected them quite well for several years.

On our way back in the car, I told Ferruccio that I did not believe anything about the moon phase, or that the woodcutters paid any attention to it either, but he continued to insist that it was of the greatest importance and that certainly the woodcutters took it into account in their operations. I began to laugh and Ferruccio did too, and so we reached a tacit understanding that we would agree to differ on the subject. This did not stop us teasing each other about it over the years: he poked fun at what he considered my reliance on book learning, while I teased him for believing in old wives' tales.

I later discovered that he and other people in the area also took into account the phases of the moon in a wide range of farm activities, including winemaking. For example, it was important when racking wine from one barrel to another. If the timing was wrong, the wine would turn to vinegar, they said. Later, when I had built a modern winery with stainless steel tanks and the like, I happened to find an old chart showing what the moon phases should be for various winery operations. With my tongue firmly in my cheek, I framed it and hung it on the wall for customers to look at. Since many of them were local people, I hoped that it would help them to think that the modern equipment all around them was mitigated by some traditional approaches to winemaking.

However, the last laugh was on me. Several years after Ferruccio and I had first discussed the moon phases and the cutting of chestnut poles, and after I had repeatedly told him I believed nothing about the effects of the moon phases in farming or winemaking, I came across an article in an agricultural magazine that described some experiments carried out in Australia. The seeds of a certain type of plant had been sown at different moon phases, but with all other conditions such as soil, temperature, moisture, and light controlled to be the same. The researchers were surprised to find that the phase of the moon at the time of sowing affected the plants tendency to bolt, or run to seed. When I told Ferruccio about this research he pushed his hat back from his forehead and chortled with delight.

Working and being with Ferrucio was always fun. His humour was boundless and varied. One would never have imagined, if one had not known him so well in his family context, that he could be so chauvinistic and domineering, especially towards his daughters. The younger one in particular, Francesca, had problems with him. She was an independently minded child and had frequent shouting matches with him. They were so loud that their voices carried easily over the 300 metres (1,094 yards) or so between our houses. Francesca did well at school and followed it with a hotel and tourism training course. She wanted to become an air hostess. She had grown into a bright and attractive girl with the physical attributes and height required for that job, for she had inherited her grandfather Armando's tall, slim build.

All Francesca needed to fulfil her ambition was to learn English beyond her basic schooling in the language. She asked for my help and I made contacts for her to go to England to become an au pair. But, even though she was almost eighteen, her father was adamant in his refusal to let her leave home.

Her older sister, Maria Lisa, was small, taking after her grandmother Mariolina. She was a sweet-natured and calmer child than Francesca, and I also watched her grow into an attractive young woman. When she was about nineteen, she fell in love with her first cousin, Lamberto. He was a radar technician working at a military airbase in northern Italy, but he seemed to spend most of his time travelling to and from Castel Sabino by train and bus to spend long weekends at home.

Lamberto always seemed tired, which he probably was from his long nights spent sitting up on trains. But even so, there was a general listlessness about him. He would often lean languidly against a wall or doorframe rather than stand upright, and he had a slow, deliberate way of speaking. This and his work with electronics caused Ferruccio, with his comic creativity, to distort his name of Lamberto to the nickname of *Lampo,* which means a flash of lightening.

I once asked Ferruccio about the budding relationship between Maria Lisa and her first cousin. I was wondering what his feelings were about her marrying someone so closely related.

"Ah, that'll come to nothing," he said. "Lampo would need an electric wire up his arse to make him hump!"

But the joke was on Ferruccio, for a few months later Maria Lisa became pregnant. She and Lamberto duly got married and had three children.

9

Planting at Last

I was eagerly awaiting the arrival of the first 5,500 grafted vines from the nursery near Pisa that Pino Manzo had recommended. The area of two hectares that we had marked out with bamboo canes during the *squadro* was ready and we wanted to plant in mid-March. This would be good timing because, depending on the temperatures, the bud-burst on vines in the area was usually about four or five weeks after that, in the last ten days or so of April.

The vines were delivered on a weekday, and when I got to the property at the weekend, Ferruccio had followed Pino Manzo's instructions and placed them in a shallow trench with their roots covered in soil. They were packed in bunches of twenty-five, and each bunch carried a yellow label which identified them as Sangiovese grafted onto 420 A rootstock. This rootstock is a classic workhorse in viticulture. It was first developed in France in the 1880s and is selected from a cross between two American vines known as *Vitis berlandieri* and *riparia*. It withstands alkaline soils quite well, and Pino Manzo considered that it would be a good option for the conditions at Castel Sabino.

I had never seen grafted vines for planting before and was surprised by how unimpressive they looked; simple sticks about thirty centimetres long with a few whiskers of roots at one end. A closer examination showed where the *Vitis vinifera* upper part had been grafted to the rootstock, but they hardly looked capable of ever creating the lush green curtains of vines along each row, and the dense clusters of grapes, that were in my mind's eye.

Pino Manzo had suggested that we plant the vines in holes created by forcing a steel tubular implement into the soil. We had to have a couple of these tools made, but there was no blacksmith in Castel Sabino, so Ferruccio and I set off to see the one in Monte Nativo, the next village. As is typical of village rivalries, the people of Castel Sabino always said that the people from Monte Nativo were stupid and told a whole series of jokes about them. Ferrucio regaled me with some of these as we drove along. Many of the stories seemed to go back to the Middle Ages and were too silly even to be very funny, like the one of the people of Monte Nativo who were short of water on their hilltop. So they organized an expedition with ropes to go down to the valley and pull the river uphill to the village.

But in fact the blacksmith was not too bright. It took us a lot of time and effort to explain that we wanted two pieces of steel tube ten centimetres (four inches) in diameter and 1.5 metres (five feet) long, worked to a blunt point at one end. They should have a crosspiece of angle iron welded to the tube thirty centimetres (twelve inches) from the bottom so that the tube could be pushed into the soil by pressing one's foot on the crosspiece. He finally got the point, but when I tried to find out from him when the tools would be ready, he was vague in his response. I thought that I could perhaps telephone him to check on progress, but of course this was Italy long before everyone, and their dogs, had mobile phones.

"Have you got a telephone?" I asked.

"Yes," he replied, "but my daughter's got it, and she lives in Rieti".

Ferruccio was delighted by this daft response. It seemed to vindicate everything that the people of Castel Sabino said about the people of Monte Nativo. On the way home he told me more stories about the stupidity of the neighbouring villagers. And for years he would recount the story about the blacksmith in Monte Nativo whose telephone was kept by his daughter in Rieti, some twenty kilometres (twelve miles) away.

We began planting about ten days later, in fact as soon as the blacksmith had finished the tubes. Planting the two hectares took a little less than a week. Pino Manzo had told us to clip the whispy roots of the vines back to a length of about two centimetres (three-quarters of an inch), so each vine was even less prepossessing than it had been before. We drove the tubes into the ground and slipped the vines into the holes we had made. Then we pressed the soil around the vines with our feet and hands and scraped together soil from the surrounding surface to create a small protective mound over them. We stuck the short bamboo cane that had marked the planting place into the top of each mound that covered a pair of vines. A few weeks later, when the weather was warmer, we carefully removed the mounds of soil and exposed the few tiny and tender leaves of each vine to the air and light. After that they grew at a remarkable rate, and their thin canes in that first year of 1976 were almost fifty centimetres (twenty inches) in length.

Pino Manzo and I began to discuss the other varieties that we would plant. I was, and still am, very fond of the robust red wines of the Abruzzo region, on the other side of the high mountains to the east of Castel Sabino and stretching down to the Adriatic coast. The best ones are mellow, low in acidity, and with a strong fruit flavour. They are made from a grape known as Montepulciano d'Abruzzo. This is very confusing for foreigners trying to understand something about Italian viticulture and wines, for it has nothing to do with the town of Montepulciano in Tuscany, which is home to the famous Vino Nobile, as mentioned earlier. It was once thought that the Montepulciano d'Abruzzo grape was a Sangiovese clone that had been taken to the Abruzzo region, where it transmuted over time, but quite recent scientific tests show that it is not related to Sangiovese. It therefore seems to be native to the Abruzzo.

Whatever its origin, it was approved for the province of Rieti, and I thought that it might do well at Castel Sabino, blending satisfactorily with the Sangiovese. Pino Manzo agreed, so we planned to plant a hectare and a half of Montepulciano d'Abruzzo the following spring. Again there were lengthy discussions about the American rootstock to graft it on. In consultation with the nursery near Pisa, we decided on a rootstock known as 140 Ruggeri. This was first developed in Sicily in 1897 and is a cross between the wild *berlandieri* and *rupestris* vines. It is particularly resistant to high lime content in the soil and to dry conditions, but at the same time it provides a lot of vigour to the *Vitis vinifera* variety grafted onto it.

The canes of the two hectares of Sangiovese we had planted grew without supports in their first summer, forming low clumps of green. When autumn came we began installing the poles and wires the vines would need to be trained on as they grew in their second year. I managed to borrow a post-hole borer, a device like an enormous corkscrew that fits on the back of the tractor and is driven by the tractor's power take-off shaft. As it turns, the corkscrew – more correctly called an auger – digs itself in and brings the displaced soil to the surface.

The problem with the particular post-hole borer I borrowed was that the augur narrowed towards its point. It had evidently been designed for posts with a pointed end, whereas we wanted to use it for the square-ended concrete head poles. As a result, someone had to kneel on the ground and slightly widen the bottom of each hole by hand.

Armando, the *Presidente*, was helping with this one day, gamely lowering his creaky old frame onto its knees, and then stretching one very large and gnarled hand, fingers spread, into the hole and bringing out great dollops of moist soil. He widened the bottom of each hole in a matter of seconds. It was quite a feat to watch; a lifetime of toil on the land had made Armando as tough as old goats' knees.

"Presidente," I said after I had watched him widen the bottom of a couple of holes, "you've got hands like an excavator!" He looked up and grinned at me toothlessly.

"Yes," he said. "Moving papers around a desk doesn't harden the hands too much, does it?" I laughed, looking down at my own hands made soft by office work. Armando cackled gently, more with me than at me.

The chestnut poles we had bought to use along the rows were driven in with a huge wooden mallet that Ferruccio had fashioned. Its head was a section cut from the trunk of an oak tree, and its handle was a branch still attached to it. The people around Castel Sabino were enormously resourceful in making things they needed for their work, and also in finding ways of doing things. Their devices often appeared crude, but they functioned well. To drive the chestnut poles into the ground, Ferruccio and his helpers drove the tractor with a trailer between the rows and used the trailer as a platform to get the height they needed to wield the mallet.

10

Travails with Frost and Tractor Drivers

It was late April, just over a year after the first vines had been planted, when Pino Manzo came up one Saturday morning to see how things were going. It had rained in the earlier part of the week, and then the weather had turned clear and sunny. We knew that the new vines should just be putting out their first tender leaves from the short canes that had been left by the winter pruning. We set out into the vineyard to have a look at them, but all we found was desolation: the vines had indeed grown their first small leaves, but they had all turned to a grey powdery substance. I did not immediately realize what had happened, but then Pino Manzo said:

"There must have been a frost in the last couple of days. They could be quite common here".

I was thunderstruck. I was already concerned about the altitude and its effect on ripening, and now I had the possibility of late frosts to contend with too. Pino Manzo explained that the frost damage in those new vines was not the end of the world, because they would shoot again from secondary buds under the main buds. They would lose some vigour in this, their second, year, but the real frost problem could be in the future, when the vineyard was in production. The first buds were those that bore fruit, and should the early shoots from those buds be killed by frost, there would be almost no grapes that year: for the secondary buds produced a lot of vegetation but almost no grapes.

We were standing in the vineyard talking about this when Ferruccio and Armando, who were walking down the road, saw us and wandered over. They had not noticed the frost damage until then, and they at once showed their concern.

"*Presidente*," I asked Armando, "you've been around a long time. How often do you have late frosts here?"

"Not so often," he replied, "but sometimes they're much later than this. I remember 1959. The vine shoots were already about twenty centimetres (eight inches) long. There was a frost that killed them all completely. It was the ninth of May. There were almost no grapes that year. We drank water". He chuckled merrily, but my sense of humour failed me miserably. Armando's precise memory for years and dates never failed to impress me, but on that occasion I felt I would rather not know that there was a precedent for a frost on May 9.

The fact started me off on a quest for information about preventing – or at least reducing – the damage that could be done to the delicate young shoots by a late frost. I found out that fruit growers in Florida turned on their sprinkler irrigation systems when there was a serious frost risk. The water would freeze to ice on the trees, which would protect the buds and shoots from being exposed to temperatures below freezing point. But that was no good for my situation because I would never have an irrigation system in the vineyard.

According to the literature, the cold, still air that brings frosts in spring lies over the ground in a layer seldom more than a few metres thick. If one can punch holes in that layer with hot air, a circulation will be set up that will mix the cold air with warmer air above and raise the temperature near the ground. This could be achieved by lighting bonfires or containers of diesel oil or paraffin and old tyres distributed around a vineyard.

So in later years, once the vineyard was in production, we used the tractor to rake the large masses of the winter prunings into strategically placed piles. And after the vines had started to shoot, we added some oil drums filled with diesel oil and bits of tyres. We concentrated most of them in the lowest part of the vineyard on the assumption that it was there that the coldest air would gather. If the heat we generated could punch a hole in it, perhaps we would start a movement in the mass of air higher up the slope.

Despite these precautions, the period between the vines beginning to shoot and the historical day of May 9 always remained tense. We had to make the right decision; if we got it wrong, the crop could be lost. For example, we might decide to light the bonfires when the temperature of the air at the height of the buds reached, say, one degree above freezing. But then it might not actually freeze. If that were to happen, we would have used up our best shot, and we would not have anything in reserve should it freeze the next night.

Of course, frost did not threaten every year, but there was one late April afternoon a few years later – it must have been about 1984 – when, after several days of rain, the sky suddenly cleared and the temperature began to plummet. The vines already had shoots about five centimetres (two inches) long and there seemed to be a major frost risk in the making. I was worried sick, but then I suddenly had the idea of trying to get a weather forecast from professionals. I had piloted small aircraft for several years before becoming involved in viticulture and had often telephoned the meteorological office of the Italian air force at Ciampino airport to find out about actual and probable weather conditions for a flight.

So I called the meteorological office at Ciampino airport that threatening afternoon. I explained that I had piloted light aircraft and often used their services but that now I had a different need. I had a vineyard at 600 metres (2,000 feet) altitude in the Sabine Hills; the vines had already begun to shoot, and I was very worried about a frost that night.

"Would you be able to tell me at what altitude you expect the zero degree isotherm to be tonight?" I asked.

The meteorologist at the other end of the line immediately identified with my concern. He asked me some questions about the size of the vineyard and the grape varieties I had and, in fact, his kindly interest was much greater than when I had asked other people in that office for *en-route* flying conditions in the past. He told me to hold the line while he went to check the zero degree isotherms expected for the coming night. I wondered, while I waited, whether he was perhaps of peasant stock and therefore identified with farming problems. There has been much upward social mobility in Italy in recent decades.

"We expect it to freeze down to about 600 metres in the early part of the night," he said when he came back on the line, "but it'll get warmer later in the night. You might just be all right, but I can't guarantee it. Anyway, good luck. Call us whenever you need information. Vineyards are important!"

I went out to the vineyard and hung a thermometer on the lowest wire, the one supporting the previous year's canes on which the young shoots were growing. Thereafter, I went to check the temperature every thirty minutes. It gradually dropped from the four degrees above freezing of the late afternoon when I had called the met office to three, and then to two degrees above freezing by midnight. Thirty minutes later it was only one degree above freezing. By one in the morning, it was only half a degree above. I telephoned Ferruccio to tell him we might have to light our bonfires in the next half hour or so. Surprisingly, he was quite good tempered about being roused in the middle of the night. He said he would get dressed.

After a further twenty minutes I went to check again and I noticed that some cloud had begun to drift across the previously clear night sky. The temperature in the vineyard was still half a degree above freezing. Twenty minutes after that, the cloud cover had spread further, and the temperature had gone up by more than a degree. I called Ferruccio and told him to go back to bed. He sounded quite disappointed about not lighting up the landscape with bonfires. By two-thirty in the morning the sky had almost completely clouded over, the temperature was more than three degrees above freezing, and it was still rising. The crisis had passed and I, too, went to bed.

In subsequent years, I called the met office on two or three occasions, and they were invariably helpful and kind. In fact, we only once had to light the bonfires when a frost occurred, and they seemed to solve the problem. But in the years we did not light them, we had a ceremonial bonfire night on or shortly after May 10. It was quite a sight, with columns of flame leaping up from the many points in the vineyard where we had heaped the prunings and put out drums with diesel oil and bits of tyre in them. No doubt the Greens would have complained about the air pollution we created, but in those remote Sabine Hills no one took any notice. We would stand outside Ferruccio's house, under a spreading oak tree with glass in hand, watching the show and celebrating that another spring had passed without a late frost.

Ferruccio had never learned to drive a motor vehicle, and his mode of farm transport was a device known locally as a *traglia*, in effect a giant sledge. He had built this wooden contraption himself and he harnessed it to the pair of magnificent white bullocks he always kept. They dragged it slowly around, making a horrendous noise as the steel strip that covered the runners of the sledge screeched over the stony ground. His plough, too, was little more than a tree trunk with a short plank set at an angle to it to serve as a mouldboard. It was identical to the ploughs used by ancient Romans. Thus, his farm equipment was little better than I had so often seen in developing countries. It was low investment, low technology farming. Like people in much poorer countries, Ferruccio and his family had only a few hectares of land and little or no access to capital or credit. Self-sufficiency was the guiding principle. In fact clothes, coffee, and sugar were about all the family ever bought; the rest they produced for themselves.

Since Ferruccio could not drive, I had to find a tractor driver. My weekends would not be time enough to deal with all the needs, especially the frequent spraying of the vines against fungal attacks. These protective sprayings had to be done within a certain time lapse after rain, and this time lapse depended also on the temperature. It was therefore impossible to limit tractor work to weekends only.

My first tractor driver was Felice Targa, the youngest of three brothers who farmed with their parents a few kilometres away. Felice spoke slowly, was short and fair with a rolling walk, and he handled a tractor with great skill. He worked with me happily for almost two years. Then, one winter's day, I arrived back from a short trip abroad and went straight to Ferruccio's house to see him. Ferruccio's normally cheery expression was sombre as he told me that Felice had had an accident. I immediately imagined the worst scenario with my tractor, but in fact he had been grinding grain with a hammer mill for the livestock on the family farm when the accident happened. Whilst sweeping the few remaining kernels down the hopper he had put his right hand into the mill and he lost the tips of all four fingers down to the first joint.

I rushed to Felice's home to see him and found him in a very bad way. He was evidently still in shock, and he was deeply concerned about his future as a man who worked with his hands and had mutilated one of them. He ultimately recovered well and, being partially disabled, had preference in the selection process for a job with the road authority. There he flourished, did very little work, and put on a lot of weight. Thinking much about Felice's accident afterwards, it seemed clear that the large quantities of wine drunk by the locals dulled their sense of judgment, especially in matters of safety. Indeed, Felice and his brothers often joked that they only drank twice a day: "With meals . . . and between meals".

My second tractor driver, Michele, was Ferruccio's nephew, and he also came near to a disastrous accident. He never bothered to put the safety guard on the power take-off shaft of the tractor with the result that it was spinning in the open when an implement was being driven by that shaft. One day he stopped the tractor with the sprayer attached to it and left the engine running. Then, instead of walking around the front of the tractor or the back of the sprayer, he stepped over the revolving shaft. The cuff of his jeans caught in part of it and they were ripped off up to his thigh. Had the jeans been newer and stronger, he could easily have lost his leg, or even his life, as the jeans wrapped ever more tightly around the spinning shaft.

Ferruccio was not far away when it happened. He told me that he had heard his nephew shout and seen him beckoning wildly for him to come over to the tractor. Ferruccio was amused to see the youth stripped half naked by the incident and told the story with some glee. But it so happened that not long before, as part of my work with FAO, I had been searching for photographs of tractor accidents to use in an educational presentation I was producing on the safe use of farm machinery. There was one gruesome picture of a man who had been terribly mangled, and killed, after the sleeve of his tweed jacket had caught in a power take-off shaft. The following weekend I borrowed the photograph from the office and showed it to Ferruccio. He went quite pale under his tan. He reached for his wine glass, drained it, and banged it back down on the table.

"*Porca Madonna!*" he shouted. "That careless cretin, Michele! Just wait till I tell him."

In Michele's case it was not alcohol that made him careless, for he drank very little: unlike his father who was one of the village drunks. He was squat, red-faced, and very overweight. He had been nicknamed *Il Rospo* (The Toad). In the past, people in the village had egged him on to drink. If they found him in one of the bars, they would bet him that he could not empty a 1.5-litre flask of wine without stopping. He was able to do so but, by the time I knew him, he had calmed down somewhat, on doctor's orders.

Even so, The Toad still got carried away occasionally. One wet, windy, and cold winter's night, Ferruccio was making his way home, walking along the edge of my vineyard rather than along the road. As he drew level with the cemetery he heard a terrible moaning sound. Even he was startled. He began to wonder whether the priest had a point about not walking this way at night, but he pulled himself together and went to investigate. He found The Toad lying in a deep puddle, groaning as if an agony and about to die. In fact, he probably would have, of exposure, if Ferruccio had not managed to drag him to his feet and half carry him to the warmth of his home. When I asked The Toad about this event, he scratched his head in bewilderment.

"Yes, I did drink quite a lot of wine down at the bar, maybe fourteen glasses, and I was perfectly fine. It was the fifteenth that did all the damage."

11

More Grape Varieties

We decided to plant the Montepulciano d'Abruzzo vines close to the cemetery and running parallel to the road running up to Ferruccio's home. The area was about a hectare and a half. I ordered the vines, grafted onto 140 Ruggeri rootstock, from the same nursery near Pisa that had supplied the Sangiovese the previous year. But Pino Manzo and I were still curious to find out more about the grape variety that the locals seemed to think was native to the area and which they said used to do well there, "A sort of Cesanese," as they had described it, "with a red stalk". I decided to do more research into Cesanese to see whether it could be an option for me.

I soon found out that Cesanese is, in fact, a prestigious red grape variety in the region of Lazio. Its main home is in a hilly area about forty kilometres (twenty-five miles) to the southeast of Rome, close to the Rome–Naples *autostrada* and the spa town of Fiuggi. In a direct line, flying over some high mountain terrain, it was only about sixty kilometres (thirty-seven miles) from Castel Sabino. The reference books listed two types of Cesanese grape: Common Cesanese and Cesanese di Affile. None of the descriptions described either of these as having the red stalk mentioned by people around Castel Sabino. However, both types were listed among the recommended varieties for the province of Rieti.

I went through various books on Italian wines and found that Cesanese, especially Cesanese di Affile, was highly regarded. The books also mentioned that there were three Cesanese production areas with the status of *Denominazione di Origine Controllata,* or DOC, the equivalent of the French *appellation contrôlée.* These three DOC areas were around the villages of Piglio, Olevano Romano, and Affile. Wine produced from Cesanese was considered a top red of Lazio, although the region is probably better known for its white wines from places such as Frascati and Marino.

Poring over a map, I found that the village of Affile is at an altitude of 684 metres (2,244 feet), and Piglio at 620 metres (2,034 feet), both higher than my property, but Olevano Romano was lower at 571 metres (1,873 feet). The altitudes of Piglio and Affile delighted and intrigued me. Perhaps my doubts about the altitude at Castel Sabino were unfounded after all.

I telephoned Pino Manzo to tell him about my findings. He, of course, knew of the Cesanese grape variety, but he did not know much about the wines made from it or about the main areas where it was grown.

"We must go to Affile and Piglio as soon as possible and have a look around," Pino said enthusiastically after I had finished telling him what I had found out. So the following Saturday morning, I collected him from his home and we set off to discover, at first hand, everything we could about the two types of Cesanese and the wines they produced in that area near Fiuggi.

We drove down the Rome–Naples *autostrada* to Anagni where we left it to wind up into the hills towards Piglio. We passed through a sunlit landscape, a riotous blend of olive groves, small vineyards, and vegetable plots. It was early October, and vintage time was approaching. Many people were washing wooden barrels outside their houses. They were also standing them on end and filling them with water to swell their staves and seal the gaps that had opened when they had been allowed to dry out.

"Terrible barrels some of these people use," commented Pino Manzo as we drove past one that was even blacker and more decrepit-looking than the others we had seen. It was standing by the roadside, spurting water from many places between its staves, while a hose leading from the house and inserted into its bunghole was trying to keep pace with the water streaming out of it.

"Bad and dirty barrels can cause a lot of trouble," Pino continued. "They need a lot of care and attention. If they don't get it, they go mouldy and give the wine a disgusting taste. Small farmers seldom take their barrels seriously enough." I was able to confirm this through my own experience of drinking local wines round Castel Sabino.

One of the first things we saw as we came into the outskirts of the village of Piglio was a large building with the words *Cantina Sociale* on its façade. The cooperative winery was obviously a good place to begin our enquiries. I explained to a young man, who turned out to be the oenologist, why we were interested in knowing about Cesanese and the wines of the area, and he became instantly helpful. He told us that the wine they produced came in two styles, a slightly sweet version and a dry one.

Pino and I were not interested in the sweet version, so the oenologist drew some of the dry version for us to taste from one of the many tanks in the area behind the office and sales part of the building. It was robust and smooth at the same time, filling the mouth with fruit, but it could hardly be called a fine wine. It was pleasant but not remarkable. I later learned that wines only develop bouquet and finesse in bottle when a spontaneous process, over time, causes some of the alcohol in the wine to combine with some of its acids to produce esters, the compounds that provide the perfume.

My earlier research had told us that the wines from Affile had a better name than those from Piglio, so after a long chat with the oenologist about the time of harvest, typical sugar content of the must, and so on, we set out again.

The village of Affile sat atop a steep-sided hill, while its agricultural land lay below it in a flatter area. Even if it was below the village, however, that area must still have been higher than my property. I looked up at the village, which I remembered was at 684 metres (2,244 feet), and guessed that the flatter land could not be more than fifty metres (164 feet) lower. If they could produce fully ripe grapes here, then surely I would be able to at Castel Sabino.

We drove through a stone archway and up into the village centre. There was a bar on the square with a few chairs and tables outside it.

"Come on, Pino, it's *cappuccino* time," I said. "We can also ask in the bar who grows Cesane di Affile and makes good wine."

We ordered our *cappuccini* from a vacuous-looking young blond whose dark eyebrows betrayed the original colour of her hair.

"Tell me," I asked, "do you know of anyone here who has a vineyard of Cesanese di Affile and makes good wine?"

She shook her head and shrugged, totally disinterested, but there were two elderly men sitting at a table in the bar playing cards. As always happens when strangers appear in such a village, they were observing us carefully, and of course listening to what we said.

In the absence of a response from the blond, one of the men said, "We used to produce a lot of good wine here, but everyone has left to work in factories in the valley or in Rome. Most of the vines have been abandoned".

The other man chipped in with an aside to his companion and they talked in low voices for some time. I heard the word *l'Anticolano* several times, but most of what they said was a mumble in local dialect.

Then the first man piped up in proper Italian.

"Franco Morricone is about the only person who looks after his vineyard and makes good wine. He's about the last one around here who still does."

We asked them how to find him and they told us where he lived.

"Just ask for *l'Anticolano* if you get lost," one of them said as we left.

Back in the car, I asked Pino Manzo what had they had meant by *l'Anticolano*.

"It's probably his nickname," Pino replied. "I don't know what it means but it is probably something to do with *antico* (old). So maybe he's an old-fashioned type of person."

In fact, Pino was wrong. Morricone told us later that the nickname was because his grandparents had come to Affile from another village called Anticoli, and the nickname had passed from father to son to grandson. But even if his nickname had nothing to do with *antico,* he was indeed an old-fashioned wine-grower. He was in his late sixties, with thinning silver hair above an open, friendly face. It was deeply tanned and had laughter crinkles around his eyes. He smiled happily when we told him why we had looked him out.

"Yes," he said, "I've got about a hectare and a half of Cesanese di Affile and I'll be pleased to take you to it. But before that, come into my *cantina* and taste some of my wine".

The winery was rather dark and the equipment quite basic. While Pino Manzo and I waited near the entrance Morricone rummaged around in an even darker recess and emerged with a bottle in his hands. It was very dusty and had no label.

"This is five years old," he said as he carefully drew the cork. "It is made with only Cesanese di Affile."

Despite the rather primitive *cantina,* the wine he poured us was excellent. It had a deep ruby colour, and a strong and penetrating bouquet. On the palate it was full and chewy, but also soft, and with a persistent aftertaste. It also had that warmth that comes from a good alcohol level. It was certainly the best red wine made in Lazio that I had tasted so far. I was impressed.

"That's really good!" I said. Franco Morricone laughed with pleasure.

"Our Cesanese produces good wine. Did you know that wines from Affile won gold medals in wine fairs in Paris in the 1930s? It is a pity that no one here seems to want to keep the tradition alive. We had our DOC approved by the Government in 1973. There were still a few of us producing grapes and wine then, but the youngsters have all gone off to work in Rome. I'm one of the very few people left working the vines."

Franco Morricone's vineyard was beautifully tended, trim, neat and without a weed in sight. The berries in the grape clusters were tightly packed, and they were also small. At the time, I did not know the significance of this, for it was only several years later that I learned that almost all of the world's grapes for quality red wine look like that. This is because the small berries have a higher proportion of skin to juice than do varieties with fewer and larger berries, and it is the skin that provides the colour and many of the elements that give a good red wine most of its particular characteristics.

Pino asked Franco Morricone whether there were any special problems with Cesanese di Affile, such as susceptibility to particular fungus attacks. Morricone assured us there were none or, more precisely, that it was no worse than any other variety he knew. He told us that it ripened better at this altitude than the Common Cesanese, mainly grown near Piglio. But even more important was that it produced better wine.

I asked Morricone what the sugar level in his grapes usually was at harvest time.

"It's well over twenty per cent in most years. That wine you just tasted has more than thirteen per cent alcohol and I have almost never had it less than twelve. Only in very bad years, and even then it was 11.5."

An alcohol level of 11.5 per cent in a bad year was still quite acceptable. I told Morricone about my concerns regarding the altitude of 600 metres (2,000 feet) at Castel Sabino and what people had said about it being too high.

"They're wrong," he said. "If your vineyard is well exposed, and you limit the grape yields as I do, you'll have no trouble at all."

I was delighted, for this was an opinion based on the experience of a practising wine-grower close to Castel Sabino and even a little higher. It was already clear that I must plant a good area of Cesanese di Affile. Not only was it a recommended variety for the province, but it also seemed to be a variety that could give quality wines. Even if my main aim at that time was to sell grapes to local people, I must have known subconsciously that one day I would begin producing wine myself, and hence the grape quality was of special importance.

We wandered up and down several rows of Franco Morricone's Cesanese di Affile and plucked and tasted the occasional berry. They were already very sweet even though Morricone said his vintage was still about two weeks away. I was deep in thought about where I was going to find grafted vines of that variety. What nursery would have them, and grafted on to a suitable rootstock? But then Pino Manzo stepped in.

"Tell me," he asked Morricone, "would you be willing to set aside some of your prunings this winter for us so that we can have them grafted for planting in the spring? We would need pieces of cane about a metre long and they should be medium in diameter – not the thickest ones and not the thinnest".

"Of course," replied Morricone. "It'd be a pleasure. It would be nice to think of my vines creating new vines at Castel Sabino. I don't know who will look after these when I die, so they'll probably disappear."

On that rather sad note, we went back to his *cantina* and savoured some more of his wine while we discussed the logistics of the operation. Pino Manzo said it would be best for me to collect the prunings and take them to his Institute. Once there, he would put them in the Institute's cold room and, as spring approached, send them to the nursery in Pisa for grafting. And that is what happened. The cuttings from Franco Morricone's canes were grafted onto the same 140 Ruggeri rootstock that we had chosen for the Montepulciano d'Abruzzo. We planted just over half a hectare of my land with Cesanese di Affile. Over the coming years I was to regret not planting much more. For just as in its native village of Affile, it did excellently at Castel Sabino, even if it was not the grape with the red stalk that the locals talked about.

It is sad that outstanding local grape varieties such as Cesanese di Affile have tended to die out in recent years, but growers have been bowing to market trends that seem increasingly to recognize only the great international names such as Cabernet Sauvignon, Merlot, Chardonnay, and the like. The way things are going, this globalization of taste risks standardizing wines from all over the world, with only the factors of soil, climate, and the winemaker's art to create differences between them. It would be sad to lose some of those local varieties, for even if they are less famous, they can produce outstanding wines that are delightfully different. Fortunately, in very recent years a few traditional Italian varieties have been making a strong comeback, though Cesanese is not among them for the moment.

Most of my initial thinking about grape varieties to plant was centred on red grapes, mainly because most of the grapes grown around Castel Sabino were red, but perhaps too because I am more interested in red wines. But the time soon came to discuss which white varieties to plant on the one and a half hectares or so of the land that would remain after we had finished planting the Sangiovese, Montepulciano d'Abruzzo, and Cesanese di Affile.

Pino Manzo suggested that we plant Trebbiano. This is a very widely grown white variety in Italy and in many other parts of the world. In France it is known as Ugni Blanc. Pino said that it was a very high-yielding variety that ripened at about the same time as the red varieties we had selected. So I duly ordered the vines, again grafted onto 140 Ruggeri rootstock. This turned out to be the only piece of questionable advice Pino gave me over the years. He was right about the high yields of Trebbiano, but the wine made with it is totally lacking in distinction, at least as far as my experience of making it and drinking it is concerned.

When Ferruccio and I did the *squadro* for the area we planned to plant with Trebbiano and counted the places where vines would go, I discovered that I had not ordered enough of them. There would be a small area of the property, about a quarter of a hectare, left over. I am naturally rather law-abiding, so I am not sure how it happened, but I decided to flout the Italian regulations and plant Pinot Bianco in that small area. This, of course, is one of the world's great white varieties, of Burgundian and Alsatian fame as Pinot Blanc, but it was not recommended or authorized for the province of Rieti. I took the decision partly because the nursery near Pisa had Pinot Bianco vines available and partly because the area was at the bottom of the slope and not as well exposed as the rest of the vineyard. I wanted to see how an early ripening variety would do. In addition, I happen to like the dry, crisp wines that can be made from Pinot Bianco.

The soil in the patch we were to plant with Pinot Bianco was very clayey. This caused Ferruccio and me a major problem when he and I alone did the *squadro*. It had rained heavily, but we needed to do the *squadro* that weekend because spring was near and vines had to be planted very soon. The piece of land was extremely steep and we had to walk up and down it continuously to lay out the lines and plant the pieces of bamboo to mark where the vines would go. Within minutes of starting to walk up and down, our rubber boots grew the most enormous accumulations of sticky clay. The load on each boot weighed so much that it became very difficult to walk. We would scrape it off with a shovel at the edge of the plot, but within minutes it had grown as big as ever again.

I was fitter than Ferruccio and always managed to reach the top of the slope well ahead of him. I also had longer legs. Quite early on in this *squadro* operation, I turned to see him struggling mightily, wet clay clinging to his boots up to his knees, and his arms loaded with bits of bamboo. It was a comic sight and I could not resist teasing him.

"Come on, Ferru! Get marching, for God's sake! Hurry up!" I shouted in my most commanding tone of voice.

He stopped struggling in the mud, looked up at me and grinned. "I can't hurry for my own sake, let alone God's!" he called back.

After that, each time I reached the top of the slope before him I turned and shouted sternly at him to hurry up. By the time we finished doing the *squadro* we were caked in mud and almost helpless with laughter. For years afterwards I only had to shout commandingly at him, "Get marching, Ferru!" to bring back the memory of that day, and we would start to laugh again.

With that last plot of Pinot Bianco, the planting was complete. Of the total seven hectares of the property, more than a hectare and a half were taken up by land near the house for a garden and part of the slope below Ferruccio's house that was too steep to work as a vineyard. This left about five and half hectares of vineyard. Ultimately, and at Pino Manzo's suggestion, I planted hazel nuts on that steep slope. He rightly said that they were a valuable crop, but he was also personally attached to them because, as already mentioned, he came from Avellino where the European hazel nut originated. (Its Latin name is *Corylus avellana*.) I must admit, however, that I never looked after the hazel nut bushes properly, for I became totally enthralled by the enigma of wine-growing and simply did not have the time.

12

Bugs and Fungus

Vines produce their first grapes in the third year after planting, although they do not reach full production for another three years or so. The Sangiovese in its third year was growing marvellously. By late May it reached to the top wire of the trellising system, about 1.8 metres (six feet) from the ground, and formed magnificent green curtains that marched across the land in straight lines. It has remained one of the wonders of nature for me to see how the drab vineyard of winter, with its unprepossessing, stumpy vine trunks and hard-pruned canes tied to wires, bursts into an exuberant display of enormous quantities of lush greenery by the summer. That nature also turns those miniscule green clusters of flower buds, which appear with the first shoots in late April, into magnificent bunches of golden or purple grapes by October is just as remarkable.

I was very proud of how good the Sangiovese was looking and invited Pino Manzo to come to see it one Sunday in early June.

"It's fantastic!" he exclaimed as we approached the rows. "What vigour! This must be a really good area for vines."

My delight in Pino's comment did not last for long, for as we walked between those verdant curtains, Pino suddenly stopped, reached in among the leaves, and plucked out a tiny cluster of flower buds.

"Colin, you've got an attack of berry moth," Pino said, holding the bunch out for me to examine. Many of the tiny buds that would open about two weeks later were missing. The part of the bunch where they were missing was shrouded by a fine mass of cobweb.

I was nonplussed. How was it possible that my new Sangiovese vines, so beautiful to behold and of which I was so proud, had already been hit by a pest? And what was more, it was a pest I had never even heard of. It felt like a mortal blow, but ultimately I recovered enough to ask Pino what could be done about it. He must have seen the worried look on my face.

"Don't worry," he said, laughing. "It's not too serious. You can spray against it. The berry moth has two generations, sometimes three. What you've got here is the first. As you can see, it's attacking the flower buds. The damage isn't too serious because when the buds get eaten by the larvae, more space is left in the cluster for other berries to swell and fill it. What's more serious are the second and third generations. Those grubs eat into the grape berries. The physical damage they cause makes it much easier for mould to get in and seriously damage the crop."

"When do I spray and what with?" I asked anxiously.

"You need to spray when there are a lot of moths flying around, but it's mainly a nocturnal moth, so it's difficult to know when that is. Ideally, you should set traps with pheromones, to attract males. When a lot of adult males are being caught in the traps, that's the time to spray. But keep an eye open for the moths anyway. You can sometimes see them in daylight. They have a wingspan of about one and half centimetres (half an inch). The front parts of the wings are white with an orange or yellow tinge. There's a brown stripe in the middle of the wings. It's a pretty little moth."

"I don't care whether it is pretty or not," I said grimly. "I'm going to blitz it! But I don't have the time to start messing about with traps, so I need to know when to spray on the assumption that the second generation is flying around."

"The first generation of moths is usually flying in mid-May, and the flight lasts about three or four weeks while they mate and lay their eggs on the grape clusters. Moths of the second generation hatch from the chrysalis in late June, so I would spray twice, at about two week intervals, beginning at the end of June."

On the following weekend I went to look at some other people's vines around Castel Sabino. I found attacks of berry moth in almost all of them. It was therefore hardly surprising that my vineyard was also infested. Curiously, none of the locals had any idea what was causing the attack on the flower buds of their grapes and creating the cobweb-like mass. When I told them what I had learnt from Pino Manzo, only a few took the matter seriously enough to ask what insecticide to use. The rest shrugged fatalistically as if to say it had always been like this and always would be. Ferruccio did take it seriously, however, and asked me to buy the insecticide for him too.

I never did have the time to set traps, but thereafter I solved the problem of berry moth by always adding the appropriate insecticide to the normal vineyard sprays in that period. Perhaps that word "normal" will attract the wrath of fans of organic farming, but in truth, the fight against pests and funguses in a vineyard seems to be never ending, and complex too, for there are some eighty different funguses that can attack vines and grapes.

The commonest enemy in this army of pests is downy mildew. Grape-growers worry about it constantly because it is usually the most serious, routine pest in a vineyard. Given the right conditions, it will invariably attack. Grape-growers need to be constantly vigilant and take pre-emptive action.

Downy mildew attacks the leaves and canes, and the grape clusters too, both before and after flowering. It can be so aggressive that it destroys the crop completely. The commonest attack is on the young leaves. It first appears as yellow, semi-translucent patches on them, and a little later, one can usually see the typical filaments of white fungus on the underside of the leaves. The patches then go brown as the stricken parts of the leaf die. In a bad attack, most of the leaves will be killed. When it attacks the delicate grape clusters before flowering they turn black and, of course, are lost. Attacks later in the season can shrivel the ripening bunches.

Downy mildew is a truly malevolent and permanent presence in a vineyard. Its spores overwinter in the soil on bits of rotting vine leaf. In the spring, when the weather conditions are right, the zoospores emerge and, carried by wind, land on the young vegetation and enter it through the stomata, or minute pores, in its surface. Once inside the plant cells, it absorbs the cells' sap until they die. And those white filaments that appear on the leaves have spores, called conidia, which get blown around by the wind and start new infections. Such organisms are among nature's most virulent forms of biological warfare.

Like so many plant pests, downy mildew was brought to Europe from North America, almost certainly when wild vine material was being brought in for the search for rootstocks that could defeat the phylloxera beetle. This mildew was first noted in Europe in 1878, after which it spread like lightning and did enormous damage. It was only the invention of the famous Bordeaux mixture that made it more or less controllable. This mixture is a kilogram (2.2 pounds) of copper sulphate and a kilogram of lime dissolved in a hundred litres of water and used as a spray. Copper is toxic to most fungal organisms and, if applied at the right moment, Bordeaux mixture will create a layer on the vine leaves and grape clusters that will prevent the downy mildew from getting in.

Many other compounds have been invented since to fight downy mildew. Many still contain copper, but downy mildew remains the bane of a grape-grower's life, even if it cannot attack without what are known as "The Three Tens": vine shoots more than ten centimetres (four inches) long with temperatures higher than 10°C (50°F) and ten millimetres (0.4 inch) of rain within a twenty-four hour period. However, it is very common in the Mediterranean area for those "Tens" to occur, so the war against downy mildew begins early and goes on for the rest of the season, or at least until about a month before vintage, when the vines are no longer forming new leaves.

The essence of defence against downy mildew is choosing the right moment to spray, in effect pre-empting it by a decision based on that combination of factors that allow it to attack. For a start, it needs moisture, so whenever it has rained sufficiently to wet the land and vegetation, or when ten millimetres have fallen, the attack has been set up. But just when it will occur depends on the average temperature, for this determines the incubation period after rain before the fungus actually attacks. For example, with an average temperature of 15°C (59°F) it will be ten days before the attack happens, whereas with an average temperature of 25°C (77°F), it will be only six days. And there are variations in-between. Furthermore, the humidity in the air plays a part: high humidity can shorten the incubation period by more than three days.

The trick to fighting off an attack is to spray a couple of days before you expect it to happen. This can call for some intricate decisions. One could install a small weather station to keep track of rain, humidity, temperature, and wind, but I had so many other calls on my resources that I preferred to ask Ferruccio over the phone about the weather conditions. So during the summer months I would call him, even when I was out of Italy for work reasons.

"We sprayed just before I left, on June the thirteenth," I might say, "and today's the twentieth. We have to decide when to spray again. Has it rained at all?"

"It rained yesterday morning for about an hour, and then it cleared up."

"What's the weather like today?"

"There's a *scirocco* blowing and it's a bit cloudy."

"Does it look as though it's going to rain again?"

"No, I don't think so."

The *scirocco* brings moist air across the Mediterranean, so I guessed the humidity would be high.

"And the temperature, Ferru?"

I could almost hear his thoughts down the telephone line. He was thinking what a pain all this technical stuff was. I remembered the trouble he had had learning to read the min-max thermometer I had installed under the porch of my house, but in the end he had learnt.

"It was twenty-two degrees at about nine o'clock this morning," he said.

I could only make a guess that this temperature at that time of the morning would be about the average for the twenty-four hour period.

"Well, Ferru, that means that with high humidity the incubation period will be about five days. It rained yesterday, on the nineteenth. Plus five days would take us to the twenty-fourth so you had better organize the spraying for the twenty-second or twenty-third, that's Tuesday or Wednesday."

"Yes, Signor Colin," said Ferruccio, the relief in his voice betraying that he was happy that all this mumbo-jumbo was over. I am not sure that he ever truly understood the concept of an incubation period and its length being affected by several factors, but he always gave me the information I needed and followed through on the decision. And we never had a serious attack of that dreaded downy mildew. Nor did we resort completely to those systemic fungicides that first came on the market in those years. They are absorbed by the vine and are translocated into every part of it, so protecting it from within. In theory, they give fourteen days of protection, so one only needed to spray at those intervals throughout the season.

I was discussing these systemic fungicides one day with Pino Manzo. They attracted me because they seemed to offer a solution that would eliminate much of the worry and decisions about spraying.

"I'd be rather careful with those systemic sprays," he said. "They may be fine in theory, but if you use them all the time, sooner or later resistant strains of mildew are sure to develop. What I would do is use a systemic if you have to spray while the vines are flowering, because the toxicity of the copper-based sprays reduces the fruit set. After the flowering and once the fruit has set, I would go back to the normal copper sprays. And for the last spraying in the season, somewhere about mid-August, I'd use a good old Bordeaux mixture. In fact, in general, I think you should use several different types of product during the season to reduce the chance of creating resistant strains of mildew."

That was precisely the advice that I followed, and Pino Manzo's words came back to me many years later when, during one July, I was talking to a friend who had a small vineyard to produce wine for home consumption. He told me that he had an attack of downy mildew. When I asked him what sprays he was using he mentioned one of the best-known systemic products. He assured me that he had used the correct doses and that he had never let more than the stipulated fourteen days go by between sprayings. He also mentioned that he had been using the same product exclusively for several years. By August, he had lost the complete crop to downy mildew and was threatening to tear out his vineyard and buy wine in future. It might have been just bad luck, but I have my suspicions that Pino Manzo's prediction about resistant strains had been right. His wisdom about crop protection served me well.

Downy mildew is only one of the common pests that hit vineyards. There is another called powdery mildew. This was first described in the USA in 1834, and it did not take long to reach Europe. It first struck in Margate, England, in 1847 where it was discovered on vines in a greenhouse by a gardener called Tucker, hence one of its Latin names *Oidium tuckeri*, though it is more correctly known as *Uncinula necator*. In less than five years it had reached France, Germany, and Italy in epidemic proportions.

Powdery mildew is second only to downy mildew in its destructiveness, but it requires significantly different conditions to develop. It becomes active at much lower temperatures, around 4–5°C (113°F), and it does not require rainfall to be able to flourish. It attacks all of the green parts of the vine and shows as a light grey powder on the surfaces. In fact, the local name for it around Castel Sabino was *cenere* (ashes). When it attacks grape berries in July and August, usually in hot and humid conditions but with no rain, it makes their skins go hard, with the result that as they continue to ripen and swell, they split open.

The classic product to fight powdery mildew is sulphur, dusted on the vines as a fine powder or added in soluble form to the sprays that are being used to protect against downy mildew. Since powdery mildew overwinters on the buds of the vines and becomes active at very low temperatures, one must dust the young shoots with sulphur when they are about six centimetres (2.5 inches) long. This is therefore the first treatment of the season in the vineyard. More modern products than sulphur were developed during my years as a wine-grower, some of them systemic. I used one of them occasionally but alternated it with soluble sulphur too.

In sum, the phylloxera beetle, downy mildew, powdery mildew, and various other plant and tree diseases must join chewing gum, Coca Cola, and rock music on my list of pernicious North American exports to Europe.

Bunch rot also had to be fought off in my vineyard. Known as *Botrytis cinerea*, this is the Jekyll and Hyde of fungi: it can destroy a crop or, in certain conditions, become the "noble rot" that is the basis of delectable sweet wines such as Sauternes and Tokaji. There are various legends as to how this first came about, beginning with the one of a priest in Central Europe in 1650. He was prevented from harvesting his grapes by a Turkish military attack, and when he finally went to bring them in they were covered with mould. He vinified them anyway, and the most astonishing sweet wine resulted. The mould had extracted much of the moisture from the grape berries, so concentrating the sugar. When the fermentation finished, some of that sugar remained in the wine.

Another legend is that the owner of Château d'Yquem, in the Sauternes region of France, went away, either to Russia or on a hunting trip, and was delayed in returning for his vintage. He too found his grapes mouldy, but he ended up producing the first vintage of the most prestigious of all sweet wines, Château d'Yquem. Another version of that story is that the German owner of a nearby château introduced the noble rot approach in winemaking to Château d'Yquem in 1847.

Whatever the origin, it is only when there is dew and humidity during the night and early morning, followed by warm, drying sunshine, that the fungus becomes "noble", drawing the moisture out of the berries and thereby concentrating the sugar and acids. Furthermore, the grapes have to be in perfect condition, almost ripe, and of an appropriate white variety, commonly Riesling, Sémillon, Sauvignon Blanc, Chenin Blanc, or Gewürztraminer.

There are some geographical locations where the climatic conditions that produce noble rot are much commoner than elsewhere, for example near Lake Balaton, in Hungary, where sweet Tokaji is made, and of course in Sauternes. But without all of these special conditions, the *Botrytis* simply causes grey rot or bunch rot which, in a wet autumn, can spread quickly through a vineyard, covering whole bunches with a nasty-looking mould. The same fungus can also attack the very young clusters before flowering and kill them.

Fortunately, among the vines I had planted, only the Montepulciano d'Abruzzo and the Pinot Bianco were rather susceptible to *Botrytis*. In the case of the Pinot, it ripened so early that it was normally harvested before the autumn rains could help the rot to spread – and could spread like wildfire. In one particularly wet autumn, I saw the grapes that had been my pride and joy one week heavily afflicted by the grey mould the next. It was very upsetting and I could never grasp that such an ugly thing could ever produce "noble rot"; to me it was just simple "rot". I found that that the Latin name for one of the family of fungi that causes it is very apt: it is called *Sclerotina fuckeliana*.

There was a spray to prevent bunch rot that had to be used early in the season and at predetermined intervals. It was very expensive, however, and it could affect the fermentation of the must if used too soon before the vintage. I used it occasionally, usually in a year after I had had an attack of bunch rot, and usually only on the Pinot and the Montepulciano d'Abruzzo. In a typical season, we would have to spray in the vineyard about ten times between early May and mid-August, that is to say about once every ten days. And in one particularly wet year we sprayed thirteen times.

Spraying a vineyard is not something you can do surreptitiously: the tractor engine must be kept at high revolutions to drive the pump on the sprayer and anyone passing by can see a mist of spray emerging above the tops of the vines. And in my case, a public road passed around two sides of the vineyard.

One day, over a glass of wine, Ferruccio said to me:

"Signor Colin, I was in the bar the other evening and someone said that *l'inglese* uses too many chemicals in his vineyard. They say we are always spraying."

"What do they know about it?" I asked, already irritated. "When did they ever protect their vines and grapes properly?"

"That's true. People round here often lose their grapes because of an attack of something. But the serious thing is that the word's getting around, and people are saying they won't buy grapes from you because there are too many poisons on them."

"What cretins!" I was so upset that I was almost shouting. "Do they think those grapes that come in on those trucks from Abruzzo and Vignanello have been sprayed any less? Don't those half-wits understand that when you are trying to produce grapes commercially you can't risk having your crop wiped out by some fungal attack? Every commercial grape-grower does what we're doing."

I calmed down and began to speak in a normal tone of voice again.

"Ferru, please tell anyone who you hear talking that way what I have said, but don't shout at them like I just did. Tell them that it always rains, usually very heavily, between the last spraying and harvest time, so the grapes will be washed clean."

Ferruccio nodded in agreement, and then said, "Talking of cretins, as you were just now, do you know what we say here in Italy about them?"

"What? That there are too many of them?" I asked facetiously.

Ferrucio pushed his hat back of his forehead and his eyes twinkled. "Something like that. We say that the mother of cretins is always pregnant."

As I was walking home from Ferruccio's house through the vineyard, I thought again about how suspicious rural people can be about methods they do not themselves use or know. In most cases, when it is for their own enterprise, one can understand that they may be cautious about introducing something new because of the possible risks of failure. And if that innovation was something expensive that they had to buy, they would be doubly out of pocket if the results did not bring benefits in increased returns. But in this case, their suspicion was about something that I was doing. It was not a good omen for being able to sell grapes to the locals.

13

Into Winemaking

Afghanistan may not seem the likeliest place for my first serious introduction to winemaking, but in fact that is where it happened. I was there during one of several visits concerning a radio broadcast project for farmers. During a meeting in some office of the Ministry of Agriculture, I met Martin Rumovic, a specialist in viticulture who was also working for FAO. It was 1975, before the Russian invasion, the war, and the internal strife that together have had such a horrific impact on what was then a magnificent country. Its proud and highly competent people were living peaceably together, and although the country was poor, it was progressing well.

Martin Rumovic was in Afghanistan because grapes are widely grown there. Most are dried into raisins, for the dry air of the continental climate is perfect for drying many different kinds of fruit. Rumovic, a Yugoslav, was advising on improved methods of viticulture and, of course, I told him about my project in Castel Sabino. He immediately invited me to his home for dinner.

It was a crisp November evening when I arrived at Martin Rumovic's house carrying a bottle of wine as a gift. The wine was made in Kabul by an Italian who had built a winery and who bought grapes from the local farmers. The expatriates living in Kabul drank this wine, branded Castelli, in considerable quantities. It was rather good, although perhaps I was so delighted at finding any wine in such an unlikely place that my judgment was affected. I have often wondered, since my visits to Afghanistan of those years, at what point during the process of the country's disintegration, the Italian was forced to abandon his lucrative enterprise. I also wondered what use the Taliban might have made of his winery.

I rang the bell and Rumovic opened the door. He came outside, glanced at the thermometer hanging on the outside wall, muttered something about my waiting for a moment, and beetled off around the side of the house. I was left standing there like an idiot with the bottle of wine I had brought with me in my hands.

He was soon back, apologizing profusely for having abandoned me on the doorstep. His heavily accented English was good, but like so many people who have a Slavonic language as their mother tongue, he tended to drop definite and indefinite articles, and a few verbs and pronouns as well.

"You see," he said as we went into his sitting room, "this is first evening we have frost. I must open doors of garage".

I was puzzled. "Sorry, but I don't understand what frost has to do with your garage."

Martin Rumovic grinned, showing a silver eye-tooth in his friendly face.

"I have my new wine in garage in demijohns," he explained. "Is very important expose new wine to cold. Helps clarify wine and precipitates tartaric acid as crystals. The more cold wine gets in first winter the better. It makes more stable."

My curiosity was fully aroused. "What do you mean by stable?"

"Well, if you not precipitate tartaric acid when wine is still new, it precipitates later when wine is in bottle . . . if bottle is exposed to cold. Have you never had bottle of wine and found crystalline stuff in bottom? You may also see some little crystals on cork if bottle stored lying down. Crystals are tartaric acid. It's natural acid in wines, but to make wines smoother on taste and prevent deposit of crystals in bottles, is best get rid of as much as possible by exposing wine to cold while is still young. You have seen wine cartons with *Protect From Cold* printed on side? Is to prevent precipitation of tartaric acid in bottle."

With dinner we drank some of his previous year's wine. It was very good, better in fact than Castelli's. I had been spellbound by his account of tartaric acid and the importance of cold on new wine. I longed to know more about winemaking, and I realized how totally ignorant I was. I asked him to outline, step by step, how he did it. He was obviously delighted to share his knowledge and launched into an animated description of the process. By this time we had repaired to his garage, where there were six demijohns, those large and bulbous bottles with a narrow neck, standing in a row near the open door.

"I bring here grapes I have bought and crush them. At home I have mechanical crusher that breaks skins of grapes as they pass between two rollers. But here I use old method. I take off trousers and stamp on grapes in big tub."

He stomped up and down to illustrate the action before going on with his description.

"Very important to add small dose of potassium metabisulphite to crushed grapes. This releases sulphur dioxide. Has been used in winemaking for many centuries."

"What does it do?" I interjected.

"Sulphur dioxide is sterilant in grape must and wine. Ripe grapes in vineyard are always covered with wild yeasts, micro-organisms that ferment the sugar in grape must and produce alcohol. When they work they make by-products of heat and carbon dioxide gas. You can see yeasts on ripe grapes, like delicate powder. I think what you call in English 'bloom'. When you crush grapes, wild yeasts start fermentation process, but problem is that wild yeasts not always very efficient. Maybe they will produce less alcohol than good yeasts do, and may also give unusual flavours to wine.

"Luckily, sulphur dioxide affects wild yeasts more than good yeasts. So putting in small dose of potassium metabisulphite holds back bad yeasts and lets good yeasts work. So if grapes healthy, I put in twelve or fifteen grams potassium metabisulphite for every hundred litres of crushed grapes. Potassium metabisulphite gives about half its weight in sulphur dioxide, so I am adding about six or eight grams of sulphur dioxide for hundred litres. If grapes not healthy, say mouldy, I increase dose."

Martin Rumovic went to a shelf at the back of his garage and came back with a small plastic bag in one hand and a small tin can in the other. The plastic bag contained a rather lumpy white powder. Rumovic opened the neck of the bag and shoved it under my nose. I recoiled involuntarily as I sniffed the acrid aroma of sulphur dioxide. It was like having my nose close to a match just after it had been struck.

Martin Rumovic laughed at my reaction. "Yes. Sulphur dioxide has very strong smell. Other sulphur compounds exist that release sulphur dioxide in wine but potassium metabisulphite is commonest in small wineries. Big wineries use sulphur dioxide compressed into liquid form."

The small tin can contained a light brown granular substance, rather like fine sand but obviously less heavy from the way it moved as Martin Rumovic shook the tin for me to see.

"Selected yeasts," he explained. "During many years, yeasts have been collected, identified, and tested. Most efficient ones have been selected and reproduced. These in this can are dried. About twelve hours after I have crushed grapes, and when the sulphur dioxide from potassium metabisulphite has had time to control wild yeasts, I add selected yeasts, maybe fifteen or twenty grams for hundred litres. Precise amount not too important. Some people also add small amount of ammonium phosphate, which is nutrient for yeasts and helps them work. But I don't unless fermentation not going well."

Martin Rumovic then showed me the tubs in which he fermented his red wine. He explained that the carbon dioxide, a by-product of fermentation, always brought the grape skins and pips to the surface where they formed a floating cap. This cap had to be broken and submerged at least twice a day. If it was not, there was a risk that it would go mouldy. It would also be a home for those tiny flies, which always seem to assemble in their millions when wine is being made. These flies carry bacteria on them that turn alcohol into vinegar, which is why they are sometimes called "vinegar flies". Moulds and bacteria from the cap could pass into the wine. In addition, breaking and pushing down the cap regularly helped to extract the colour and tannin from the skins and pips.

"How many days do you leave the juice and skins fermenting together?" I asked.

"What is it you say in English? That is question like, 'How long is piece of string?' No?" He chuckled. "All depends what sort of wine you making. Some people leave together for two weeks or more. They want to extract maximum colour and tannin from skins to make wines with much body. They wait before pressing until some skins in the cap start falling to bottom of vat. But more usual for fresh wines for drinking young is maybe four to eight days. Depends on when you have colour you want. And that depends on many things, like temperature and quantity of sulphur dioxide. Because sulphur dioxide helps release colour from skins."

"What about rosé wines?" I asked.

"Ah!" he exclaimed. "Many people think rosé is mixture of red and white. Not at all! Not at all! Proper rosé is red wine that is separated from skins when colour of must is still pink. After maybe twenty-four or thirty-six hours of fermenting together. Some wine producers make rosé so to have more skins to put with their red wine while is fermenting. Like that, they have more colour and body in their red wine. Rosé can be very good wine but often has bad image."

"Do you make white wine as well, Martin?"

"Not here in Kabul. Good white wine much more difficult to make. Usually, must is separated from pips and skins immediately and fermented alone. Needs to ferment at temperature below 20°C to produce wines with fine bouquet and fresh taste. So needs cooling system of some sort. Also white wine does not clarify easily like red. Usually needs be filtered to make really transparent and brilliant. We have saying in my country, and I have heard in Italy too, that red wine is made in vineyard because if grapes are good, red wine makes itself. But white wine is made in the winery. Needs much more equipment and skill to make good, fresh, white wine. And it is continuous fight to stop air getting to white wine and oxidizing it. Which makes it lose freshness, and colour goes more yellow."

How well I was to remember those comments about white wine by Martin Rumovic in later years as I struggled to keep the fermentation temperature of my white wine under control with simple but rather primitive means. I also had to try my hardest to protect it from oxygen at all times until it was safely in bottles.

"After four or five days I take my red wine out of fermenting tubs and pour through press to separate liquid from solid part of pips and skins. Then I press the skins to extract liquid. That is my press."

He pointed to a traditional hand-operated wine press in a corner of his garage. It was the usual cage of vertical wooden slats on a steel base. A threaded shaft rose from the base and at the top of the shaft was a screw and ratchet mechanism that, when turned, pressed two half-moon shaped wooden discs down on to the mass in the cage. It was a small press; it probably would not have taken more than forty or fifty kilograms (88–110 pounds) of fermented skins, but it was certainly big enough for his needs when making the six demijohns of wine sitting near the garage door to get chilled by that first frost. They were the biggest demijohns available, fifty-four litres each, so he was making about three hundred litres of wine, enough to keep him and a few of his friends in Kabul happy until the next vintage.

When I got back to my hotel room in Kabul after that informative session with Martin Rumovic, I immediately wrote down everything I could remember of what he had said. It was my primer in winemaking. Of course, I had to add a lot more information to it over the years, but it was an excellent beginning. I could have got similar information from Italians nearer home, and I later consulted Rome-based oenologists extensively, as well as reading whatever I could find on winemaking. For it was a much more complex field than Rumovic let on, but that fortuitous meeting with him, in such an unlikely place, was an invaluable introduction.

That encounter with the Yugoslav in Afghanistan was the first of dozens I had with other winemakers over the following years. I discovered that wine-growers are part of an informal worldwide fraternity, and that they love to meet other members and chat about their work. If I saw someone working in a vineyard in Spain, or Yugoslavia, or Chile, or Australia – or in fact anywhere where wine is produced – I would stop, greet them, and tell them I was a wine-grower in Italy. The reaction was always the same: they would drop whatever they were doing and enter into a long conversation during which we exchanged notes about how we did things, our problems, and the like. More often than not the conversation continued over a glass or two of wine. There seemed always to be a great desire to be informed and to inform, and these wine-growers were invariably congenial company.

Back in Italy after that trip to Afghanistan, I suddenly realized that I could make a few demijohns of wine, just like Martin Rumovic in Kabul. There was no need to wait until my own vines were producing grapes; the following October I could buy some grapes, just as the locals in Castel Sabino did. My rebuilt house had two garages in what had once been cow stalls below the living space. One of the garages was supposed to house the tractor, but winemaking suddenly took priority. Even if the overall plan was to sell grapes to the local people, how would it be possible to grow grapes and not want to produce some wine as well? Especially with my love for it. The result was that the tractor was put where my car was supposed to be, because tractor drivers – including me – are reluctant to sit on the wet seat of a tractor that has been left out in the rain. My car stayed out in the open so that the tractor's space could be made into a primitive winery.

The main items I had to buy for my first winemaking venture were three *bigoncie* (large black plastic tubs). A typical *bigoncia* holds about seventy litres of liquid. I would ferment my bought grapes in them. I only intended to buy a hundred kilos (220 pounds) or so of grapes and two tubs would probably have been enough. However, I tend to be obsessional about waste, even before it has happened, and I had read that you needed at least twenty per cent of headspace in any fermenting vessel. This is because the carbon dioxide released by the fermentation creates foam that will overflow the vessel if there is not enough headspace.

One Saturday morning around the middle of October, almost a year after my session with Martin Rumovic in Kabul, I went down to the small square in Castel Sabino to wait for the first truck loaded with grapes to arrive. One had arrived the previous weekend, and I knew more would arrive that day. I did not have to wait long for the first one to nose into the square and park. Its number plate showed that it was from the province of Pescara in the Abruzzo region. The driver climbed down, lit a cigarette, and leaned against his truck. He was a surly-looking man and he hardly answered my *"Buongiorno"* as I wandered over to examine the grapes. They looked excellent. They were an even and deep purple, without any of the green, unripe berries so common among the Castel Sabino grapes at harvest. And there was no mould to be seen.

"What variety are they?" I asked.

"Montepulciano d'Abruzzo."

I turned over a few bunches to look at the underside. There was still no sign of unripe berries.

"Do you know the Babo level?"

"More than nineteen . . . so the grower said."

I pulled my calculator out of my pocket. Multiplying the Babo by 0.65 gave me a potential alcohol of 12.3 per cent.

I asked the grape merchant whether I could pick some berries off different bunches to measure their sugar content myself. He looked surprised but nodded his agreement.

As I went to my car to collect my *mostimetro,* sieve and jug, I reflected that perhaps the man's un-Italian grumpiness might in fact be just wary reserve towards a strange foreigner. In fact, when I came back to the truck and started chatting to him about how the season had been, and how he was getting on with the sales, he became less surly and came over to watch my antics with the *mostimetro*. When it was floating in its tube filled with must he peered at the scale with me. It showed almost 19.5, a level that should give wine of more than 12.5 per cent alcohol. We haggled in a friendly way about the price. Once we had agreed, I went to fetch my tractor and trailer and transported 120 kilograms (264 pounds) of fine Montepulciano d'Abruzzo grapes up to the house.

I had told Ferruccio of my plans and I had hardly parked the tractor by the garage when I heard the unmistakeable sound of his *traglia* as it runners screeched over the stony ground of the vineyard. The giant sledge soon appeared, pulled by his two magnificent white bullocks. Ferruccio was standing on the sledge, reins made of an old rope in one hand and a whip made of a bamboo cane and a long piece of baler twine in the other. He looked like a rustic version of some Roman chariot driver.

"Ferru," I said, "you look like Ben Hur. You should drive that *traglia* down to Rome and race it round the Circus Maximus".

I did not think he would know who Ben Hur was, but I underestimated the power of television. The film had been shown again only a few weeks previously.

"Yes, and I might win too if the chariots were loaded up like this is," he said, pointing his whip at the grape crusher and wine press he was transporting on the sledge. "What's the point of making a chariot with wheels if it isn't used to carry things? Those ancient Romans understood nothing. Anyway, if I looked like that actor who was Ben Hur in the film I'd be in the film studios in Cinnecittà, not here in Castel Sabino."

He had brought the equipment over from his *cantina* to process the grapes I had bought. He would not need it for another ten days or so because his grapes would ripen later at Castel Sabino than the ones I had bought, which had come from a lower altitude.

We set to work surrounded by several plastic laundry tubs into which we had tipped the bought grapes. We placed the crusher that Ferruccio had brought on top of the first *bigoncia* and filled its hopper with grapes. Ferruccio turned the handle that drove it. The bunches of grapes passed between to counter-rotating steel rollers set a little less than a centimetre (0.5 inches) apart, the distance needed to break the berries without crushing the stalks or the pips.

This was the simplest of hand-driven crushers. Martin Rumovic had told me that it was generally better to remove the stalks before fermentation, and that more up-to-date crushers also did the de-stalking. I had looked at such a crusher/de-stalker one day in a wine-equipment shop in Rome. It had a revolving shaft under the crushing rollers with a number of spikes protruding from it. This shaft was set above a concave steel channel with perforations large enough for juice and skins to pass through them, but not big enough for a typical stalk to pass through. As the crushed grapes and stalks fell onto the shaft, the spikes caught the stalks, whereas the juice and skins fell into the concave channel and through the holes into a tank at the bottom of the machine. From there the crushed mass could be pumped away. The spikes in the revolving shaft were set in a spiral arrangement so that they conveyed the stalks to one end of the concave channel and ejected them on to the ground. The whole contraption was driven by a small electric motor.

However, we did not have such a crusher/de-stalker at the time, and after the crushed mass, including the stalks, was in the tubs, I said to Ferruccio, "Let's take out as many of the stalks as we can by hand." I began to dig into the mass in one tub.

Ferruccio did not reply. He looked at me quizzically for a moment, but then silently set to work on another tub. Removing the stalks by hand was not as easy as I had thought, but we managed to remove about two-thirds of them before giving up, our arms sticky with grape juice up to our elbows. Ferruccio straightened from his work.

"No one ever takes the stalks out around here," he said. "I've always left the stalks in. That's the way it was when we didn't have crushers like this one, when we tramped on the grapes."

Although it was expressed as a statement, I recognized that Ferruccio was also challenging me to justify and explain why we had done something that was not the normal practice for him and his friends in the area.

"Ferru," I said, "I have been told, and I've read, that if you leave the stalks in during fermentation they can give unusual flavours to the wine, and that the wine's better when the must and skins are fermented without them".

I thought he was going to make one of his usual comments about my book learning, but instead he looked genuinely interested. He commented that if it were true, he would think about getting an electric crusher/de-stalker when he could afford it. Slowly, it seemed, I was beginning to gain some credibility in Ferruccio's eyes. However, my next move was going to be a real test. I was going to add potassium metabisulphite to the crush, in line with Martin Rumovic's practice of about twelve to fifteen grams (0.5 ounces) per hundred litres in order to produce about half of that amount of sulphur dioxide. I had subsequently found out, after my session with Rumovic, that adding sulphur dioxide was the usual practice everywhere when wine was being made seriously. Higher doses were used if the grapes were damaged or mouldy in order to inhibit micro-organisms that could have a negative effect on the fermentation.

The problem I was going to face with Ferruccio was that all those who produced wine around Castel Sabino would tell you with great pride that they added "nothing" to it. What they meant by that word "nothing" was chemicals of any sort. I had tasted some of their wines after the heat of summer had set in and when they were already turning to vinegar, but they would still insist that it was good because it was *genuino,* with nothing added. Of course, a small dose of sulphur dioxide could have helped protect it from the bacteria that were turning the alcohol into vinegar. I later found that it was not only around Castel Sabino that such attitudes about chemicals were current: they predominate almost everywhere where wine is made by small producers for home consumption.

How was I going to deal with Ferruccio when it came to introducing ideas to which he might be inherently resistant? Yet, there was no alternative to using modern production methods if my venture were to succeed. Another aspect of the problem was that Ferruccio might spread stories around among the local people about the methods I was using to produce grapes and wine. Given what seemed to be a common attitude of initial mistrust, or even contempt, among locals for anything they did not know, this could damage the image of my produce.

I decided that the only way ahead would be to explain to Ferruccio the rationale of what I was doing, or asking him to do. There was no possibility of doing things such as adding sulphur dioxide to wine in secret, for I would need his physical presence and help for so many tasks. I would just have to hope that he was intelligent enough to understand and to keep quiet about what we were doing.

While Ferruccio began washing the laundry tubs under a hosepipe in front of the garage, I went into the house to fetch the small plastic bag containing the potassium metabisulphite and a small set of scales I had bought. They were like a miniature set of laboratory scales and would weigh accurately down to half a gram. When I appeared with them, Ferruccio was immediately curious.

"What's that?" he asked.

As I carefully weighed out fourteen grams of the white powder, I explained that it was potassium metabisulphite and that it would release about half of its weight of sulphur dioxide into the crush.

"Why are you going to add sulphur? I've heard that wines with sulphur in them give you a headache when you drink them."

"If you drink as much as you do, any wine can give you a headache," I retorted.

"My wine doesn't!" he shot back. We both laughed.

In truth, I had quite often experienced headaches immediately after drinking open white wines from the Castelli Romani, as the hills to the south of Rome are known. These headaches began as a tight feeling across the forehead, and became progressively more intense. I believed that excess sulphur dioxide in the wine was the cause. Quality wines, such as Frascati, come from the same area, but they have been made and bottled properly and have never caused me problems.

"I think some people are careless about the quantity of sulphur dioxide they put into their wine," I said to Ferruccio. "Perhaps they don't have precise scales to weigh the potassium metabisulphite properly. Some of those carafes of open white wine they serve in *trattorie* in Rome do give me a headache. I think too many small producers who sell their wine in bulk work on the principle that if a little sulphur is good, more must be better."

I carefully explained to Ferruccio the reasoning behind adding small doses of sulphur dioxide to the crushed grapes to favour the better yeasts before fermentation began, as well as later when racking wine from one container to another to protect it from attacks by damaging bacteria.

"Some people around here have used it, but only when the wine has already gone off," Ferruccio said. "I've heard people talk about the headaches they've had from drinking wine that's been treated like that."

"I suppose that it might slow down the process of the wine getting worse, or if they added enough it might even stop it from going off completely, but it wouldn't cure the damage that had already been done."

I added the potassium metabisulphite to the crush in the tubs and started to mix it in well with a broom handle. Ferruccio grabbed the iron bar that worked his wine press and was about to plunge it into another tub.

"Don't use that, Ferru!" I exclaimed. "You should never put iron in contact with must or wine. Wine can change colour and go off because it's absorbed iron."

"*Porca Madonna!* All the things that can go wrong with wine and that I never knew about."

"There are dozens of other things that can go wrong with wine. It can also pick up tastes that are difficult to get rid of. I've read that it can even pick up a taste of paper from cardboard filter pads. You have to flush water through new filter pads to wash the taste out before the wine goes through them."

"*È una croce!*" (It's a cross!), said Ferruccio. "All this technical stuff you've been picking up. Much better not to know these things. Then you don't have to worry about them."

I told Ferruccio about selected yeasts and left him scratching his head through his hat as I went into the house to fetch them. I opened the can and showed them to him. I told him that I was going to add about twenty grams per one hundred litres to the crush in about twelve hours time, once the sulphur dioxide would have inhibited the wild yeasts.

"All these things are new to me," said Ferruccio. "I've heard about some of them, but I've never seen them used. Do they really make a difference to the wine?"

"I suppose so, or they wouldn't be used as widely as they are." I replied. "They've been introduced as innovations in winemaking over generations, and if they were no use, they'd have been dropped by now."

The preoccupied expression that Ferruccio had been wearing was suddenly replaced by a wide grin and that sparkle in his eyes. He pushed his hat back off his forehead.

"You know, Signor Colin," he said, "I like innovations. I like them very much . . . but only the ones I already know!"

Over the following days, Ferruccio or I pushed the floating cap of the skins down into the fermenting wine in the tubs twice and sometimes three times a day, breaking it up well. The foam trapped under it burst to the surface in a brilliant pink lather, releasing that heady smell of fermenting wine that was to be so much a part of my autumns over the following years.

After five days, when the wine had taken on a good rich colour from the skins, and there was almost no trace of sweetness left, Ferruccio and I poured the mass into the cage of his press. Most of the wine ran freely between the slats of the cage, down on to the base plate of the press, and out of its spout into a wide and low-sided plastic container placed below it. From there we transferred it by the bucketful, through a funnel, into some demijohns that I had bought.

When most of the free-run juice had come out, we settled the two half-moon wooden plates – with a semicircular notch cut out of their straight sides to accommodate the screw of the press – on top of the skins and pips that had remained in the cage. Various wooden blocks placed on top of the plates made up the height we needed. We wound the large screw down on to the blocks by hand until it became too stiff to turn any further. Ferruccio slipped the long steel bar into its socket on the ratchet mechanism and began to pull it slowly backwards and forwards. This produced a loud and rhythmic, metallic clinking sound as the heavy pawls dropped into their slots to prevent the screw from unwinding. I was immediately transported back to my childhood, to the sounds of the winery below the house where I had lived in Switzerland. It was a unique and extraordinarily evocative sound, but one that has disappeared in today's modern wineries with their electric and pneumatic presses.

More wine came pouring out of the press as we slowly increased the pressure. Italian demijohns come in a range of size from five to fifty-four litres. By the end of the pressing, the new wine almost filled one of the largest and another of thirty-three litres. We had extracted something over seventy per cent of the weight of the original grapes in wine, about normal for a hand-driven operation like ours. And we had not applied excessive pressure, which could affect the quality of the wine.

The wine was still fermenting and was slightly prickly on the tongue.

"We have to improvise some air traps," I said to Ferruccio. He looked blank, so I went on. "The wine's still fermenting and giving off carbon dioxide that will lie on top of it and protect it from the air, but we still have to make sure that no air gets into that space above the wine in the demijohn."

I went into the house to fetch some plastic tubing I had bought. I cut a small hole in the plastic lid of each demijohn, slipped a piece of tube through it, and sealed the joint with some masking tape. I pushed the lids on to the mouth of the demijohns and led their tubes into the bottom of a bucket half filled with water. Carbon dioxide soon began to bubble out through the water.

"Look at that, Ferru," I said, mightily pleased. "The gas from the fermentation is coming out through the tube and no air can get in. That's a simple air trap we've made."

"I see," said Ferruccio. "Are you sure it's wine you're making? With all these tubes it looks more like what you see on television when they've got some patient in intensive care and all hooked up to tubes."

"Well, from what I've been reading, wine is like a patient that needs constant care and attention if it's to get better and better."

The wine went on fermenting gently for another three or four days, and about three weeks after that, I siphoned it off into other demijohns to separate it from the lees that had settled into the bottom. This was shortly before November 11, St Martin's day, which is important in Italy for two reasons: firstly, it is the patron day of cuckolds, and secondly, it is the day that the new wine is considered to have fully become wine. It is when it is tasted seriously for the first time.

As I walked down to the tractor garage with Ferruccio on that important day, I asked him how it was that St Martin's day was cuckolds' day and new-wine day.

"I don't really know," he replied. "Maybe it's because while the men are in the *cantina* tasting their new wine, their wives are having it off with someone else."

Naturally, I had tasted my wine many times before that date, but there was something ceremonial about the St Martin's day tasting. I siphoned some of my Montepulciano d'Abruzzo into a glass and Ferruccio and I examined it. It had the purple hue of all very young red wines, and its taste was still tart. I knew absolutely nothing about how to judge a very young wine for its future potential, but to me it seemed to hold the promise of a clean, fruity taste.

During the winter months, and well remembering the example of Martin Rumovic in Kabul, I exposed the wine to as much cold as possible. By late February it had clarified almost completely, leaving a sediment that included branching and lacy structures of tartaric acid that had been precipitated by the cold.

After a final racking in spring it was a beautiful ruby colour, but still with the violet tinge of a young wine. It was full of the fruit flavours and freshness typical of Montepulciano d'Abruzzo wines. The depositing of the tartaric acid had got rid of the aggressive acidity it had had before winter. At each racking I had added ten grams of potassium metabisulfite for each hundred litres of wine. I had read that this small addition of sulphur dioxide would protect the wine from oxidation and attacks by micro-organisms. I had been washing and putting aside empty wine bottles for months, and in the early summer I bottled that first production with bought grapes.

The end result was successful beyond all my expectations. All who drank the wine exclaimed at how good it was. I was delighted; my only regret was that I had not bought more grapes. Even my sons enjoyed it. Fortunately, they had by now decided that wine was better than beer, thereby proving that a love of wine is highly inheritable.

That first experience of winemaking, however small, had fascinated me and I knew I would start to vinify some of my own grapes as soon as the vines began to bear fruit. After all, winemaking was a doddle, or so I thought after that first small success. It did not take long for me to discover how wrong I was.

14

Harvest

Vines produce their first grapes in the third year after planting, but their quantity and quality is much less than it will be after some six or seven years, when they will be fully established. Their root systems will have spread several metres laterally, and will also have gone several metres deep into the soil. Just how deep they may go in some conditions is shown in a wine producing area in Portugal called Colares. There, ten metres (thirty-three feet) of sand lie on top of calcareous clay, and the vine roots must reach that clay for their sustenance. A bonus of that particular situation was that the phylloxera bug cannot burrow through the sand to such depths, and so Colares vines still grow on their own roots instead of being grafted.

The year of 1978, when my two hectares of Sangiovese were due to yield their first fruit, was one of great expectations. The season was very favourable. The buds on the vines began to burst in the last week of April, when there was sunshine and warm winds, and no risk of frost. The leaves of the trees opened as well, and as soon as the canopy was dense enough to hide them from view, the Golden Orioles resumed their residence in the oaks at the lower end of my land. Their flute-like calls could be heard all over the vineyard throughout the late spring and early summer, but they were hardly ever to be seen. Just occasionally one might catch sight of the yellow and black flash of a male, or of a green-grey female, as it swooped into the branches.

Birds have fascinated me since childhood. A gardener in Berkshire where I was brought up was an accomplished amateur naturalist who delighted in passing on his interest and knowledge. Today, with bird life so much under pressure from human activity, particularly modern farming with its heavy use of chemicals, it is shameful to admit that one collected birds' eggs as a child. However, in those days it was common, and the gardener taught me to collect them doing the least possible damage. He made me wait until there were several eggs in the nest, and then to take one, and only one. He explained that birds could not count, so they would not miss one egg out of three or four. But if one took the first egg that was laid, the chances were that the birds would abandon the nest. On one occasion I did cause a Blackbird to abandon its nest, and I got a severe dressing down from the gardener. He also taught me how to put an egg in my mouth to keep it safe when climbing down a tree from some high nest, and how to prick a small hole in both ends of an egg and blow out its contents before putting it into my collection. I am not proud today that I had a collection of bird's eggs, but looking for nests certainly was part of the process that gave me my interest in birds.

Curiously, I have never met an Italian country person who was even slightly interested in birds . . . unless it was a *cacciatore* (hunter) whose only interest was in blasting them out of the sky. When I first mentioned the Golden Orioles to Ferruccio, in the company of the whole of his family, they said they had never noticed them. Nor had their calls from the tree canopies entered their awareness. I have found the same phenomenon in other rural areas of Italy. There is an Italian association for the protection of birds, but its members seem mainly to come from the cities. My interest in and love of birds has stayed with me all my life, and it was a delight to have the unseen but musical presence of the Orioles in the oak trees for my many summers in Castel Sabino.

That first year of grape production was seldom hot enough for the vines to suffer, and there were occasional drenching thunderstorms. This meant being very alert to ward off attacks of mildew, but the grapes developed well. I watched them as they transformed from those tiny clusters of flower buds, through flowering, and fruit set. After that, the nubby little bunches took on size at a remarkable pace. Then the first few berries began to change from green to red until, by mid-August, the vines were festooned with magnificent purple bunches. There were not very many of them, but they looked spectacular.

The locals commented on how beautiful the grapes were and began to enquire whether they could buy some. I had to be careful with respect to how many clients I promised to supply, for it was impossible to estimate accurately what weight of grapes there was in those two hectares of Sangiovese.

One day in FAO during the early part of that summer I chanced to meet an

Israeli friend, Gidon Blumenfeld. He was a large man with a large bass voice, and he was colossally amiable. He was also an outstanding agronomist who, after his retirement to New Zealand, planted the first olives there. He asked me how the vines were doing. I told him happily that we would be harvesting the first grapes in October.

"It's only the third year, isn't it?" he asked. I nodded, and he rumbled on: "In Israel, the first year's grape harvest is dropped on the ground and left to rot. The rabbis won't let people make wine from the grapes that year. They say it'd be no good anyway."

I was dismayed because I had been hoping to obtain at least some small return from the sale of grapes after all the outgoings of the previous years. But what if the quality of the grapes was so poor that it damaged my reputation among potential future purchasers?

"Well, I intend to harvest the crop, sell some of it, and keep some to make wine myself. Actually, I'm surprised you Jews throw away anything as valuable as grapes."

Gidon beamed benignly. "Isn't Fraser a Scottish surname?" he asked innocently, and broke into his booming laugh.

As soon as I could I called Pino Manzo to find out whether he knew anything about the quality of the first year's grape crop. He told me that he did not know specific details, but that it was generally agreed that until the vines were better established it was likely that the grapes would not ripen as well. However, he did not think that I should follow Israeli practice, so I decided to go ahead as planned.

There are often thunderstorms in Italy in the second half of August. These mark the end of the drought and the blinding heat of the previous month or so, and that year was no exception. But once the storms had passed, a typical September set in. There were warm sunny days and cool nights and the sugar level in the grapes began to rise quite rapidly.

By then I had given up the messy squeezing of grapes by hand and the sieving of the juice for the Babo *mostimetro*. I had upgraded my technology for measuring sugar content to a hand-held refractometer. This handy device was like a small telescope, about twelve centimetres (five inches) long, with an inclined glass surface at the end opposite the eyepiece. All you had to do was squeeze a drop of grape juice on to the inclined glass surface, push a hinged transparent plastic plate down on to it to spread the drop, look through the eyepiece, and read off the sugar content on a scale. There was also a small thermometer in the device so that one could make a fine adjustment to the reading to account for the temperature.

A refractometer measures the angle that light is bent by the dissolved substances in a liquid, giving what is called the Brix reading, or the percentage of dissolved substances. Like Babo, Brix was a nineteenth-century Germanic scientist whose name is immortal, at least among wine-growers. Not all of the dissolved substances in grape juice consist of sugar, however, so a Brix reading needs to be multiplied by 0.6 to obtain the probable alcohol content of the future wine, as opposed to the 0.65 used with a Babo reading.

The books said that, as vintage approached, one should go through the vineyard and measure the sugar content at regular, but reducing, intervals as the grapes ripened. Towards the end, it would be necessary to take the readings every couple of days. The correct time for harvest would be when there was no further increase in the sugar content over a period of three or four days.

When Ferruccio and I tried to follow these deceptively simple instructions, I began to share his doubts about book learning. We tried to pick representative rows in the vineyard and walked along them, stopping every few yards, while I plucked a berry from a bunch, squeezed a drop of its juice onto the prism of the refractometer and read off the Brix level. Ferruccio would note the figure on a piece of paper in his spidery handwriting. There was often a difference of two Brix points or more between the readings of individual berries. I took pains to be as impartial as possible in selecting the berries, taking them from the rows on the left and right of where we were walking. I also tried to take them from different parts of each bunch because I had read that the sugar content varied according to the position of the berry on the bunch. The highest sugar content was in the "ears" at the top and sides of the bunch, so obviously I could not take all the berries from there if we were to reach a true average for the vineyard on that day. In my attempts to be as random as possible, I even plucked berries off without looking at them first.

The only way, it seemed to me, to compensate for the rather large differences between individual readings was to take many of them. So Ferruccio and I tramped up and down different rows until Ferruccio had noted down seventy or eighty readings. I then sat down with my calculator to work out the average of them all. A general tendency of increasing sugar content did emerge, but on some occasions when it had rained, there was actually a slight reduction, presumably because the grapes were swollen with water. A couple of days after the rain, the sugar content had risen again.

I was waiting for those famous three or four days described in the books when there was no further increase in sugar content to fix the day to begin the vintage. The Brix level was hovering around 17.8 and seemed still to be rising. In the end, however, it was not possible to take any scientifically-based decision, for it was the pestering of the clients to have their grapes at the weekend they had chosen to make their wine that determined when we began the harvest.

That first harvest took place on a spectacularly lovely day at the end of the first week in October. There was none of the haze of humidity so common in the main months of Italian summer, and from the high part of my land the view spread over kilometre after kilometre of rolling, verdant hills and woods. The sun shone warm from a cloudless sky and the ground underfoot was dry. A happy group of about eight people, mainly local women under Ferruccio's control, cut the stems of the bunches with secateurs and dropped them into plastic buckets.

Armando, the *Presidente,* was also helping and his self-appointed task was to empty the buckets of the pickers into the numerous *bigoncie* that I had bought and which were strategically placed every thirty or so metres (100 feet) along the row. I had painted my name on the *bigoncie*; for Ferruccio had warned me that *bigoncie* had a highly developed and astounding talent for disappearing if they were not marked. In fact, they were such a commonplace item for a variety of farm needs that it would be easy to get mine mixed up with others when delivering grapes to a *cantina.* Doubtless too, there were some locals who would think that purloining a couple of *bigoncie* from *l'inglese* who was spending so much on a new vineyard would be a fair gain.

At one point, I was surprised to see Armando pick up a large round stone in his massive hands and start thumping it down on the grapes in a *bigoncia.*

"Presidente, what are you doing that for?" I called out.

"Get more grapes into each *bigoncia*. Less transport," he mumbled.

"Yes, but you shouldn't damage the grapes before they're put through the crusher. It affects the wine." I did not go into the issue of the negative effects of the oxidation of grape must that I had read about.

Everyone had stopped picking grapes to listen to my exchange with Armando. They were all aware that, although I was an agriculturist, I knew almost nothing practical about viticulture and winemaking. One of the women said:

"We always thump the grapes down into the *bigoncie*. Otherwise we'd need too many *bigoncie*, and we'd need to make too many journeys."

"I understand, but we've got enough *bigoncie* here, and we've got the tractor for transport. I don't want the grapes hammered down into them. You can just push the last few bunches down gently with your hands so that they don't fall out during transport, but no more."

The pickers went back to work, some of them shrugging as they did so. Armando scratched his head through his cap. I knew they all thought I was mad, but they had the grace to realize that I was paying the piper and could call the tune.

We brought the laden *bigoncie* out of the vineyard with the tractor for which Ferruccio, on his own initiative, had made a *tavola* (table). He was very proud of it, and justifiably so. It was large platform that he had cobbled together from two long timbers and various bits of plank he had scrounged from somewhere. The two long timbers, which protruded from under the front of the platform, were slipped under the rear axle of the tractor, and the rear end was rested on the hydraulic lift arms, to which an implement was normally attached. The whole contraption was so big that eleven *bigoncie* fitted on it, a load of almost a quarter of a ton of grapes. Ferruccio had also fitted the platform with four uprights of round timber so that the *bigoncie* could be roped securely on to the platform. It was hardly beautiful, but it was a masterly piece of improvisation. Certainly, I could have bought a similar platform made of steel from a farm implement supplier, but the models generally available were far smaller. Ferruccio's *tavola* served us for many years, and when it began to creak and groan to the point where I thought it was going to fall apart under its load, Ferruccio renovated it with some extra cross pieces.

A central point for the first, and for all later, harvests was a small store I had illegally built in the vineyard to keep fertilizer and anti-fungal sprays. It was next to an electricity pole from which power was taken to the submersed pump in the borehole. When I first thought about building it, the mayor of Castel Sabino was a lady. She owned one of the food shops.

"Signora Romina," I had said to her one morning as I was buying bread, "is it all right if I build a hut next to that electricity pole near the cemetery to house the electricity meter for my water pump?"

"How big do you want it?" she asked

"Oh, I don't know exactly. Big enough for the meter, and maybe one or two other things."

I truly did not know at that point, so my vagueness was not a ploy to have her agree and then build something enormous. But I suspect that she thought that it was, for she merely shrugged silently and smiled. There were other people in the shop, but no one could ever say she had given her approval. Nevertheless, I had a tacit green light. Of course, by the time we finished the building it was a fair-sized store with an even bigger lean-to shed attached to the back under which to park farm implements. The electricity meter occupied a little space on one wall. No one ever complained, and in fact the *casottino* (little hut) as Ferruccio christened it, was decently rustic with a roof of old tiles that I had managed to buy from Mario Ricci.

In the end, however, my *abusivo* (illegal) building caught up with me when one of Italy's revolving-door Governments was creatively looking for sources of revenue. This is, of course, a chronic situation in Italy, in good part because of tax evasion. Indeed, one of the events that fascinates, and irritates, ordinary citizens the most is the annual press coverage of what leading personalities have declared as their annual income. The fairy stories are quite astonishing. For example, it can be learned that the owners of a large and successful shop declared less income than the individual wages of their sales' staff.

To return to my *casottino*, a Government decided that it would regularize all existing illegal buildings. It passed a law under which *abusivi* builders like me had to have proper plans drawn up of what they had built, lodge them with the authorities, and pay a fine. The whole process was rather tedious, and the commonly expressed opinion was that architects and *geometri,* like Roberto Paoli who did my paper work, made more money out of the exercise than did the Government.

The *casottino* was the headquarters for the vintage and all major operations in the vineyard. Ferruccio found an old table and chair from somewhere and installed them there, so I called it his office. It was where the vineyard workers gathered and also sheltered from the rain if necessary. It was also where we weighed the grapes when the tractor brought the full *bigoncie* out of the vineyard on the *tavola.* Ferruccio had heard of someone who had a used weighing scale for sale, and I had bought it. We weighed two full *bigoncie* at a time on its platform subtracting three kilograms (6.5 pounds) for each *bigoncia.*

Some of the purchasers of the grapes hung around while we weighed their load, perhaps thinking that we would cheat them out of a few kilograms. Sometimes they transported their purchases with their own means, but more often than not, I delivered them. If the consignment was more than the eleven *bigoncie* that would fit on Ferruccio's wooden platform, we loaded them onto a trailer. I often had to summon all my old skills as an instructor in farm machinery to reverse the trailer up the medieval alleys of Castel Sabino and around narrow corners to reach the door of a client's *cantina.* After humping the loaded *bigoncie* into the *cantina* and helping to tip their contents into the client's crusher, I was invariably asked to taste some of the previous year's wine. By the end of the day, my tractor driving showed more verve, but somewhat less precision.

The first vintage set the pattern for many others, although some were far less pleasant. For example, during several vintages it rained, and picking grapes slogging around in sticky mud is a miserable task. Furthermore, I was always worried that the rainwater on the bunches would dilute the sugar content, so I insisted that the pickers wait until they had at least dried to a reasonable extent. And when there was mud stuck to the bottom of the *bigoncie,* many clients complained that our tare weight of three kilograms per *bigoncia* was no longer correct and I would have to knock a considerable number of kilograms off their total consignment to stop their moaning. But it was usually good-natured banter and everyone remained cheerful.

15

First Wine from my Vineyard

Flushed with the success of the wine that I made with those bought Montepulciano d'Abruzzo grapes, I began preparing for that special day when I would bring in some of the Sangiovese from the first harvest to vinify myself.

I converted the tractor garage into a primitive winery by building a wide plinth along one wall on which I could stand some tanks. Along the opposite wall, I built a higher and narrower shelf on which to place demijohns. It was high enough to be able to siphon wine from one fifty-four-litre demijohn into another on the ground. I bought three 600-litre fibreglass tanks. They were fermenters for red wine. All such tanks have a large opening on their side, close to the bottom, through which the pips and skins can be brought out for pressing once the free-run wine has been pumped off. My fibreglass tanks had an oval opening at the bottom that could be closed by screwing home a stainless-steel plate with a rubber seal.

Of course, the tanks could also be used for storing wine, and for this purpose they had a floating lid. The lid was a loose fit in the tank, and the gap between it and the side of the tank had to be sealed off because the surface of wine, when exposed to the air, grows all manner of bacteria that form a nasty white scum. The normal way to seal off the surface of the wine exposed between the lid and the side of the tank was to float a layer of oenological oil about a centimetre (0.5 inch) thick in the gap. This oil is an odourless and transparent paraffin oil. Over the years, I was to find it rather messy to use and clean up, but it was certainly effective.

An alternative way to prevent spoilage of the surface of wine exposed to air was to use small wax disks that have been impregnated with a chemical called in Italian *isosolfocianato di allile*, a name that was completely meaningless to me, but the substance, whatever it was, had a very strong smell that was vaguely familiar. However, I had used the disks many times before recognizing the smell as that of strong mustard. Perhaps the manufacturer of the disks used a synthetic form of it, but it was certainly mustard.

One of my favourite tricks with friends helping me with wine operations for the first time, and who asked me what the disks were for, was to stick one under their nose and say, "Smell that!"

If it was a new disk, and therefore had a very strong smell, they jerked away from it. It was like getting too much really strong English mustard in your mouth and feeling the acrid fumes waft into the back of your nose. Strangely, not many people identified the smell as that of mustard, which made me feel better for the many times I had used it without realizing what it was. Then, when I was writing this book, I realized that my ignorance about the substance could not continue. I found out that it is called "allyl isothiocyanate" in English and that it contains sulphur and nitrogen. It is extracted from black mustard seeds, and it is also used as an emetic to make people vomit if they have swallowed a poison.

The first harvest of Sangiovese amounted to about four tons of grapes. I sold most of them to local buyers but brought about a ton and a half into my tractor-garage winery. I wanted to make between 1,000 and 1,200 litres of wine. This would more or less fill two of my 600-litre tanks and leave one empty for racking the wine.

I had bought a small electrically driven crusher/de-stalker and it made short work of turning the grape clusters into mush. I followed exactly the same procedures as I had for making wine with the bought grapes in the previous year. I was brimming with confidence that wine made from my own grapes would be as good or better and that I would not run into any problems. Those expectations turned out to be very rash, for my beginner's luck left me.

All seemed to go well initially with the fermentation, the pressing, and the rackings from one tank to another to separate the wine from the lees that had settled to the bottom. Then, in the spring, I began to notice that the wine had a marked smell of rotten eggs. From what I was able to find out from books and asking around, the cause was that the yeasts, running out of oxygen, were working on the sulphur dioxide in the wine, or more especially in the lees, and turning it into hydrogen sulphide. The problem was quite common and it seemed that it could be prevented by earlier and more frequent rackings to avoid wine being left on its lees for too long.

Once hydrogen sulphide was present, one way to get rid of it was said to be letting the wine cascade from a height while racking it from one tank to another. The aeration would let the hydrogen sulphide disperse into the air. That at least was the theory. Indeed, in that first year I was able to get rid of the smell in that way because I caught it very early.

In fact the hydrogen sulphide problem occurred in several batches of wine in those first years, and earlier and more frequent rackings did not prevent it. It was sometimes very difficult to eliminate by aeration. Furthermore, too much aeration of wine causes the loss of important aromas, with the result that the final product suffers.

Ferruccio said that the problem was very common locally and that the treatment used traditionally was to swill the wine around in a copper tub. Some books also mentioned this because the hydrogen sulphide will combine with the copper and be eliminated. Dumping some copper turnings or many pieces of copper wire into the wine was also suggested. In one way or another, we usually managed to solve the problem; on only one occasion was a small batch of wine beyond recovery.

In practice, hydrogen sulphide can be very easily removed by a small dose of copper sulphate. I once talked to a winemaker in Australia about hydrogen sulphide in wine, and he told me that he had also experienced it quite often.

"But it's no problem," he remarked laconically. "Just put in a small dash of copper sulphate, swirl it round a bit, and whoosh, it's gone. No worries, mate!"

No worries for him, maybe, but in Italy the addition of heavy metal salts like copper sulphate to wine is strictly prohibited. Out of pure curiosity, I did once experiment with a fifteen-litre demijohn of wine that had a strong smell of hydrogen sulphide. I added a tiny quantity of copper sulphate, and sure enough, the smell went immediately. But that was not the end of the story because the wine had developed a bitter taste. Even the tiny amount of copper sulphate I had put in was probably too much, and the bitter taste was probably due to copper in the wine. I had read that there were ways of removing metals like copper from wine using some cyanide compound, but I considered such processes were going into the occult, quite apart from being illegal and possibly dangerous.

My experiment with copper sulphate was at about the time that several people in Northern Italy had died after drinking cheap wine that they had bought in two-litre bottles in a supermarket. The reason was that the wine contained high levels of methanol, which is also called methyl alcohol, and is present in methylated spirit. Methanol is poisonous, as anyone who has followed the sad fate of the down-and-outs who drink methylated spirit will know. On the other hand, the alcohol that results from fermentation is called ethyl alcohol: it is safe to drink – or relatively so, at least in appropriate doses.

In Italy, the full facts of scandals, such as the one involving methanol, or acts of terrorism, or the disappearance, or death in unexplained circumstances, of people who might have important information, never seem to come completely to light. Years and years of official investigations and hearings, and thousands of pages of testimony, obfuscate the truth until the whole episode is silted over, or *insabbiato* as the Italians say. To many people, this obfuscation is a deliberate tactic to protect the entrenched interests of the powerful, including State bodies.

Be that as it may, the story going around in wine circles after the methanol scandal had a strong ring of probable truth about it, at least for me. In essence it was that the supermarket wine containing very high levels of methanol was the indirect result of an attempt to defraud the European Union. It was in the years when the Union was buying up large quantities of excess wine of low quality and distilling it to produce alcohol for industrial uses. The price paid for that wine was based on its alcohol content. Some nefarious producer of poor wine, probably from some vineyard giving very high yields and where the sole intention was to sell the wine for distillation, realized that methyl alcohol for industrial use could be bought very cheaply. If he added large quantities to the wine he was going to sell for distillation, he could get a higher price for it. So he did just that.

Then, a wine company that was engaged in buying up inferior produce and adjusting it, before putting it into large bottles for low-price sale in supermarkets, needed some high-alcohol wine for blending purposes. Probably as a result of a mistake, they bought the wine that contained methanol and had been intended for distillation. More people could have died but for some fortuitous circumstance: one of the people who drank the wine was taken to a hospital in Milan where a recently qualified doctor had written his thesis on methanol poisoning and immediately recognized the symptoms.

That sort of scandal made honest wine producers even more honest, me included, so I was not about to start fiddling around with copper sulphate and cyanide compounds in my operations. In any case, a couple of years later I started to use a different type of selected yeasts and the problem of hydrogen sulphide disappeared.

The shop in Rome where I had bought my crusher/de-stalker was hardly the sort of agricultural emporium you would expect to find not far from the centre of a major city. It was quite large and filled with an unimaginable variety of items. If you wanted anything from gumboots to chicken feed, fertilizer, garden insecticides, sprays for vines, potassium metabisulphite, wine bottles, corks, brushes for sweeping the yard or, above all, if you wanted to have your wine analysed, Valentino de Angelis would smilingly look after you. He and his wife, in their forties, presided over this amazing collection of items, a collection that almost filled the floor area with boxes, bags and drums, as well as being hung from the walls and ceilings.

Valentino de Angelis was quietly competent and unfailingly helpful. He was knowledgeable enough about wine production to be able to give good advice after he had analysed a sample. I was very disappointed in my first home-grown Sangiovese wine, even after I had rid it of its hydrogen sulphide. So in the spring, I took a sample of it to Valentino de Angelis. I knew it tasted too acidic, and it had very little body, but I wanted to know how this would show up in the laboratory.

There are said to be as many as 200 different identifiable components in red wine. Indeed, I once met a university professor of biochemistry in Australia who used highly sophisticated tests on wine as the practical work assigned to his postgraduate students. But Valentino de Angelis just did the few simple tests the amateur winemaker needs: alcohol content, volatile acidity, total acidity, and quantity of sulphur dioxide in milligrams per litre.

I still have the report of that analysis of my first Sangiovese. Looking at it now, I am surprised that I did not pull out the vines and plant walnut trees, cherries, or whatever. The alcohol was only 10.3 per cent and the total acidity was almost 8.5 parts per thousand. Most red wines have an acidity level that ranges from about five to seven parts per thousand. The taste of wines with high levels of acidity can be brought into balance if the alcohol level is also high, but low alcohol and high acidity produce a disjointed wine. The only good thing about the analysis was the low level of volatile acidity. In simple terms, this is a measure of the acetic acid and gives an indication of the wine's tendency to turn to vinegar, and therefore of the health and stability of the wine. A low level of volatile acidity is also an indirect indication that the grapes at harvest were undamaged by fungal attack, and that the hygiene in the winery was good. Levels of volatile acidity below about 0.5 per cent are considered safe, and my Sangiovese had less than 0.3 per cent. However, that changed nothing of the basic fact that the wine was very poor.

I was alarmed by the situation. It brought back all of my worries about the altitude. Or were the Israelis right that the first year's crop was inferior? Or should I have waited longer before beginning the vintage, despite the clamouring of my grape clients? An additional factor was that there appeared to be two different clones of Sangiovese in my two hectares. Their leaves were slightly different and one type had grapes of a noticeably higher sugar content than the other. And those vines had been bought from what Pino Manzo considered to be a serious nursery. I was later to discover that many nurseries, even ones with a good reputation, often acted irresponsibly. If my Sangiovese were an inferior clone, or clones, that would be serious, for I had more area planted to that variety than any other. My uneasiness was not much helped by the fact that friends showed no reluctance in helping me to drink the poor wine of that first vintage. Indeed, the thousand or so litres I had produced soon went, helped by locals who began to buy the wine in demijohns.

16

Unwelcome Visitors in the Vineyard

Hail is the dreaded scourge of all fruit farmers. In the Mediterranean area, with its extremes of weather, hailstorms are more common than they are further north. Most grape-growers, at least in Italy, take out insurance against hail damage, and I did so as soon as the vineyard began to produce. The system was quite simple. The insurance company, which was a parastatal organization, decided in the spring what value it would set per quintal (100 kilograms/220 pounds) of grapes for that season. The grower then declared how many quintals of grapes he wanted to insure. In my case, Pino Manzo had told me that we should be aiming for 120 quintals of grapes per hectare, so with about five hectares under vines, I chose to insure 600 quintals, or sixty tons.

In point of fact, Pino was wrong in his estimate. I eventually discovered that to produce the sugar levels I wanted, some seventy quintals per hectare were about the maximum yield in the conditions at Castel Sabino. But how I achieved lower yields is a story for later.

My vineyard seemed to lie just off the main route of the violent storms that brought hail. We would often see them swirling blackly past to the south or north and hear later that they had left a path of destruction not very far away. But occasionally one would visit us and do some damage. The procedure then was to send a telegram within forty-eight hours to the insurance company. During the next few days, the company would send an inspector to assess the damage as a percentage – no damage would be zero per cent, and total loss would be 100 per cent.

The hail insurance issue brought all of Ferruccio's cunning to the fore. There is a delightful saying in Italian to describe natural peasant craftiness: "Coarse boots – fine brain!" It fitted Ferruccio perfectly.

There were two hail inspectors who quite often came to my vineyard to assess the damage. I never met them, for I was seldom in Castel Sabino during the week, unless it was vintage time, so it fell to Ferruccio to deal with them. After he had sent the telegram, he would wander around the various parcels in the vineyard to see which rows showed the greatest damage. Of course, when the inspector arrived at Ferruccio's house, he would accompany him and, without appearing to do so, guide him into those rows. Then when the inspector pronounced that the damage in that parcel was, say, eight per cent, Ferruccio would remonstrate mildly, saying that he thought it was much higher, more like fourteen or fifteen per cent, and pointing out the damage on the worst affected bunches he could see at that moment.

After the trek around the vineyard, Ferruccio always invited the inspector into his home, gave him wine, bread, and ham or salami. The discussion about the hail damage continued in these convivial circumstances, and Ferruccio invariably wrung some extra percentage points out of the inspector. After several years of this performance, Ferruccio was on such good terms with the two inspectors that one of them, who was rather fat and disliked slogging around the vineyard on a hot day, did not even bother to do so. He sat in the kitchen of Ferruccio's home and fixed the percentage of the damage on the basis of Ferruccio's estimate. And Ferruccio was astute enough never to produce a figure that would have been so incredible that the inspector would have to rouse himself to go out to make his own assessment.

There were occasions when I wished that Ferruccio could have used the same skills he applied in handling the hail insurance inspectors to handling the inspectors from the Rieti office of the Ministry of Labour. The trouble was that he never had the opportunity, for unlike the hail inspectors who went to his house first and allowed him to entertain them to wine and ham, the inspectors from the Ministry of Labour arrived unannounced and directly into the vineyard, like hail itself and as equally feared.

In the first year or so after I had bought and started to develop the property, the casual labour market for agricultural workers was indeed very casual. At the end of the month I simply paid them the agreed wage per day for the number of days they had worked, and that was the end of the story. Rightly, however, the Italian State then began to enforce existing laws that they had never bothered about before, or to introduce new ones, and to enforce them, too.

In practice, I had to go to the Rieti office of the Ministry of Labour and ask to have certain people assigned to me for casual work throughout the year. I had to present the persons' *libretti di lavoro* (employment cards) when I made the request and wait several days before being given the approval of the office in the form of a flimsy slip of paper. Every three months I would have to declare how many days each had worked and pay their social contributions. No one could work more than 180 days during the course of any year, for if they did, they would gain the right to become a full-time and salaried employee. And no small farming operation could afford that, or the high severance pay they would have a right to when they left. The simple and widely used solution was to fire them formally in December, re-hire them formally in the following spring, and never have anyone work more than 180 days in the year. Most of the workers had their own piece of land, or were pensioners, and they were quite happy with this arrangement. And even Ferruccio, who worked with me more than anyone else, never got close to that total of 180 days, while most of the others did no more than fifty or sixty days.

One problem was that in the early years when these provisions were being applied with increasing strictness, many of the people who came to me for casual work did not want to be recruited according to the regulations. They said they were worried that they would have to pay tax, or that their own or their spouse's pension might be reduced. In fact, they did not need to worry because, in general, their earnings were low enough not to affect any pensions they were receiving. In all probability, their real concern was about becoming involved with officialdom, a concern that is easy to understand in Italy where the arbitrary application of Byzantine regulations can sometimes ride roughshod over an individual's rights.

In any case, I did not initially insist that people who came to work for two or three days tying the vines to the support wires be properly recruited. To do so was a hassle, apart from anything else, for I had to go to the office in Rieti to make the request for someone five days or so before I actually needed the person. And I had to go there again to collect the authorization. Because I was working in Rome during the week, and quite frequently abroad as well, this was often difficult to arrange.

One evening Ferruccio telephoned me in Rome to tell me that two Ministry of Labour inspectors had arrived in the vineyard that morning while he and several other people were tying the vines. He and two of the others had been properly recruited, but three more had not. The inspectors had left a formal request for me to present myself at their office within ten days.

When I read the request the following weekend, I found that it had a very peremptory tone. It challenged me harshly to explain and justify why the people named were working in my vineyard without the authorization of their office. It was an alarming summons, and when I presented myself meekly before the functionary of the Ministry of Labour in Rieti that Saturday morning, I was frightened that they would slap some heavy penalties on me. I explained that it was often difficult to start the recruitment process five days before I needed people because vineyard work was not easy to predict precisely; that I could not start recruitment too long before I needed the people and then not have them work; that as a part time-farmer, like so many others in the area, I couldn't just leave my work in Rome and come all the way to Rieti twice, the first time to make the request and a second to collect the authorization.

The functionary sat impassively behind his desk, apparently unmoved by my explanations. Unnerved, I stumbled to a close of my discourse, feeling like a delinquent teenager before a magistrate.

The functionary stared at me for a while in silence, then cleared his throat and said:

"The sanctions for not conforming to the labour regulations are very heavy," and he mentioned some figure that I can't remember, but it was certainly zillions of lire. "How many days had those people been working in your vineyard before our inspection?"

"It was their first day," I lied. "I intended to come here and recruit them properly as soon as I had a chance."

The functionary stared at me in silence again. I was sure he had not believed a word I said. I expected the worst.

"All right," he said finally. "Give me those *libretti di lavoro* you've got there and I'll have the authorization issued. But just remember how serious it is to have people working for you who are not *in regola* (in order)."

I passed him the *libretti di lavoro* I had been holding, hoping that my sweaty palms had not marked them too badly. I thanked him profusely and left before he could change his mind.

The inspectors appeared again the following year: again they found a couple of people who were not *in regola*, and again I had to go and talk my way out of being penalized. Fortunately, the functionary who listened to my excuses was not the same as on the previous occasion, so my task was easier.

We later found out – as ultimately everything is known in small rural communities – that the inspectors' second visit was the result of a *denuncia* (denunciation) that I had people illegally working for me. The informer was a man in the village who was disaffected because Ferruccio had refused to have him work in the vineyard. Such a *denuncia* could happen again at any time, and I was very frightened of the inspectors from the Ministry of Labour. I laid down the law with Ferruccio and told him that, in future, I would have absolutely no one in the vineyard whose recruitment was not completely in order. He should refuse any request for work from people who did not want to be formally recruited, blaming the refusal on me.

The inspectors continued to plague us at least once – and quite often twice – a year. After their early finds of irregularities, they probably expected to catch us out again, but they never did because everyone working was *in regola.* Ferruccio told me that they always went away looking disappointed.

"You'd think those *stronzi* (turds) were being paid a bonus for every worker they find who's not *in regola.*" Ferrucio sniffed in contempt and took a deep draft of wine. "And just think . . . one of those bastard inspectors was originally from Castel Sabino. He still has family in the village. He's no right to make problems here."

I laughed. "He's doing his job, Ferru. You can't expect him to go easy on people here because his family is from here. That's not the way things should work."

"Well, it's the way they do work . . . usually, even if it's not like that in England."

"No, it's not like that in England. You Italians get away with things that would be unthinkable there."

Ferruccio pushed back his hat. "Ah! Now I understand why you like living here, Signor Colin," he said.

Then a man called Marco Amici began working with me on a regular basis. He had worked in the building trade, but he also had some land and a small area of vines to produce wine for family consumption. And his wine was usually much better than the average for the area. He had come occasionally to help with the pruning in winter, when building was frequently at a standstill, but when he formally retired, he came to work with us throughout the year.

Marco was in many ways the antithesis of Ferruccio. He was thin and quite tall, and his face was lined and always deeply tanned. He never wore a cap or hat, and he kept his curly, grizzled hair very short. His small bristly moustache was always neatly trimmed as well. He was taciturn and serious, and there was a quiet dignity about him. He had a mannerism that was peculiar to him. When replying in the affirmative or agreeing with something that you had said, he would tilt his head quickly upwards, and slightly to one side, and emit a small grunt.

Like most men in the area, he drank a lot, but apparently without effect, for I never knew him to slur his words or walk anything but steadily, unlike Ferruccio. When I once teased Ferruccio because he had been unsteady on his feet the previous evening, he replied that his shoes had been hurting. And one morning, after I had been a little unsteady the previous evening, he asked me innocently if I had just bought some new shoes. But it would never have been possible to have such an exchange with Marco.

Ferruccio always referred to Marco by his nickname, "*Scrocco*". That Italian word normally means a scrounger or a freeloader, but I could see no relevance in it to Marco. After some months I asked Ferruccio why Marco was called *Scrocco*.

"You told me you've worked with sheep in England. *Scrocco* is what we call a ram round here. You must have seen what a ram does when it wants to mount a ewe? It comes up alongside her, nuzzles its face against her head and neck, and it keeps tilting its head and grunting."

He imitated the action and sound, and it was a perfect copy of Marco's mannerism. And of course I had often seen rams do just the same. I marvelled at rural people's capacity for observation and at their inventiveness over nicknames. In a neighbouring village there was a municipal policeman who had the nickname *Buzzichetto*. This was the term in local dialect for one of those small oil cans with a pump operated by one's thumb to squirt oil through its spout. The policeman had inherited the nickname *Buzzichetto* from his father; and he had earned it because he was a messy feeder with constant greasy stains on his shirtfront.

The summer that Marco joined us, he was in the vineyard with Ferruccio and four other people tying the vines to the wires. All were *in regola* apart from Marco. I had requested permission to recruit him, but the five days had not gone by. He was already working because there had been a strong wind the previous night and many vines had to be retied, as a matter of urgency, to let the tractor and sprayer through the next day. Of course, the inspectors from the Ministry of Labour turned up. The vines were almost fully grown and formed dense curtains, but the inspectors found the group of workers quite quickly by homing in on the chatter and laughter that always accompanied them as they progressed steadily through the vineyard, three rows at a time.

The group had almost finished tying three rows, and so were quite close to the ends, when the inspectors appeared on the scene. They began to take down the names and dates of birth of the people nearest them. Marco was several metres away and went on with his work, pretending to ignore them and keeping his head well buried in the vegetation. However, he was also working his way surreptitiously, but quite rapidly, towards the end post. Ferruccio was watching him out of the corner of his eye and trying to keep the inspectors' attention on himself. When Marco thought the inspectors were looking the other way, he straightened suddenly, scuttled round the head pole, and disappeared.

But one of the inspectors had glimpsed the movement.

"Who was that?" he demanded of Ferruccio.

"Who was what?"

"That person who was working further up the row."

"I don't know who it was. Whoever it was has probably gone into the next row. We can't stop work every time you arrive here."

The inspector hurried to the end of the row and looked along the headland. But by then, there was no one to be seen, for Marco had run past the ends of several rows, plunged back into the vineyard, and was rushing down to the other end to disappear completely off the property. Marco's presence of mind saved me. By then, the third occasion when I had transgressed, I am sure I would have been heavily fined.

Ferruccio told me the story of how *Scrocco* had outwitted the inspectors and of the speed he had shown as he beetled away and disappeared.

"*Porca Madonna*, Signor Colin," he said gleefully. "You should have seen him go! You'd have thought there was a flock of ewes waiting for him somewhere."

The image of the dignified Marco making such an undignified exit, as described by Ferruccio, was very funny. But when I raised it with Marco to thank him for his quick wits, he just half smiled and tilted his head with a grunt.

Overall, the inspectors from the Ministry of Labour were on a par with hail in terms of fearsomeness. The worst hailstorm of all was about five years after I had planted the Sangiovese. It was in October and during the vintage. A violent storm with hailstones the size of walnuts hit one night when only about half of the Sangiovese had been harvested. Walking along the rows and seeing the top half of every bunch of grapes smashed to pulp was hard to bear. Ten minutes of nature in a homicidal frenzy had undone months of tender and expensive caring for the vineyard. In addition, bunch rot would quickly set in if we did not harvest the damaged grapes as soon as possible. Furthermore, we had to get the hail inspector in rapidly too. Luckily, and exceptionally, he came the same day after I had called the insurance company and pleaded urgency. None of Ferruccio's manipulatory skills were needed to get him to rate the damage at sixty per cent of the grapes not yet harvested.

The problem remained of what to do with the unharvested and damaged grapes. Unfortunately it was a Monday, and the chances of selling the grapes quickly to locals were slim, for they always wanted to make their wine at weekends. The solution turned out to be to mobilize the local truck owner, Renzo Bertini. He transported almost all of the building materials used in the area around Castel Sabino, and I knew him well because he had transported load after load of stone when I was rebuilding the house. He had also bought grapes from me.

I telephoned him to tell him of my plight with hail-damaged grapes, and he was immediately concerned. We scheduled two trips over the next two days to a cooperative winery. It was about an hour's drive away, towards Rome. We filled all of the eighty *bigoncie* we had with damaged grapes, and when Bertini's truck arrived for the first trip, we spread a large sheet of plastic in its enormous carrying body and tipped the grapes into it.

Bertini's son, Luigino, was driving the truck that afternoon. He was in his early twenties, small and agile like his father. I went with him in the truck to the winery. On the way we talked about flying, his great interest and also one of mine because of the pilot's licence I had held before starting my project at Castel Sabino. So, as on earlier occasions when we had met, there was plenty for us to talk about. As a teenager Luigino had worked with his father whenever possible and saved all the money he could to take flying lessons. He had gained his private pilot's licence and occasionally buzzed my property in one of the aircraft belonging to the flying club in Rieti, waggling its wings in greeting.

On the way to the cooperative winery, Luigino told me that he was in a selection process for being taken on by Alitalia as a trainee pilot or a flight engineer. However, he was not optimistic because there were more than 800 applicants and only a dozen would be selected from among them, six to be trained as pilots and six as flight engineers.

"I'd be delighted even to get selected for training as a flight engineer," he said with his infectious grin as we swung through the gates of the enormous cooperative winery.

We were beckoned to park on a large weighbridge above which, dangling vertically from an outstretched mechanical arm, was a stainless steel tube about a metre (three feet) long and about ten centimetres (four inches) in diameter. As we climbed out of the truck, a man in a glass box high in the wall of the building manoeuvred some levers that brought the dangling tube over the grapes and lowered it so that it probed quickly into them, liquidizing a core of grapes and sucking up the juice. A few seconds later he lifted the tube smartly out and lowered it in a different part of the load, and then again a third time. On the wall of the building below the glass box a screen lit up with red letters reading, "BABO 16.8".

A winery employee then pointed to the large hopper let into the ground into which the grapes had to be tipped. Luigino reversed quickly up to it, pulled a lever, and the body of the truck slowly rose until the grapes slid down into the

Low Sabine Hills

The low Sabine Hills are gentle and mild.
Olives flourish here and give excellent oil.

High Sabine Hills

The conditions in the high Sabine
Hills, near Castel Sabino, are wilder
and harsher at the upper-altitude limit
for olives. However, grape vines
abound, although no respectable,
commercial wines have ever been
produced from them.

The original land

Seven hectares of abandoned land in the high Sabine Hills were bought in 1974…

The old house

…with its abandoned house.

Rebuilding the house

Reconstruction and additions to the original building.

The finished house

The end result after the major rebuilding.

New vineyard

The initial planting of two hectares of Sangiovese vines.

Ferruccio – trusted right-hand man, and provider of comic relief.

Pino Manzo – adviser and friend – in Franco
Morricone's vineyard at Affile.

The vineyard in high summer

View from the garden

Only guests had time to enjoy the deckchair in the shade!

Montepulciano d'Abruzzo vines

The Montepulciano d'Abruzzo grapes formed a good blend with the Sangiovese and Cesanese di Affile.

Colin and Ferruccio

Admiring the vineyard – clean and orderly after the spring cultivation.

Poggio Fenice from the air

The winery in the foreground is dug into the slope below the house. The pink house in the top-left corner is Ferruccio's home.

Tanks in the winery

Four 5,000-litre tanks; on the plinth to the right, the small fibreglass tanks first used in the tractor shed winery and the 7,000-litre fermenting tank.

The grotto

The grotto for storing and ageing bottled wine. Its impeccable concrete, domed roof was created at breakneck speed by a few simple workmen of peasant stock.

The labeller

The second-hand labeller; effective but often cantankerous.

Mighty oak

The mighty oak, described in 1974 as being worth more than the rest of the abandoned property put together, still flourishes in 2004.

Colin in the vineyard

Examining grapes, in 2004, in the vineyard that was planted some thirty years earlier.

The cups

Trophies for the Poggio Fenice wines that the author founded and went on to win.

The bottles

The author's end product, the first commercial wines from the high Sabine Hills. The stages in the development of the label design over the early years can be followed, from left to right.

hopper. Then he drove back on to the weighbridge, after which I was handed a chit with the information that we had delivered 38.8 quintals (8,536 pounds) of red wine grapes of 16.8 Babo. That was only the beginning of the paperwork, for I had to go into an office with the chit and fill in all manner of forms about myself and from where the grapes came. The formula for paying me, sometime the following year, was a combination of the Babo level and the quantity: in effect, they were paying for grape sugar.

As we drove back, Luigino and I discussed cooperative wineries like that one. The Italian and European Union authorities had been promoting them and financing them for years, but they seldom seemed to produce decent wine. The reason was obvious: they had no control over the quality, or even variety, of the grapes brought to them by growers, so however good their winemaking technology, their end product would always reflect the quality of the raw material. Indeed, the only cooperative wineries to have survived in recent years and produce good wines seem to be the ones that impose strict standards on their members. They simply refuse to accept grapes of low standard, or pay so little for grapes of low sugar content that the grower is forced to do better next year.

I ruminated about the 16.8 Babo of those grapes we had brought in. That was the equivalent of less than eleven per cent alcohol. The grapes were all Sangiovese, and by then those vines were reasonably well established. It could no longer be an issue of poor quality in the first year. Nor was it one of harvesting too early, for I had learned to fight off the demands of clients wanting their grapes before they were really ready. The Sangiovese was letting the side down, but there was too much of it to think seriously about grafting a better clone on to it. There were no experienced grafters in Castel Sabino, as there probably would have been in an area with more commercial vineyards.

About a month later, however, I was cheered from these worries by a call from Luigino. His voice was ecstatic as he told me that he was among the six out of the 800 applicants selected for pilot training by Alitalia. Less than a year later, after intensive training in Sardinia, he was first officer on DC9s flying routes in Europe. What a delightful case of upward social mobility! A truck driver's son from a rural backwater, without any help from friends in high places, whose sheer enthusiasm and singlemindedness had turned him, literally, into a high flyer.

17

Progress

The Cesanese di Affile and Montepulciano d'Abruzzo vines, once in production, proved far superior to the Sangiovese. Their grapes reached higher sugar levels and gave much more colour to the wine. That was especially true of the Cesanese, with its bunches of tightly packed small berries. I began to be more optimistic about the possibility of producing good wines.

Most of the information I gathered had indicated that red wines made from more than one variety were generally more interesting than single variety wines, known as varietals. This does not mean, of course, that varietals made from particularly high-quality grapes are not excellent. For example, there is the Italian variety Nebbiolo, which alone goes into famous Piemonte wines such as Barolo and Barbaresco in northwest Italy. And there are Cabernet Sauvignon, Syrah, Merlot, Chardonnay, Sauvignon, etc., that are used alone to make outstanding wines in many parts of the world. However, even these prestigious grapes are often mixed with others, or their young wines blended. This is the case with the famous clarets from Bordeaux that are blends of Cabernet Sauvignon and Merlot. Taking this into account, and based more or less on the proportion of the vineyard planted to the three red varieties, I decided to produce a red wine that would be made up of about half Sangiovese and a quarter each of Cesanese and Montepulciano.

Over the five or so years that I mainly sold grapes and vinified relatively small quantities in the tractor garage, I continued working with my red from the three grape varieties, but I also tried making a varietal Cesanese. It turned out with an alcohol content of over twelve per cent, and it was well balanced and full of fruit flavour. Montepulciano d'Abruzzo is often used to make an excellent rosé wine, so I experimented with that too, and added the fresh pressings to the three-variety wine. That added depth of colour and flavour, but I was still having trouble with low levels of alcohol in the three-variety wine. I had set a target level of twelve per cent alcohol but it seldom reached even 11.5 per cent.

In France and in most other wine producing countries in Europe, legislation allows the addition of sugar to the fermenting wine to increase its alcohol, a procedure known as chaptalization. In theory, however, it is only done under controlled conditions, after the winemaker requests permission from the local authorities and provides details of how much sugar he wants to add. One might assume, therefore, that permission is only granted in unfavourable years, but a Bordeaux wine producer told me once that he and his peers routinely added at least a kilogram (2.2 pounds) of sugar per 100 litres of must every year, whether the season had been favourable or not.

In contrast, adding sugar in Italy is strictly forbidden, except in some very limited areas in the extreme north, at high altitudes. Chaptalization is banned in almost all of the country because it considerably increases the amount of wine that can be produced with an acceptable alcohol level. Indeed, a late 1990s article I recently came across stated that chaptalization was enabling Europe, as a whole, to produce twenty million hectolitres more wine than it could without the practice. A hectolitre is one hundred litres, so those twenty million hectolitres equate to almost 2,700 million bottles of wine in which the alcohol level is fully satisfactory only because sugar was added during fermentation.

In any case, there can be no doubt that the climatic and soil conditions in most of Italy are among the best in the world for wine production. It was not by chance that the ancient Greeks gave it the name *Oenotria* (Land of Wine). It is inherently far superior to cooler areas of Europe, where, more often than not, it is only chaptalization that makes it possible to produce decent wines. Nevertheless, even if chaptalization is forbidden in most of Italy, it is said that the sales of sugar in the northern parts of the country start to climb during the summer months, peak in the early autumn, and decline again from November onwards. I do not know whether this is true, but it could be.

In my days of winemaking in Italy, one could produce up to fifty hectolitres, i.e. 5,000 litres, without becoming subject to the numerous declarations, paperwork, and regulations as to what one was allowed to do. The output from my tractor-garage winery was much less than that, so I considered that I could add sugar without infringing the law. I readily found out that 1.6 kilograms

(3.5 pounds) of sugar added to one hundred litres of wine will normally increase its alcohol by about 1 per cent, and I took action accordingly. Nevertheless, I felt the guilt born of a repressive British education when I bought packets of sugar, so I spread my purchases over several days and different supermarkets. Ridiculous really, because it is not part of the Italian culture to blow the whistle on anybody – except in football. The principle of "live and let live" is deeply entrenched in Italian social behaviour.

As an alternative to sugar, I could have added concentrated grape must. This is must from which much of the water has been evaporated. It is a dense, treacly substance, sold in drums, that is either red or yellowish according to the colour of the original must. However, there would have been an inherent problem in using it, for in addition to its colour, it carries much of the taste of the original must. There would have been no point in trying to produce wines that were characteristic of the grapes I had planted if their taste were changed by the concentrated must I had added at the time of fermentation. I therefore decided against using it.

In those years of the early eighties, when I was covertly buying sugar and adding it to my fermenting wine in the tractor garage, a large industrial plant was being built near Anagni, south of Rome, and close to the home of my Cesanese vine cuttings from Affile. It looked something like an oil refinery with its chimneys and tanks. Its purpose was to produce Rectified Concentrated Grape Must, or RCGM. The raw material for the process would be ordinary concentrated grape must, complete with its colour and flavour, but the plant would rectify it, in the sense of purifying it. The final product would be a transparent syrup of grape sugar and water with no taste, apart from sweetness.

Several such plants to produce RCGM were eventually set up with financial support from the European Union. The reasoning was that there were too many grapes, and too much wine, being produced and that a good way of absorbing the excess was to convert it into RCGM. This would be used to raise the alcohol level of wines being made in cool areas where grapes ripen less well. Furthermore, the purists were saying that it was wrong to use sugar made from beet to increase alcohol levels when RCGM was an "all-grape" alternative. In Italy, RCGM would provide, for the first time, a technically viable and legal replacement for the sugar that was being used illegally and which the authorities must surely have known about.

Most of the grapes that would go to produce RCGM would come from the central and southern parts of Italy. It would in the main be from grapes of inferior quality for winemaking. For example, there were large areas planted to Regina dei Vigneti, a white grape variety that was very high yielding, up to forty tonnes per hectare. This was considered to be a variety that was both suitable for eating and for making wine, even if it was uninteresting to eat and made very inferior wine. (It is still around, but it has been banned for use in winemaking.) The European Union would subsidize the use of RCGM by reimbursing some of its cost to the wine producer.

In principle, the RCGM initiative appeared to be one of the more sensible ones in the European agricultural sector. Its ultimate aim was to replace sugar with RCGM in winemaking everywhere in Europe. However, even today, years later, the process of eliminating the addition of sugar is very far from being complete; wine producers in the cooler areas have been strongly resisting the change to RCGM. For example, I raised the question of RCGM with the Bordeaux wine producer I mentioned earlier and who said that he and his peers added sugar to their fermenting wines every year. We were talking in his winery. It was early September, with the vintage expected to start in a week or so, and behind him were sacks of sugar piled high on pallets.

"What do you think about using Rectified Concentrated Grape Must instead of sugar, something Brussels wants us all to do?" I asked.

The French language lends itself to a very particular tone of voice and way of emphasizing words that denotes deep scorn. He hit the pitch perfectly as he replied, with the full gamut of facial expressions needed to emphasize his protest.

"*Mais c'est con!* We've used sugar here for generations and it works fine. Why should I risk my wine by adding some concoction that Brussels says I must? I know nothing about the stuff. It's produced somewhere else, and how am I to know that it won't damage my wine, even if it does add to the alcohol? And what's more, I've been told it costs more than sugar."

I am not claiming that such arguments were necessarily typical of the reason in some regions for the resistance to adopting RCGM, but what he said resonated with me.

My first production of wine from the Pinot Bianco that I had planted more or less illegally seemed to me to show promise. The first year that the vines bore fruit, I harvested just enough to make about 200 litres of wine. Ferruccio and I put the grapes through the crusher/de-stalker and then transferred the mass immediately into the press, for I wanted to ferment the must without any contact with the skins. This is the normal process for making those light-coloured, fresh and fragrant white wines that most people want today. Ferruccio was surprised because he and the local people normally fermented their white wine on the skins for several days before pressing. I had tasted some of these wines and they lacked any of the delicacy and aroma that I liked in a white wine. They were also too dark in colour, as well as being cloudy, or even muddy on occasion.

We transferred the must of the Pinot Bianco into large demijohns to ferment and I gave it the usual treatments of potassium metabisulphite and selected yeasts. The fermentation went quite slowly because the weather was cool, and because the quantities – about forty litres in each fifty-four-litre demijohn – were so small that the heat created by the fermentation process was easily dispersed. After exposure to the cold of winter and some rackings, the wine was completely transparent. This surprised me because I had read that white wine always needed to be filtered, contrary to red wine that cleared more easily.

I regularly tasted that first small batch of Pinot Bianco, and by the late spring it seemed as good to me as many professionally produced wines made from similar grapes that I had drunk. Or was my ambition and enthusiasm causing me to deceive myself? I needed to find out from independent and knowledgeable people whether my first Pinot Bianco was as good as it seemed to me.

It so happened that about a year before I had been asked to write two articles on Italian wines for FAO's staff magazine. Shortly after their publication, I received a phone call from a man called George Khudin, an African from Benin. I knew him only by name, but he was friendly and charming as he congratulated me on the articles. He went on to suggest that we set up a Wine Study Group in FAO, alongside many other special interest and leisure groups for staff covering things such as dogs, tennis, fishing, yoga, and so on. I said that I thought it an excellent idea: I had received many comments and questions from people who had read my articles, and I knew that there was a lot of interest in wine in that large and heterogeneous international group of people that made up FAO Headquarters staff. George Khudin said he would start organizing a first meeting to start the ball rolling.

A few days later I had to travel to Asia for work. When I got back, George Khudin called to tell me that the first meeting had taken place. It had been attended by more than thirty enthusiastic people who wanted to learn more about wine through courses and through visits to vineyards and wineries.

"Oh, and by the way," he said, "you know that French saying about 'the absent always being wrong'? Well, in keeping with that, we elected you chairman of the group while you weren't there".

It turned out to be a pleasant task and the group's activities and contacts helped me to learn more about wine. In fact, at the time of my first Pinot Bianco, the group was being instructed in the techniques of wine tasting at a weekly evening session. Our mentors were two people from the Italian Association of Sommeliers (AIS). Few members of AIS actually work as sommeliers in restaurants or hotels; the vast majority are amateur but very knowledgeable wine buffs who have successfully completed a course run by AIS. They are happy to help others acquire better knowledge about wine and how to combine wines with different types of food. I decided that I would take a couple of bottles of my Pinot Bianco to a tasting session that the group was to have under the guidance of the AIS sommeliers.

One of the people from AIS leading us through these sessions was a retired general. He looked more British than Italian with his erect posture, blue blazer with brass buttons, clipped moustache, and authoritative but courteous manner. And he was a stickler for detail in wine tasting.

We examined and tasted four wines the evening I had brought my Pinot Bianco. As the session was drawing to a close, I reached down to my briefcase on the floor and extracted the insulated bag with my two bottles inside it. Earlier in the day I had persuaded the manager of a nearby bar to let me leave them in his refrigerator until I passed by to collect them on my way to the session. I was relieved to feel that the bottles were still well cooled as I passed them to the general.

"I'm thinking of buying a couple of demijohns of white wine," I said, "and the producer gave me this sample to try before deciding. Could we taste it together? I'd like to know what you think of it".

Some members of the group clamoured to know where the wine was from, but I just laughed them off and said that these experts from AIS should be able tell us. The general's AIS colleague deftly drew the corks from my bottles, which of course had no labels, and poured the wine into the glasses. The group began holding their glasses over a piece of white paper placed on the table in front of them to examine the wine's colour and transparency.

"*Signora!*" It was the general's voice, with such an edge to it that we all looked up from our contemplation of the physical appearance of the wine in our glasses. The general was looking rather sternly at a woman member of our group who was cuddling her glass of white wine in her hands. She was a middle-aged English woman who loved wine, but she was not over-inclined to take it – or anything else – too seriously.

"*Signora*" he repeated, lowering his voice to its usual tone of courtesy and reason. "Please allow me to remind you that you should always hold a glass of white wine that you're going to taste by its foot, and not by its bowl. If you hold it by the bowl, your hand will warm it. And white wine has such delicate aromas that if you have washed your hands with scented soap or have perfume on them, it will not be possible to evaluate the bouquet properly."

The lady looked slightly embarrassed, but only for a moment.

"Yes, general!" she said, giving a mock salute and repositioning the glass to hold it by its foot. Everybody laughed, including the general. I don't know whether anyone noticed that my laughter was rather nervous, for I was very on edge to hear what would be said about my Pinot. So much depended on the outcome of the tasting. Would I be able to produce fine wines at Castel Sabino as the Tuscan consultant had said when he urged me to buy the property?

"So, what do you think of its appearance?" asked the general, tilting his glass to one side and peering down through it.

People around the table began to offer their judgments based on the marking form we all had in front of us. Was it brilliant, transparent, cloudy, opaque, or turbid? The majority verdict was that it was somewhere between brilliant and transparent, a verdict that was endorsed by the general.

"Now," he said, "let's examine its arches, or what in England wine tasters call its 'legs', I believe".

We each swilled the wine around in our glass, tipped the glass to one side, straightened it, and held it up to the light as we did so. We were looking to see how the wine flowed down the inside of the glass. Did it appear slightly oily and viscous, leaving narrow arches as it flowed down, or did it appear more liquid, spreading out over the glass and leaving wide arches? From previous sessions with the general we had learned that wine with a viscous appearance and narrow arches had a high level of glycerine, an alcohol that naturally occurs in wine. Glycerine is sweet and oily and gives a wine smoothness. After some discussion in the group, guided by the general, it was decided that the wine did not have much glycerine. It was also agreed that its colour was "pale straw".

Now came the moment to agree on a mark for the appearance of my Pinot. The marking system we were using accorded a maximum total of thirty points for a wine, of which six were for appearance, twelve for bouquet, and twelve for taste. The appearance of the wine was judged to be good but not outstanding. It earned four points out of the possible six.

"Now the bouquet," commanded the general. The group diligently swilled the wine around in their glasses to release its aroma and bent their noses for two quick sniffs, one into each nostril, and waited for a short while before repeating the process. This was the way AIS did it, for the general had stressed that too long, or too frequent, sniffs overwhelmed one's sense of smell, with the result that it lost its power of discrimination.

There were murmurs of appreciation from the group as they sniffed.

"Quite extraordinary!" declared the general, and there were murmurs of agreement from the group. I could hardly contain my excitement.

After many further minutes of discussion and sniffing the conclusion was that the bouquet was intense, persistent, fruity, fragrant, and fresh. It contained scents of pineapple, anise, lime, and golden delicious apples.

"Why do you think it smells of apples?" the general asked.

"That's the smell of malic acid," replied several of the more diligent members of the group together.

"Very good! Yes, and remember that it gets the name malic acid from *malum,* the Latin word for apple. And now, what mark are we going to give the bouquet?" the general asked.

In the marking system we were using, the bouquet was sub-divided into three sectors with a maximum of four marks for each. These sub-sectors were persistence, general assessment, and characteristics.

"I'd give it four for persistence," said the general's AIS assistant.

"So would I", said several members of the group.

"Yes," said the general. "It's outstanding, and I'd also give it top marks for its overall quality. Its fruit and fragrance are exceptional."

After some further discussion about its characteristics, which were also agreed to be of top level, the bouquet of my Pinot Bianco was awarded the maximum mark of twelve. Somehow, I managed to maintain a slightly disinterested air as the proceedings went on, but inside, I was seething with excitement.

"Now the taste," said the general. He and the group took a generous sip of the wine, sloshed it around in their mouths, and breathed in over it, as we had been taught. The taste strongly filled the mouth and nasal cavity, and after swallowing it, the aftertaste persisted well, or so I thought. But of course I made no comment.

The marking system for the taste allowed a maximum of six points for the balance and overall taste, and a further six for the persistence and quality of the aftertaste. Again the group was murmuring in appreciation.

"Elegant and well balanced," the general said. "Slightly astringent, I find, and that's good."

The discussion that followed ended with the wine being awarded the top mark of six for balance and overall taste. The aftertaste was found to be good, without being exceptional, and it was marked four out of six.

Thus my first Pinot Bianco, made in my tractor garage, in demijohns, had been given twenty-six points out of a possible thirty. By any standards, this was a success. If I'd had the equipment to filter the wine it would have got a higher mark for its appearance. By this time I was grinning widely, overjoyed with the result.

"Well, now tell us about the wine?" the general said.

"Yes, and where we can buy some!" said a member of the group.

"You tell me first what you think it is," I hedged.

"Let's begin by deciding what it can't be," the general began thoughtfully. "It's much too elegant and delicate to be anything like Trebbiano." He took another sip. "It's not a Chardonnay because that has a very particular taste. So does Müller-Thurgau. And it's got a much better bouquet and is fresher and fuller than either Sauvignon or Pinot Grigio. I would say it's a Pinot Bianco, possibly from the Oltrepo Pavese."

The mention of this prestigious wine production area near Pavia, on a range of hills that emerge improbably from the plains of the Po Valley, delighted me.

"You're right about it being a Pinot Bianco," I said, "but it comes from the Sabine Hills, a place called Castel Sabino, and I made it myself, in demijohns in the garage. The grapes were from the first harvest of some Pinot Bianco vines that I planted illegally in my new vineyard three years ago."

"*Per Bacco!*" exclaimed the general. "I'd never have thought it. The Sabine Hills are renowned for good olive oil, but not for wine. And certainly not for a wine like this."

"I know." I said. "In fact, some people told me that Castel Sabino was too high for grapes to ripen properly, but that wine's got 12.5 per cent alcohol without adding any concentrated must or sugar."

The group was gathering around me, calling out compliments and congratulations and patting me on the shoulder. It was a fine moment. The general asked me about the vineyard, and I told him about it and about the varieties of grapes I had planted.

"Well, my compliments," he said. "If you can produce other wines like that Pinot, you'll do very well."

Ferrucio, too, was delighted when I told him about the twenty-six points out of thirty. I am not sure he had ever known that people sat around tasting wines and awarding them points, so I explained the whole process to him in some detail. His face was a study in shock and horror when I mentioned that tasters confronted with many wines spat out each sample after swilling it around in their mouths. He was so taken aback that he could not even comment; he just sat there shaking his head in disbelief.

18

Grafting and
Pruning for Quality

The success with my first Pinot Bianco showed that quality wines could be
produced at Castel Sabino, at least if the grapes ripened early. The Pinot for that
first wine had been harvested on September 26, whereas the red varieties and the
Trebbiano took at least a further two weeks to ripen. Even in an unfavourable
year, early ripening varieties such as Pinot Bianco, Riesling, Merlot, and Cabernet
Sauvignon would be ready by mid-October. That was a cut-off date in my mind
because it seemed that it often rained heavily in the second half of that month.
But none of my varieties, with the exception of the Pinot, were early ripening;
they were all classified as mid-range in their ripening date.

Somehow I would have to try to obtain better quality grapes from the vines
that I had. They were all inherently capable of producing grapes for quality
wines, with the exception of the Trebbiano. Indeed, I had already decided
that the Trebbiano was a major problem: it had given me a very indifferent
wine in its first year. I discussed the matter with Pino Manzo. We were together
for dinner in Rome and we had just tasted some of my first Pinot Bianco. I did
not have much of it left, but I had put some aside for occasions like this. I also
wanted to see how it would withstand its first year of life in bottle. I did not
expect it to keep all of its qualities for much more than that, but even delicate and

fresh white wines must be able to hold up for at least a year or eighteen months in bottle.

"Those AIS people were right," Pino Manzo said after tasting the Pinot. "This wine's outstanding. Of course, Pinot Bianco is a far better variety than Trebbiano. Don't forget, though, that our original idea was to sell grapes. The locals would probably be very happy with Trebbiano. And it yields a lot more than Pinot."

"I know, but I've become more interested in producing wine, and the market for grapes in Castel Sabino seems to be reducing. Some people who've bought grapes from me have given up making their own wine. Too much work, they say."

"Why don't we graft Pinot onto the Trebbiano? Are there any good grafters at Castel Sabino?" Pino Manzo asked.

"No. There's a man, one of Ferruccio's uncles, who has a reputation for being able to graft fruit trees, but he is pretty ancient and I've heard he's not well."

"That's one of the problems of being in an area where there are no other commercial vineyards. If Castel Sabino were in a prestigious wine producing area, there would be gangs of grafters you could call in. They would do the lot in a couple of days."

We discussed the problem further, and the outcome was that Pino Manzo would use his contacts in the Castelli Romani to see if he could find some grafters. In the meantime, I got out my viticulture books and read up about grafting. I was surprised to find that there were references to various grafting techniques that went back to the Romans in the fourth century AD. I was also surprised to learn that grafting was commonly used in vineyards to change varieties according to market demand. Furthermore, in some vineyards aiming for high quality, grafting may be a process repeated over time; each year, cuttings are taken from the best vines and are grafted on to inferior ones, so that the overall quality of the vineyard is gradually raised.

I also discovered that there are many different grafting methods used at different times of year. Those during the summer months, when the vines are growing, required very careful timing. Because grafters were not available locally, this would present logistical complications for me. Grafting in spring before the vines began to bud would be easier to arrange.

As usual, Pino Manzo was as good as his word. He called me in January to say he had found two grafters near Frascati who would be willing to come to Castel Sabino in early April. I had already told Ferruccio to leave some of the canes un-pruned on the Pinot Bianco to provide cuttings for the grafting.

The grafters duly came two weekends in a row. They began by sawing off the trunks of the vines, about thirty-five centimetres (fourteen inches) above the ground, in the hectare or so of Trebbiano. The grafters had brought a lot of raffia with them and they bound it around the trunk just below the cut. Then, using a special knife, they made a vertical cut across the top of each stump. They pruned the canes that Ferruccio had left on the Pinot vines and cut them into lengths of about ten centimetres (four inches) with two buds. Then, using a special knife again, they very carefully sharpened the lower end of the cutting into the shape of a perfectly symmetrical wedge and gently pushed the piece of cane down into the vertical cut they had made in the trunk. They explained that the angle of the wedge was critical because its surfaces had to lie flush against the inside surfaces of the cut in the trunk. The cuttings, two of which were inserted into each trunk, also had to be positioned so that the cambial layer just below the bark on the cuttings coincided with the cambial layer of the trunk. To achieve this, the cuttings were set at the edge of the trunk, opposite each other, so that they stuck up like two erect ears. More raffia held them in place, and the top of the sawn-off trunk was daubed with some blackish gunk to protect it.

The bandaged stumps looked hideous, and I wondered what disaster had been perpetrated. However, the grafters assured me that if all went well, about ninety-five per cent of the grafts would take. In the event, about ninety-three per cent did, and so I had more than a hectare of Pinot Bianco, a variety that I knew for certain could produce excellent wine in the conditions of Castel Sabino.

Grafting could have been a way of improving other parts of the vineyard, especially the Sangiovese, but the lack of grafters in the area would have made it virtually impossible. I suggested to Ferruccio that he might like to learn the skill by going down to Frascati and spending a couple of days with the grafters. He was not enthusiastic.

"Grafting needs more patience than I've got," he declared.

"Good, Ferru," I said. "I'm glad to see you know yourself so well." I was remembering the occasions I had seen him working on some task that was not going precisely as he wanted and hearing the profanity and invective that punctuated his efforts.

"Why don't you learn to graft, Signor Colin?"

"I'm not very patient either, and besides, I don't have the time. What about Maria Lisa or Francesca? Perhaps they'd like to learn. It must be quite a satisfying thing to do. Or one of the women who work in the vineyard with you? Women are much better than men at doing fiddly precision jobs."

An expression of astonishment crossed Ferruccio's face.

"I don't believe it. Neither Maria Lisa or Francesca could ever learn to graft. And nor could any of the women who work with me. Grafting is a skilled job. I've never known a women who can even cut bread straight."

It was a waste of time persisting along that line, for I well remembered a discussion I had had with Ferruccio some years earlier about the wages being paid to the men and the women who worked in the vineyard. The people were all casual agricultural labourers and at peak times, such as tying the fast-growing vines to their support wires, there could be half a dozen or more men and women at work together.

The first time I made out the pay packets for such a mixed group, I paid the women the same daily rate that I had agreed for the men. Within an hour Ferruccio turned up at my house, very concerned.

"The men have asked me to talk to you," he said. "They're very upset because you've paid the women the same as them."

"Of course. They're doing exactly the same job. There's no special skill or knowledge needed. They should get the same wage."

"It's not like that here. Women never get paid as much as men, even when they're doing the same work."

"I've no wish to throw money away, Ferru. You know that. This operation's costing me a lot of money, and if I could save on labour costs, I'd be happy. But it's a question of principle."

"Men get paid more because they've a family to support. That's normal."

"Well, there are some widows in our lot who have miserable pensions and need money as badly as anyone," I retorted. "And the married women are helping to support their families, too."

Nothing I could say convinced Ferruccio. He was adamant that the women be paid less, adding that the men would refuse to work for me if it were otherwise.

"All right," I finally said. "You know the people round here better than I ever will. But only a token difference. The men get twenty-eight thousand lire a day. You get an extra thousand because you're the foreman, and I'll pay the women a thousand less."

"I think it should be two thousand less," Ferruccio said. "Then everyone will be happy."

"Why should the poor women be happy? I'd be furious if I were one of them. And what are they going to say when I tell them I'm taking two thousand lire off their daily wage in future?"

Ferruccio laughed.

"Signor Colin," he said, "just tell them they're lucky they can keep the extra they've had for the last month. They'll be happy."

And to my amazement, he was right. The women also thought it perfectly normal that they be paid less than the men, and they seemed grateful to have had the little extra that particular month.

It was a pity that Ferruccio would not go along with my idea of learning to graft, or of letting his daughters or some of the other women learn, but I sensed that the perceptions among local men about women's limitations were so deeply ingrained that to insist would cause trouble. The men also considered that pruning was a job only for men. They would be happy to have a couple of women to help, tying the pruned canes to the support wires or replacing a pole, but the actual task of deciding what to prune off and using the secateurs could only be done by a man, they claimed. However, over the years, two men in their seventies who had helped with the pruning left to enjoy a full retirement. Then, Ferruccio's nephew Michele, who was also the tractor driver and who had been taught to prune, left for a job at Rome airport.

"What are we going to do about the pruning next winter?" I asked Ferruccio. "Do you know anyone else who's any good at pruning?"

"Don't worry," Ferruccio said. "Last winter I began teaching Maria Lisa how to prune. She's quite good at it already."

I burst out laughing. "What's happening to you? You've always told me pruning was a man's job. I'm not surprised that Maria Lisa's learned to prune. What makes you think women are incompetent? Where would you be without Giuliana and all the work she does, and does well, around the place, with the pigs, chickens, and so on? And that's in addition to the cooking, washing, and everything for your comforts. You're a terrible male chauvinist, Ferru!"

Ferruccio looked a bit abashed for a moment, but quickly recovered.

"*È una croce con le donne!* (Women are a cross to bear!) Maybe they can sometimes learn to do something properly. They're only useful in one place . . . and you know where that is. There's not much they do that a man couldn't do better, with a bit of practice. Even me."

"What about bringing children into the world?" I asked, somewhat aggressively.

"Yes, but what man would want to do that? I wouldn't. Too painful!"

With that oblique recognition that women tolerate pain better than men, the subject was dropped. Convincing men that women were just as competent as they were, at least for the lighter tasks on the land, was as difficult as convincing them that the urine-coloured white wine they made and drank was as bad – or even worse – than the liquid it appeared to be.

Thus, women became gradually involved in the winter pruning of the vineyard. The way it was pruned was of great concern to me, for it determined to a great extent the quantity of grapes produced, and hence their quality. Shorter winter pruning would produce fewer grapes with higher sugar content. So also would removing some bunches during the growing season from vines that had too many. But the very idea of cutting off already existing bunches was a sacrilege in a rural society as poor as that around Castel Sabino. It would be easier to adopt shorter winter pruning, or so I thought. But even applying that strategy turned out to be a major and long-lasting battle.

There are many different pruning and training systems used in vineyards. They have been developed over centuries in the context of different climatic and soil conditions, the density of planting, and the variety of vine. In general terms, the more favourable the conditions, the more expansive the pruning and training system, whereas in cold or very dry conditions, each vine is pruned short. That is why, for example, the vines after the winter pruning in Switzerland, and in many parts of Burgundy, are mere stumps with three or four very short canes emerging upwards from them. The same system is used in hot, dry areas of southern Italy and Spain; it is known as *alberello* (bush) in Italian and "head-trained vine" in English.

At the other extreme are high trellises, and systems that create a large ceiling of vegetation almost two metres (6.5 feet) above the ground, known as *tendoni* (awnings). Tractors can criss-cross beneath them to work the ground. They can produce forty tons of grapes, or even more, to the hectare. This may be acceptable for table grapes, which have a lower sugar content than wine grapes, but no decent wine can be expected from a *tendone* system. Thus, with the emphasis on quality rather than quantity that has slowly taken over the wine industry in Italy in the last couple of decades, *tendoni* have been going out of fashion. Some high trellis systems, but not as expansive as awnings, are still used for special reasons. For example, in flat and low-lying areas where late frosts are common, the purpose of high trellises is often to lift the budding vegetation above the layer of cold air that does the damage.

In between the two extremes of short and expansive training are the systems known as *filari* (rows). This uses rows of poles and horizontal wires and allows the vegetation to be trained vertically upwards and tied to the wires. There are usually three wires. The vine is pruned to create a trunk that reaches the lowest one, normally about sixty to seventy centimetres (twenty-four to twenty-eight inches) from the ground, while the two higher ones support the summer vegetation and grape clusters. The height of the top wire may vary, but in most of central Italy, including the great vineyards of Tuscany, it is set about 1.8 metres (six feet) above ground. Pino Manzo recommended that we adopt this system, the commonest in Italy.

However, the pruning and training story does not end there. Many different methods exist even within *filari,* each with its name, such as horizontal spurred cordon, Sylvoz, Cazenave, Leyvraz/Simon, Geneva double curtain, Guyot, and several others. All of these systems are conditioned by one vital fact: vines bear their fruit on the canes produced in the previous season, and any pruning system must provide one or more such canes for the following year.

Pino Manzo and I discussed at length what system to use, and in the end we decided on a classic method, the Guyot. This method has been known since the days of ancient Rome, but its name derives from a French nineteenth-century scientist, Dr. Jules Guyot. He was an eclectic who studied many things, from the effect of heat on the healing of wounds, to steam engines and the motion and pressure of air. But his name lives on in the pruning system that he described and began promoting in the 1850s and which is now used worldwide. His name is also perpetuated by the Jules Guyot Institute, the oenology and viticulture faculty of the University of Burgundy.

The Guyot method develops the trunk of the vine to the height of the first wire and then, at each winter pruning, a single cane of the previous year is left and tied horizontally along that wire. The shoots that emerge from it will bear most of the fruit, and they are trained upwards and supported on the higher wires. In addition, a short spur with two buds is left near the trunk, mainly to provide a good cane to be bent along the wire as the main fruit bearer in the following year.

In favourable conditions the Guyot system can be double, or bilateral, that is to say that after pruning there are two fruit-bearing canes, one going left from the trunk and one going right. In my case, since the vines were planted in pairs, we planned to use a single Guyot system, with one vine trained to the left and the other to the right.

How many buds to leave on each fruit-bearing cane was another issue that Pino Manzo and I discussed in detail. Normally the Guyot system leaves 6–12 buds on the cane. Pino said he thought we should leave from 8–12, but the number within that range would need to be adjusted according to the vigour of the individual vines. This decision would, in practice, depend on Ferruccio and others pruning with him, for I did not have the time to become directly involved.

However, even if I did not prune myself, I walked around the vineyard with Ferruccio at weekends in winter to see what progress was being made and how the pruning was being done. About five years after the planting of the Sangiovese, I began to find that there were many pruned vines with fruit canes that had far more than the maximum of twelve buds mentioned by Pino Manzo. In fact, there were very few within that limit of twelve, especially in the Sangiovese. The fact concerned me, but I had never pruned a vine in my life, whereas Ferruccio and his helpers had pruned their own vineyards for decades. So I hesitated to criticize what he was doing. Nevertheless, during one particular walkabout in the vineyard on a cold but fine January day, I began to express my concern. I stopped in front of a pruned vine that had a second fruit cane laid along the middle wire.

137

"Ferru," I said, "I'm worried about the length of the pruning we're doing. We're well over the twelve buds on the fruit cane that Pino Manzo mentioned. And I see that this year you're often putting a second cane along the next wire up, like this one here".

I ran my finger along the canes of the vine in front of me, counting the buds aloud. I reached nineteen on that vine, and several others with a second cane had a similar number, or even more.

Ferruccio followed me in silence. After counting aloud the buds on a few more vines – there were nearly always between fifteen and twenty-two – I stopped and turned to look at him. He scratched his ear thoughtfully before speaking.

"Doctor Manzo also said we had to adjust the number of buds according to the vigour of each vine. These are very vigorous, Signor Colin. They can give a lot of grapes. It'd be pity not to take advantage of what they can produce."

We wandered up and down a few more rows, with our inspection only interrupted at the end of one row by a familiar announcement from Ferruccio, one that always amused me. "Must take Willy for a piss!" He stumped off to the nearby hedgerow to relieve himself before we resumed the inspection.

I was still in doubt about the pruning, but I had no criteria by which to judge the situation. Pino Manzo had said the vineyard as a whole should produce about twelve tons of grapes per hectare, but parts of it were still too young to be producing fully, and we were nowhere near the total of sixty tons of grapes we expected to produce from the five hectares or so of vines. Nevertheless, letting it produce too many grapes was almost certainly causing the low sugar content, especially in the Sangiovese.

The vines grew very vigorously, and over the next two years the production rose. Of course, there were still problems with low sugar levels. It seemed that we had not yet found the right pruning and production level for the conditions of climate and altitude. I talked repeatedly with Ferruccio about the problem. On one occasion he asked me why it worried me so much when none of our customers for grapes had ever complained about their quality.

"That's because no one round here knows what ripe grapes and good wine are like," I replied. But that was not really true because locals had also bought good, ripe grapes off trucks that came to the village, as I once had. Indeed, in those years I often wondered why they bought grapes from me when they were essentially inferior in quality to those being brought in from Abruzzo. I did not, of course, want to put a flea in their ear about the quality of my grapes by asking them, but I suspected that the reason was because they preferred grapes from a local vineyard; they could actually observe the grapes growing and ripening every time they walked or drove along the road to the cemetery. In addition, Italians are greatly influenced by *campanilismo*. This word derives from *campanile*, the bell tower of the church, and it means pride in, and loyalty towards, things local. This is perhaps a logical sentiment in a country with such a turbulent history as a series of small States and a relatively short experience of nationhood. Better the local and known than the unknown from outside, even if it might be better. Furthermore, almost none of my grape clients had the means of measuring sugar content.

The season after the pruning that I had discussed with Ferruccio, when there were often two fruit canes and around twenty buds on many vines, the vineyard produced sixty-two tons of grapes, the target set by Pino Manzo. I had such faith in Pino's enormous knowledge and experience that I had taken this target as gospel. However, the results in terms of sugar levels were catastrophic. I had to visit a number of supermarkets over several evenings to buy all the sugar I needed to add to the fermenting wine in the tractor shed. And there were a few rumblings from some of our customers about the number of bunches that were showing green berries. Furthermore, we had to scurry around to find extra customers to buy all of the grapes that we had produced.

The whole vintage was fraught with problems and I was deeply unhappy about the situation. Above all, the wine I had produced was much too acidic, which was another indication – in addition to low sugar content – that the grapes had been unripe. A reasonably high level of acidity in wine is very important in terms of its stability and capacity to mature well: in fact, acidity is often described as "the backbone of a good wine". In the relatively cool climate of Castel Sabino, a shortage of acidity was never going to be the problem it can be in very hot areas, but in that year of the sixty-two tons of grapes, the acidity in my wines was way over the top. There are approved methods for reducing the acid in wine using, for example, potassium bicarbonate. I carried out tests on small quantities of my wines before treating the bulk of it, but the results did not satisfy me. The taste of the wine suffered.

My concerns were not assuaged by my eldest son, Stuart. By now, he and his brother Iain were greatly enjoying wine, and during their visits from England, we always tasted my wines and others and commented on them. They gradually became informed wine drinkers and supporters of my wines, but also its critics. That year, after trying my new wines, Stuart said, "You know, Dad, the best red wine you've ever made was that first one with the Montepulciano grapes you bought." I could easily have wrung his neck!

Both boys helped me in the winery on occasions, and Iain with his scientific bent – he later became a doctor – was particularly helpful with technical aspects. They also brought school friends to stay, and I like to think that their visits gave them some appreciation of the work that goes into producing grapes and making wine. They certainly appreciated the wine itself, and we would all start drinking it as an *aperitivo* while I was cooking dinner in the large kitchen. Stuart would take over as the sommelier pouring wine for us all, but he also took on the task of making *bruschetta* (toasted coarse bread rubbed with garlic, salted, and liberally anointed with good olive oil). This was originally peasant fare, but it has become a favourite starter or snack in central Italy. I introduced innumerable non-Italian guests to it, and when they returned months or years later, they would ask if we could eat that delicious thing they had eaten the previous time. They could not remember its name, so I would exert my mind to remember the dishes that I had cooked for them the last time. I take some pride in my cooking so I would ask them whether it was a pasta dish, or a curry, or was it perhaps a *boeuf à la bourguignone*? And they would say, "No, no, nothing like that. That toasted bread with garlic and olive oil, whatever it's called." So much for my efforts to produce culinary delights at a higher level, I would think, and feed them up on *bruschetta*.

So Stuart would take up position by the open fire in the corner of the kitchen and toast the bread, which demanded a certain amount of attention and sometimes made him forget to see how our glasses were faring. On one such occasion, when my glass was empty as usual, George, a school friend of Stuart's who was with us, said in a loud stage whisper:

"Stuart, fill your father's glass. Can't you see he's drying out?" The expression "to dry out" when one's wine glass is empty has remained part of our family lexicon ever since.

Stuart's comment about the wine made from those bought grapes being the best I had produced was true. I knew it and I was peeved by it. My father had a saying he used to deliver, putting on a Scottish accent, to the effect that it was not the lies that hurt: it was the damned truth! By now, I was harbouring a great ambition to produce quality red wines from my own grapes, and Stuart's comment focussed my attention on the fact that I was still well off target. The Pinot Bianco was still working out very well, for it ripened early and regularly produced wine with more than twelve percent alcohol and a good acid balance; the problem was with the red wine.

I consulted at length with Pino Manzo. He said that his original estimate of the yields per hectare we should aim for could well have been too high. He confirmed my view that we should prune the vines harder, especially the Sangiovese where the problem of low sugar content and high acidity was by far the most serious.

In early December and before the pruning was started, I sat down with

Ferruccio in the kitchen of his house to discuss the problem of yields and pruning.

"We've got to reduce the yields," I said. "This year, for the first time, we averaged over twelve tons to the hectare. I've been over the figures of the grapes we sold and the Sangiovese produced more than sixteen tons to the hectare. You must prune shorter this year.'

Ferruccio looked perplexed. "But Signor Colin," he protested, "you took in more money from the sale of grapes this year than ever before. I know how expensive it is to run the vineyard. Aren't you happy with all the grapes we sold?"

"Of course the money's important, but if we go on like this we'll lose customers. It was difficult enough to sell the grapes we had this year. And I want to go on trying to produce good wine. That won't be possible with yields as high as we got last time."

The familiar twinkle came into Ferruccio's eyes. "We should prune a part of the vineyard short for the grapes you want to make your wine, and prune the rest long for the grapes we're going to sell. No one's complained about the wine they've made from our grapes this year."

"Come on, Ferru, apart from the fact that it wouldn't be honest, you know it wouldn't work. Someone would notice the difference in the pruning, find out the reason, and then people would create hell during the vintage. They'd all want grapes from the short-pruned part. No, you have to prune the whole vineyard shorter this year, especially the Sangiovese. Keep the number of buds on the fruit cane down to twelve. Maybe fourteen if the vine looks really vigorous.'

Ferruccio agreed, rather grudgingly it seemed. This impression was confirmed a couple of weekends later as I walked around in the pruned part of the vineyard to check progress. I found many vines that were pruned longer than I wanted. I remonstrated with Ferrucio, but it had little impact. He tended to blame the three others who were pruning with him, at which I reminded him firmly that he was in charge.

The struggle went on over that pruning season and the next. I was evidently up against a traditional way of doing things that was difficult to change. I would go through the vineyard, sometimes alone and sometimes with Ferruccio, counting buds and shortening canes that I thought were too long. One day, when I was complaining about too many buds on a vine, Ferruccio said quietly, "We don't count the buds. When you've pruned as long as we have, you just look at a vine and know instinctively how long or short the pruning should be".

I suddenly realized, after all the struggle, what the problem was. I put my hand on Ferruccio's arm, hoping to give emphasis to what I was about to say. "Ferru, I now understand. You've always pruned the way you absorbed from the people you pruned with when you were a youngster. People like the *Presidente* and your uncles. They never counted buds. They just looked at a vine and knew how to prune it, but they were pruning it to get the most grapes possible, within reason. They weren't too worried if the grapes didn't ripen properly. They just boiled some of the must to concentrate it and added it to their fermenting wine.

"What I want you to do, please, is to change the way you see a vine when you are going to prune it. Try to imagine really ripe grapes on it. Not that many, but really ripe . . . every bunch, with not a single green berry in sight. Try to think that we are going to produce fewer grapes, but better grapes. And for God's sake, I want no more of those second canes on the middle wire, the 'second floor' as you call it. We're going for quality, not quantity. Look at a vine with that in mind as you prune it . . . and count the buds if in doubt!"

A couple of weekends later I was again checking the recently completed pruning with Ferruccio. It appeared to be shorter and more in line with what I had been wanting. But then I saw one of his "second floors" on the middle wire. I was very angry.

"Ferruccio!" I exploded, "I told you I don't want any of your 'second floors'. I pay you to do the pruning as I want it done, not as you want to do it. I'm fed up with your stubbornness. For the love of God, what's the matter with you? Give me your secateurs!"

With secateurs in hand I marched over to the vine to cut off the offending second fruit cane. When I got to it, I found that although it was carefully tied to the middle wire to hold it in place, it was already cut through at its base. The whole thing was a hoax, and I had fallen for it. I turned to look at Ferruccio who was standing where I had left him. He began to laugh, and he went on, helplessly, till the tears were rolling down his cheeks. He was justifiably delighted with the joke he had played on me, and I had to laugh with him. For several years thereafter, Ferruccio loved to recall my anger that day.

"You were white with rage, Signor Colin. You were so angry your beard was trembling." And he would start to laugh all over again at the memory.

Gradually I got my way about the pruning and as the yields began to come down, there was a commensurate improvement in the sugar levels. I was buying less and less sugar to add to the wine fermenting in the tractor shed. I then found out that yields of grapes for quality wines in central Italy seldom exceeded about seven or eight tons to the hectare and that they are often considerably lower. It seemed we were on the right track.

In summer, there was another pruning issue, and again I found myself in a long battle against traditional attitudes and practices. When Ferruccio and his team were tying the vine shoots to the wires, they also removed a lot of vegetation.

After they had been through the vineyard, the space between the rows was thickly littered with the leaves and shoots. There was a veritable green carpet of them. This operation was called the *potatura verde* (green pruning).

I had grave doubts about the severity of what they were doing, for it seemed illogical to me to remove so much leaf area when it is the leaves that perform the photosynthesis that enables plants to grow and ripen fruit. As an agriculturist, I was on sure ground about that piece of basic knowledge, but I had no idea of how it applied in practice to the green pruning of vines, which I was assured by Ferruccio, and to some extent by Pino Manzo, was an essential operation.

I began reading everything I could on the subject, and in doing so I opened a Pandora's box. I found that it is normal practice to remove suckers growing from low on the truck of the vine, and I had no quarrel with that. But in addition to removing suckers, it is also common to remove shoots that are not fruit bearing, and shoots that grow from the base of the leaves on the fruiting canes. Furthermore, leaves are often removed to improve the flow of air around the clusters to help combat fungal attacks; and finally, the tops of the vines are often trimmed as well.

The books I consulted were frustratingly imprecise in providing practical guidance. They expounded generalities to the effect that all of the green pruning measures may have their uses in particular circumstances. Such a circumstance, as described in one book, was when "very short winter pruning was being practised, the vegetative growth of the vine must be adapted to the climatic conditions to improve the quality of the crop." This illuminating statement was not followed by single example of any climatic conditions requiring different vegetative growth or how the quality of the crop would be improved.

I had noticed in Italy, and some other Latin countries, a certain incapacity in ordering and presenting information in such a way that it can be easily understood. This may well be the result of the greater circumlocution in Latin languages compared to English. In addition, however, information that is deemed officially or academically necessary may have no practical value. For example, until quite recently, candidates for their first driving test in Italy had to learn about the inner workings of an engine, clutch, gearbox, and differential of a car, and they had to successfully answer questions about these technicalities before being granted a driving licence. But at the same time, no knowledge was, nor still is, required about how to jack up a car and change a wheel. This perhaps explains why distraught women stand on the roadside by their car with a flat tyre hoping that some man will stop to help them.

The books I studied on green pruning proved useless, confirming my impressions about some Italian communication. Some of the books skimmed over the topic quite briefly, but others rambled on for page after page about all the types of summer pruning. They cited numerous experiments with different types of summer pruning, in different parts of Italy, on different varieties of grapes, and under different winter pruning systems. The amount of data they had gathered was impressive, but there was no attempt to draw conclusions. The authors appeared to have been carried away by their own erudition, and what they had written was completely useless in communicating any advice to a grape-grower. Hard as I tried, I could draw no firm conclusions about the practical value of the different aspects of summer pruning in my particular vineyard, or about what level of severity to apply.

However, the inconclusive texts I consulted did seem to agree, at least partially, on one point: there were negative effects of removing too much leaf area in a vineyard. So even if there was no indication of what constituted "too much", my general idea of treating the vines rather gently was confirmed. So I started insisting with Ferruccio that the women only remove suckers and the leaves that were hiding the clusters so that the sprays could reach and protect them. There could also be some very light trimming of the tops if the growth had become so exuberant that it was beginning to overhang the space between the rows.

It took many exhortations from me, spread over a couple of years, before the workers began to do as I was asking. I repeatedly told them that the vines needed most of their leaves to ripen the grapes. The event that finally clinched the argument was that, one day in early summer, a woman with a sickle in hand idly lopped off a cane above its two bunches of grapes, leaving just a single leaf. The cane and its grapes were in full view next to one of the head poles in the vineyard. I watched them as the weeks passed; the two bunches never filled and ripened properly, while the others elsewhere on the same vine ripened well.

When vintage came, I took the harvesters, who were mostly the same people who had done the summer pruning, to look at those two unripe bunches close to the chopped off end of the cane. I asked them to look at them and made a little speech about how excessive removal of vegetation in summer was bad for the grapes, and that here they had the proof before their eyes. They began to nod in understanding. They had, in fact, been increasingly heeding my requests to go easy on the summer pruning, with occasional reminders from me, but after that I never had to raise the subject again.

I have since learned that severe green pruning of vines is also a tradition among small grape-growers in other parts of Italy. However, I never discovered why they were so merciless, often removing a third or more of the vegetation and lopping off the tops of the vines too. Certainly, it makes the rows look tidier – like well-trimmed hedges – but as I found out, it is not easy to make people realize that this tidiness is often at the expense of grape quality.

The vine shoots grew so fast that Ferruccio and his team had to go through the vineyard every eight or ten days, from mid-May to late-July, to tie them to the wires and to do the small amount of green pruning I wanted. The traditional material used for tying in the area was osier, and there were two willow trees on the property that had probably been planted many decades earlier specifically to provide shoots for tying. The shoots had to be clipped off in winter, stored somewhere, and put to soak before they could be used.

The people were very adept at tying with osier, or sometimes with broom, but it seemed to me that there must be a quicker and easier way, and one that did not depend on gathering and preparing shoots from trees or bushes. Furthermore, the two willow trees on the property could never provide enough shoots to tie all of my vines. The obvious alternatives were various forms of plastic tying materials that were available on the market. Some of these were hollow tubes of flexible plastic that came in two diameters, the larger, about as thick as a pencil, for tying the trunk of the vine to its supporting pole, and the smaller, about as thick as household string, for tying the canes and shoots to the wires.

When I first bought a supply of these tying materials and gave them to Ferruccio, he took them from me in silence. But then he began a rambling discourse, "There's plenty of osier around here, Signor Colin. Everyone's got willow trees on their land, and they never use all their osier". He began mentioning people he knew who had willow trees and said he would talk to them about buying their osier for a nominal amount, and he would go and collect it, and so on.

I had an immediate – perhaps unjust – vision of him disappearing with the tractor and trailer into the countryside, he and the tractor driver enjoying lengthy refreshments in the house of a friend, clipping off a few willow shoots and throwing them into the trailer, moving on to another friend to repeat the performance . . . and so on, for days on end. I would have to pay his and the tractor driver's time, plus the nominal amount for the osier. I told him shortly that it was much cheaper to buy the plastic ties then to spend time collecting osier around the countryside.

However, no one liked using the plastic ties and grumbled that it was easier to use osier because they were used to it. So we changed to that thin plastic-coated wire now used worldwide by gardeners, and even by manufacturers of electrical goods to tie the appliance's cord in a neat bundle. The women were happy enough using it, but the winter pruning gang, led by Ferruccio, moaned that the wire, even if very thin, blunted their secateurs.

I chose to ignore the complaint and we continued to use the plastic-coated wire for summer tying. However, I remained on the look out for other solutions for the winter fixing of the canes to the wires until one day, an advertisement in a farming magazine caught my eye. It was for a device made in Japan called a Max Tapener. It was, in effect, a very large stapler with a roll of plastic tape about a centimetre wide held in a container on one side of the handle. You placed the jaws over the vine cane and the wire and squeezed the handle. As you did so, the device wrapped a strip of plastic tape around the cane and the wire, put a staple through it to fix it, and cut the tape.

I immediately rang the importer in Milan and had one sent to me. I took it up to Ferruccio to give to him over dinner in his home on a Wednesday evening.

"I think we should try this," I said, pulling it out of its box.

Ferruccio looked at it suspiciously. "What sort of an *accrocco* is that?" he asked. The word *accrocco* was a derogatory term for some botched-up device that would be unlikely to work, or if it did, not for long. Ferruccio used the term quite often, as well as an *americanata* to describe something showy, modern, and probably useless. I doubt, though, that he really felt the contempt those terms would normally imply, for he was always grinning when he used them. More likely was that he was acting the retrograde peasant to make fun of me and of my desire to introduce innovations into the way he did things.

"Well, at least you can't call it an *americanata*, Ferru, because it's made in Japan. Hold your hand out and I'll show you how it works."

He stuck his hand out. I made him extend his forefinger and middle finger held together, slipped the jaws of the device over them, and in a flash, stapled a ring of blue plastic tape around them.

"*Porca Madonna!*" Ferruccio exclaimed. He held his encircled fingers up to the light and twisted them to look at them from all sides. He pushed his hat back from his forehead. "Well, it may be all right for binding my fingers together here in the kitchen, but I don't know whether it'll be any good for tying canes to the wires in the vineyard."

I deliberately resisted rising to the bait and starting a discussion with him. "Try it in the vineyard tomorrow," was all I said. Ferruccio looked quite disappointed at his failure to wind me up for one of my friendly rants about how old-fashioned he was.

When I saw Ferruccio next, early on the Saturday morning, the first thing he said was, "That *accrocco* you brought for tying isn't bad. I think perhaps you should get another one for work in your vineyard". He paused. "And while you're ordering that one, please order one for me too. I want to use it on my vines."

"Oh! So it's not an *accrocco* or an *americanata* after all?" I asked, laughing.

But Ferruccio was not going to admit total defeat. "Well, it's still an *accrocco*, but until it breaks it's quite good."

Within the next two or three years, everyone in the area was buying Max Tapeners. A small company near Rome had signed an agreement with the original manufacturer and was turning them out by the score. I should have become a partner in the business. It might have been more profitable than growing grapes, for Max Tapeners and similar devices became very popular in viticulture. And there was a rich replacement market for them too, because Ferruccio was right in one respect: they did not last very long – no more than a season or two in our experience. But they were so efficient that the cost of buying new ones was well worth it.

19

Great Leap Forward

About eight years after planting the first vines, I realized I needed to take some hard decisions, for selling grapes to local people had gradually become less viable. In the first year that I harvested grapes, a quintal (100 kilograms/ 220 pounds) of them paid for two days of a vineyard worker's time. However, inflation was much sharper in wages than it was in grape prices, so by the early 1980s, a quintal of grapes only paid for about one day of work. The costs of all of the other inputs, such as fertilizer and sprays against pests, had also risen strongly. Had it been possible to produce sixty tons of high quality grapes, as originally thought, the sheer quantity would have brought in reasonable revenue. However, it was clear by then that the yields had to be continuously reduced if we were to reach the level of quality I wanted.

The solution was rather obvious: I had to turn more and more of the grapes into wine and sell it at a good price. However, that would mean building and equipping a winery, a daunting prospect because the investment would be significant. In addition, scaling up my wine production from the tractor shed into a proper winery, with modern equipment that I knew nothing about, and with no neighbours that I could call on for advice, could be tricky. It could also be expensive if I made any major mistakes.

It was clear that a great leap forward into full-scale wine production would also be a risky leap into the dark. It could be as much of a failure as Mao's vaunted Great Leap Forward had been in China. On the other hand, the figures spoke for themselves; the gross value of the produce from the vineyard could be more or less tripled, even if I sold most of the wine in demijohns rather than in bottles. If I were able to produce wines that were worthy of bottling and labelling, the added value would be even higher.

Of course, there would be many extra costs involved, but even so, the most viable option appeared to be to build and equip a winery. I deluded myself into thinking that I had not really taken such a major decision while I started to gather basic information about suitable types of equipment, likely costs, the size that the building would need to be, and so on. But in my heart I knew the die was cast. Almost nothing was going to deflect me from setting up a proper winery, for by then my interest in winemaking had become a passion. I was going to indulge it, despite the risks. Perhaps I could resign from FAO, use my accumulated pension funds to finance the winery, and become a consultant in my professional field? That would also give me more flexibility to have time free at important moments for the vineyard and wine operations. I was by then reasonably sure that the property could produce good wines, for they had been steadily improving as I learned more about the practicalities of winemaking. However, the predominant factor in the improved wines was the progressive reduction in the yield of grapes as I won the battle for shorter pruning.

My search for information for a winery began with a visit to the famous annual wine fair, Vinitaly, in Verona where there was one building taken up by manufacturers of winery equipment. It was a bewildering display and I hardly knew where to begin. There was everything from huge presses and stainless steel tanks, to pumps, filters, corking machines, and complete space-age bottling lines. I poked around and picked up brochures, hardly daring to get into conversation with the manufactures' staff manning the stands. I doubted that my piffling needs would warrant their attention.

I finally approached a young man on the stand of a manufacturer of steel tanks to ask about the prices of the various sizes of tank they made. He turned out to be very amiable, and so I told him what I had in mind to do. I told him about the size of the vineyard and that I thought I would be able to produce about forty tons of grapes, more or less equivalent to 30,000 litres of wine. He suggested that if I was going to have to build a new winery, it would be as well to make it big enough for 50,000 litres, for I might even want to buy in additional grapes. The added cost of a building rather bigger than my immediate needs would not be very significant. He did some sketches for a layout that included some 5,000-litre tanks and few smaller ones of 3,000 litres. From this, and adding working space for pressing, bottling, storage, and the like, we concluded that the winery would need to be about sixteen metres (fifty feet) long by eleven metres (thirty-six feet) wide, and five metres (sixteen feet) high inside to accommodate the cylindrical tanks.

I went away with plenty of food for thought, and also with the address of the agent in Rome for that particular make of tanks. That agent, I was informed, was a highly respected oenological consulting group called Vinconsulting. It had been founded by one of Italy's top oenologists. I was initially surprised that a consulting group providing advice to wine producers could also be an agent for winery equipment: it seemed to create a conflict of interests, but these details do not seem to matter too much to the majority of Italians. For example, few Italians are as indignant today, as they would have every right to be, about Prime Minister Berlusconi directly owning, or indirectly controlling through his political position, about ninety per cent of Italy's TV channels, plus a raft of press outlets, and using them or influencing them to his political advantage. In any case, the tanks that Vinconsulting were agents for appeared to be among the best I had seen at Vinitaly, and they were competitively priced.

I telephoned Vinconsulting and made an appointment with one of their staff, Andrea Guidoni. He turned out to be a young man with an open face and a slow, friendly smile. He was from Piemonte, and he was a graduate of the famous school of oenology in Alba. I came to know him well over the coming years. His knowledge and friendly advice became as crucial to my winery project and winemaking as Pino Manzo's had been for the planting of the vineyard and its care in the early years.

During my first meeting with Andrea Guidoni, we discussed my vineyard operation, and the dimensions of the winery I would need. He agreed that the estimates made by the person I had spoken to at Vinitaly were approximately correct.

"But there is one problem," I said. "There's no level land anywhere on the property that's not planted with vines where I can put up a building that size."

"So much the better. Dig it into the slope. That way it will also keep a more even temperature."

Andrea Guidoni was very encouraging at that first meeting and I went away with my mind buzzing about all of the possibilities. Back at Castel Sabino, I began to think about where I could build the winery. There was a sloping area very close to the house, given over to scrub and a few olive trees, and it seemed to be the natural place. It would also have good access from the entrance drive to the property. However, the slope was very steep and an enormous hole would need to be dug.

I called on Roberto Paoli again, the local *geometra* who had helped with the purchase of the property and the rebuilding of the house. Together we walked around the property and he agreed that, indeed, the slope near the house was the best site. We sat down together over several of the following weekends – and over several bottles of wine – to discuss the layout of the floor plan based on the information and I had been given by the man at Vinitaly and by Andrea Guidoni.

We needed a covered entrance area for unloading and crushing the grapes, with a large doorway into the winery itself through which a tractor or truck could pass. Inside, the main body of the building would be for fermenting and storage tanks, but with enough open space between the tanks for pressing, pumping, filtering, and the like. A separate and quite large room would be needed for bottling and labelling. A small room with some storage space for small equipment, paperwork, winemaking ingredients, such as yeasts and so on, and with a sink for washing glasses would be necessary. Off that, there would be a toilet and washbasin.

One Saturday evening, when Roberto Paoli and I were discussing the plans, he said, "We'll need to do something to stop the infiltration of water into the building from the back and from the parts of the sides that will be underground".

From that, it did not take us long to realize that the best solution would be to build a cool cellar out of reinforced concrete, like a bunker, along all of the winery walls that would be in contact with earth piled against them.

"It should be lower in height than the main part of the winery itself so that it could be buried under about two metres of soil," Roberto said. "It would need a domed roof to withstand the weight of soil on top of it. The reinforced concrete would keep the water out, and if we made it about three or four metres wide and about two and a half high, it would be a perfect cool area for storing and aging wine. As you know, people here often dug cellars into slopes to store wine and other things that need to be kept cool. They call it their 'grotto'. You'd have a very good artificial grotto."

We became quite enthused by this notion and talked long into the night about it and about other details. "You realize, don't you, that it's not only the grotto that will have to be built of reinforced concrete?" Roberto Paoli said at one point. "The structure of the main part of the building will have to be in reinforced concrete as well. We could never get the height and the spans you need with any other form of construction, especially in this area which is officially classified as an earthquake zone."

He went on to inform me that, as a *geometra*, he would not be allowed to do the calculations for the reinforced concrete and sign off on the plans for their submission to the authorities for approval. That required the work of a civil engineer, but he had a friend in Rome who could do all that. He, Roberto, would be able to supervise the actual construction, a task that his engineer friend would not be interested in.

Step by step the project took on form in my mind, but an important aspect about which I was totally ignorant was the bureaucratic and legislative requirements for becoming a commercial wine producer. I asked Andrea Guidoni about them and he advised me to go and talk to the *Ufficio Repressione Frodi* (Office for the Repression of Fraud), a unit of the Ministry of Agriculture.

"They're the people that all wine producers fear like the plague," Andrea Guidoni said cheerfully. "You don't have to be doing anything truly fraudulent to get into trouble with them. If they drop in to inspect your winery and they find, for example, that the quantities of wine you have in your tanks don't tally precisely with the quantities you've got entered in your registers, that's trouble. Or if they come in during vintage and find that you haven't kept your register right up to date with the quantity of grapes you have brought into the winery each day, that's trouble too."

"What registers are you talking about?" I asked.

"Go and see the head of the *Ufficio Repressione Frodi*. He'll tell you. Wine producers have to keep on top of a horrendous amount of paperwork. You'll see. The man in charge is a *buon cristiano* (good fellow). He's trained as an agronomist, and as a lawyer, a perfect combination for the job. His name's Baroni. Ring him up and make an appointment."

The Office for the Repression of Fraud was far less impressive than its name. It was in an area of Rome built during Italy's economic boom after World War II, when a vast amount of construction was completed. Most of it, however, was of utilitarian intent and of unattractive design. The entrance to the building was rather grubby to boot, and so was Doctor Baroni's simple office, but he was as cordial as Andrea Guidoni had said. He was in his mid-forties, a relaxed and self-assured man without any of the apparent arrogance that it is so easy to encounter in public officials when they are dealing with ordinary mortals. Furthermore, in contrast with some Italians, he possessed a remarkable talent for being concise, lucid, and articulate in explaining complex issues.

I began by telling him what I was planning to do, and he listened carefully. This was also rather unusual, for while most Italians have exceptionally well-developed verbal skills, and enjoy the sound of their own voices, their listening skills often remain less developed. So I finished my presentation to Doctor Baroni without being interrupted, even once, and asked him what bureaucratic steps I would have to take.

"Perhaps I should explain first what this office does. We try to prevent fraudulent and illegal practices in wine production. The Italian Government and the European Union have set up a whole range of regulations that are basically to protect the consumer from wine that might contain toxic chemicals, and to ensure that grapes, and only grapes are used to produce it. This is also to prevent malpractices in the industry that could give dishonest producers an unfair economic advantage.

"So, a commercial grape-grower and wine producer, like you want to be, has to record the grapes he has brought in every day during vintage and make a declaration every year of how much wine he has produced. He also has to make a declaration at the end of August of the wine stocks on hand. He must keep a stock register in which he records every operation in the winery that increases or decreases the stocks, beginning, of course, with the increase produced during vintage.

"Then every reduction has to be recorded, including losses when racking and filtering, accidental loses, sales in bulk or in bottles, even wine taken out of the winery for family consumption. At any given moment, the stocks in a winery should tally with what's written in the register.

"You'll need a bottling register too. Every time you bottle wine, you have to record the details of what tank the wine came from and how many bottles or demijohns, of what type, were filled. The number of that register has to be printed on all of your labels and corks. It's like the identity card number of your wine. And of course, when you bottle wine, you have to record in your stock register that the hectolitres of wine you had in a tank have now become so many thousand bottles of wine.

"And then there are the VAT capsules. The capsules that go on to bottles are controlled. Each time you need them, you have to get authorization from us to have them made, and then you take that authorization to a specialist supplier. If you are putting wine into demijohns, you have to stick an adhesive strip of paper, called a VAT strip, over the lid. You have to get authorization from us to get these printed too, and they have a different code printed on them according to the size of the demijohn. You have to keep a stock register of these VAT capsules and strips as well."

The good Doctor Baroni went on to tell me, in his ordered and methodical way, about the regulations for different types of dockets required to accompany any grapes or wine that were being transported, and various other legislative aspects, such as having to take one's pressings to a distillery.

Then he told me that all of the registers I would need had to be stamped and approved by his office before I began to use them. He explained the penalties for not keeping one's registers correctly. For example, the stock register had to be completed within one working day of an entry of wine, and within three working days for an exit. Penalties for incorrect completion of the stock register, and quantities that did not tally with the reality, ranged from Italian lire 1.2 million to 30 million, about £550 to almost £14,000 at the time.

"Oh, and another thing," Baroni went on. "Of course, you'll have to have your winery approved before you start making wine for sale."

He reached into a drawer and pulled out several photocopied sheets of a Government law describing the requirements and handed them to me. I glanced down the document and my eyes hit on a clause that said that fly screens were required over the windows.

"Excuse me, Doctor Baroni," I said, "but why are fly screens on the windows necessary? Surely, the winery doors are open during much of the vintage, and I don't see how those little vinegar flies can possibly be kept out. There are always clouds of them in and around any winery I have been in during vintage".

"Yes, you're right. But those regulations I've given you apply also to buildings in which other things, like sausages or cheese, are to be made." He smiled. "This is Italy, and many laws don't make sense, but you'll have to install fly screens to get approval for the winery, as well as complying with all of the other regulations. For example, you and anyone else who is to work in the winery will need annual health certificates. We can't have you and your workers spreading disease and pestilence through your wine, even if the risk of that is practically non-existent."

I was totally overwhelmed by the complexity and number of regulations, and I was later to find out that there were others that Baroni had not mentioned.

"Doctor Baroni," I said, "this is all very, very complicated. Is it actually possible to keep within the letter of the law with all of this?"

Baroni laughed. "Listen, this office covers the whole region of Lazio. There are hundreds of wineries. I know for certain that if I visited them all, I could find something wrong in every one of them . . . yes, in *every* one. In reality it is very difficult to have everything completely right by all of the regulations."

We laughed together, and I rose to leave, thanking Baroni for his help and time. He shook my hand, and cordially wished me luck with my project.

"Call me or come and see me any time you need advice," he said. "There is, in fact a monthly magazine dedicated only to wine legislation, but it's a bit complicated for your needs. It will be simpler to talk to me."

I walked out of the building, still half stunned by what Doctor Baroni had told me. If the legislation around growing grapes and making and bottling wine for sale could justify a specialized monthly magazine on the subject, I was about to enter a minefield. I came to the conclusion that if I had come to see Baroni before I had advanced so far with the planning of the winery, I would probably have abandoned the whole project.

20

Digging a Big Hole

By early 1984, about eight years since I had started planting the vineyard, the winery project had taken on form in my mind until it had become undeniable. Any hesitations I still felt were finally swept away by an offer from friends. They owned a consulting company that was undertaking assignments for many development agencies, and they invited me to join them as a partner. I therefore decided to resign from FAO, withdraw my pension fund, and invest it in building and equipping the winery.

From that moment, events began to snowball quickly; the plans were finalized, with all of the calculations for the reinforced concrete by the Rome engineer attached, and they were approved by the local authorities in record time. Quotes from builders were obtained and one day, before I had really had time to reconsider my decision or go back on it, an excavator started digging a hole in the slope close to the house and to the entrance drive of the property. Over the following days, as the hole got bigger and bigger and deeper and deeper, the size of what I was embarked on became clearer. It was one thing to see the plans of the winery on paper, but by the time a very large level place had been excavated in the slope, leaving a hole some six metres deep at the uphill side, the true size of the building became evident. Indeed, the area of the flat roof of the completed winery and the landfill against its rear and one side wall was so great that I later built a tennis court on top of the structure.

Several people from the village came up to the property for various reasons in those days and saw the enormous hole. Their astonishment was evident, and even more so when I told them I was building a winery. The news travelled rapidly, as I soon found out from Ferruccio.

"People are saying you've gone completely crazy," he told me one morning.

"They may be right. But they said the same when I planted the vineyard, didn't they?"

"Yes, but then they thought you were just slightly crazy. Now they're saying you're completely crazy and that you'll soon finish your money."

"What do you think, Ferru?" I asked, laughing.

"I've always thought you were a bit crazy, Signor Colin, but most of what you do seems to work out all right, so I don't know anymore."

"You've just reminded me of something my stepfather used to say to me: 'You're the sort of lucky person who could fall into the farm dung heap and come up with a handful of gold coins'."

"But you don't have a dung heap here," said Ferruccio. "If what people are saying is right, when you've finished your money you'll have to come over to my place and fall into mine. I'll only charge you a small commission on the gold coins. Anyway, if the winery doesn't work out, you could always turn it into a villa for your sons. You could leave a tank of wine in a corner to keep them from drying out when they're here."

Many things in Italy are disorganized and badly run, but when it comes to building, Italians can be astoundingly efficient. This is particularly true when they are building new reinforced concrete structures, or major public works, for they seem to have a particular flair for that type of construction. When it comes to small things and renovation of old buildings, they seem to be fired by less enthusiasm and are about as unreliable as builders anywhere.

Even though the firm that built my winery was quite small, they proved highly competent and reliable. It was a pleasure to watch as the men prepared the shuttering for the concrete, and as they cut, bent, placed, and fixed the steel reinforcing rods. Within a matter of days, the first of many gigantic trucks came grinding up the hill with its slowly revolving concrete mixer. It parked next to the hole, extended a long beam and tube outwards and started pumping the concrete for the foundations into the channels between the shuttering. The builders' men ran up and down spreading it and making sure it filled the spaces between the reinforcing rods properly. Within a very short time, the columns of the reinforced concrete frame of the building were also shuttered and poured.

The most astonishing part of the construction, however, was the preparation of the domed roof of the storage and ageing area, the artificial grotto. The carpenters built the whole wooden structure, onto which the steel rods would be laid and the concrete poured, with breathtaking speed. They sawed and hammered ceaselessly to create numerous identical semicircular formers of the shape of the inside of the domed roof, and fixed them all in position. Across these they nailed the stringers, dozens and dozens of long planks fitted closely together so that concrete could not pass between them. They also had to turn the domed roof through a ninety-degree corner. I thought this would be complicated, but one of the carpenters I asked about it merely shrugged and said it was *un lavoro di tutti giorni* (an everyday job).

In effect, they built a wooden replica of the inside of the domed roof and placed the steel reinforcing rods for a structure more than twenty-five metres (eighty-two feet) long in less than five days. In the years to come, whenever I was in my artificial grotto and looked up, I marvelled at the perfect vault of the roof, at the impeccably regular longitudinal lines in the concrete made by the edges of the stringers, and at the change of direction in the dome at the corner. It was a thing of quiet elegance, put together at breakneck speed by three or four simple workmen of peasant stock in dirty shorts and tee shirts and wearing hats made of newspaper. Watch Italians doing a job for which they have *passione* and you will realize that they are *geniali* (inspired). I will not dwell here on Italians doing jobs they do not like.

While all of this frenzied activity was in progress on the new winery, I was meeting regularly with Andrea Guidoni to discuss the equipment I would need. He suggested at one point that it would be possible to find quite a lot of second-hand equipment from wineries that were upgrading their facilities. He put me in touch with several other oenologists in the Rome area. I made a point of going to see them to tell them about my project, and to get to know them. One was the young man who first taught me the original recipe for pasta sauce *alla matriciana* in his home village of Amatrice, as described earlier.

I was rather surprised by the help and support I was getting from Vinconsulting. It took the form of Andrea Guidoni's time – and occasionally the time of his colleagues – but without any mention from their side of consultancy fees. It was also surprising, I thought, that Andrea Guidoni had put me on to the track of second-hand equipment, for that would cut Vinconsulting out of any commissions.

One day, during one of my evening visits to Andrea Guidoni's office, I said: "Andrea, I realize that there are no second-hand stainless-steel tanks around and, of course, I'll buy new ones through you, but I am taking up a lot of your time on other things, and Vinconsulting isn't charging me anything. I don't feel really at ease about the situation."

"Don't worry," he said with a laugh. "We take a long-term view. For example, a wine producer in Sicily contacted us about five years ago for advice. He's quite a large producer and he wanted very much to improve his quality. Since then, our senior partner has been flying down to Sicily about once a month on average. All the company has ever received was the cost of the trip. But about three months ago, the producer got some grant to improve his winery. He's going to spend more than a million dollars on equipment . . . through us!"

"Don't think I'll ever be in that league," I said. "I can't imagine ever being in a position to spend more than a fraction of that sort of money on a winery."

"It makes no difference," he replied, smiling. "Money isn't everything. We like working with wine producers."

The contacts with other oenologists in the Rome area paid off. Occasionally one or other of them would call me and say that he knew of a piece of equipment that was being replaced, and that the item being disposed of was in good condition. This was how I came to buy a small, electronic press made by the French firm Vaslin. It was clear in the winemaking fraternity by then that improvements in presses could improve the quality of the wines produced, as well as being much faster and more convenient to use than the traditional press, like Ferruccio's. What was needed were more repeated and relatively soft pressings, with a loosening of the cake of skins and pips between each, rather than a less pressings at higher pressure. The Vaslin presses were designed to provide this soft pressing, though in more recent times, even more sophisticated pneumatic presses do the job even better.

The horizontally rotating cage of the Vaslin press I was buying had a capacity of over a ton of fermented skins and pips when making red wine, but less than half of that for whole, fresh grape bunches being pressed for white wine to be fermented without skin contact. A fixed, threaded shaft ran through the cage from one end of the press to the other. A pressure plate was threaded on to the shaft so that, as the cage and pressure plate revolved, the plate moved along inside the cage. It gradually reduced the space between itself and the fixed plate at the other end of the press and squeezed the grapes. There was a pneumatic cushion on the pressure plate to measure the pressure being exerted on the grapes. It automatically reduced the speed of operation of the electric motors as the pressure increased, or stopped them when the maximum pressure selected by the operator had been reached. It then put the press into reverse so that the plate began winding back to the open position. There were slack chains between the pressure plate and the fixed plate and as the press opened, these chains flailed around to break up and spread the cake for the second and third pressings. The must ran down through the slots in the revolving cage into a large tray under the press, from where it could be pumped into tanks in the winery.

This second-hand Vaslin press was for sale several months before my new winery would be ready, but it was too good an opportunity to miss. I bought it and had it delivered to my tractor-shed winery. Ferruccio was mightily impressed when he first saw it. He had never been into a modern winery, and he did not know that such ingenious presses existed. And even if it was one of the smallest models made by Vaslin – the largest was ten times bigger – it still seemed very large in the tractor shed.

Ferruccio looked at it from a distance before approaching it and running his hand over the perforated cage. "How's it supposed to work, Signor Colin?" he asked.

We opened the hatch on the cage through which the grapes or lees would be loaded and I showed him the plate and explained how it moved along inside the revolving cage. For once, he seemed to be at a loss for some droll comment, and over the coming months as other items of equipment began to arrive, I noticed that he seemed to be rather subdued. I had also noticed that he was not drinking as much wine as usual.

"Are you all right, Ferru?" I asked him one day. "You've been looking a bit pale recently."

"I've not been feeling too good," he said. "A doctor at the hospital in Rieti told me a couple of weeks ago that my liver is swollen. Said I must stop drinking. What's the good of being alive if you can't enjoy wine? He wants me to come back for some tests, but I don't think I'll go."

"C'mon, Ferru, that's not very sensible. Go and have the tests done. If they show that your liver is damaged you'll just have to go easy on the wine."

He looked glum, and then grinned. "There's a saying around here. "The wine drinker lives longer than the doctor who forbids it'."

Some of his old cheerfulness returned, but I was concerned about him and continued to urge him to return to the hospital for tests, which he finally did. The results showed that he indeed did have damage to his liver. He was told to give up alcohol completely. That, of course, was a tall order for him, but he did drink far less over the following months. He began to look better and recovered much of his cheerfulness.

Work on the winery continued through the summer months and the target was to have it completed in time for the vintage. I ran around organizing all of the finishing touches that would be needed to meet the regulations, including of course the famous fly screens. In addition, the walls had to be tiled or painted with a special plastic paint that was completely washable in order to ensure hygiene. Even the small basin in the toilet for washing one's hands needed a special type of tap: it had to be operated by a foot pedal or by a long lever that one could move with one's forearm, rather than having a normal household tap with knobs that could be contaminated by bacteria-laden hands.

When it comes to creating rules and regulations, the Italians are light-years ahead of other countries, but when it comes to ensuring that they are applied, it is another story. When I ultimately obtained certification that the winery was in order, the person carrying out the very cursory inspection appeared not to notice that the plastic paint on the walls, although recently applied, was peeling off in some areas, probably because the plaster under it was still damp. Nor did he even go to look at my long-levered tap on the washbasin.

The first three stainless-steel tanks bought through Vinconsulting arrived. The largest had a capacity of 7,000 litres and was a fermenting tank. Like my first, small, glass-fibre tanks in the tractor-garage winery, it had a flat bottom and manhole hatch set flush with it. Once the free-run juice had been pumped away, the hatch could be opened and the lees be brought out for pressing. It was big enough for a person to get inside the fermenter to bring the lees toward the opening. We set the fermenter on a plinth that I had built for it and for the little glass-fibre tanks. They were dwarfed by the new fermenter, but I was sure that they would be useful, even in my much-expanded operation. And besides, I was attached to them; I had turned down several offers for them from local people.

The other two tanks were of 5,000-litre capacity and were for storage. They were on legs and had a conical bottom in which sediment would accumulate. There was a stopcock set just below the level of the manhole on the side of the tank. I had never worked in a well-equipped winery, but common sense told me that to rack a wine from one tank to another, one merely fitted the tube from one side of the pump to the flange of that stopcock and the tube from the other side of the pump to a similar stopcock on the receiving tank.

I supposed that once no more wine came out, one could open the manhole and, watching very carefully, gradually lower the suction tube from the pump into any clear wine that was left, stopping when the sediment was reached. That part at least would be similar to what I had always done with a small pump in the tractor-garage winery. The only decision that had to be taken when racking was whether to pump the wine into the receiving tank through its bottom stopcock, so that it slowly rose in the tank, or to let it cascade down by pumping it in through the hatch on top of the tank. Normally wine needs to be protected from air to preserve it and its aromas, but if it has developed an off flavour, such as the disgusting hydrogen sulphide that dogged me in the tractor shed, as mentioned earlier, a good aeration as the wine splashes down may get rid of it, but usually at the cost of losing some of the wine's desirable aromas.

The shining tanks looked very impressive in the new and pristine winery. The image that had been in my mind's eye was taking physical shape. It was very satisfying.

21

Scaling Up

The winery was ready in time for the vintage of 1984. I had just left my job in FAO and was finalizing the arrangements to join my friends' consultancy company. Although I was looking forward to putting the winery to use, I had many self-doubts about my ability to handle the scaled-up operation. One of my handicaps from the beginning of my Castel Sabino venture had been my lack of formal training in viticulture and oenology, as well as my lack of practical experience in those fields. I had been forced to rely heavily on advice and help from the specialists I had come to know, on books, and on learning by doing. The process often left me feeling very insecure.

On many occasions I was made aware of my fundamental lack of preparation as a wine-maker. One of those occasions was when I had an appointment for a chat with the manager of a large winery in California's Sonoma Valley. I was waiting in the winery for him to turn up, and I was watching two young women laying out pipes and connecting them to tanks for a racking. It was winter and they were dressed in jeans, sweaters, and gumboots. One of them was also wearing a woollen hat with the Union Jack on it, and as she hurried past me carrying the end of pipe to a tank, she called out something to her workmate. Her accent was unmistakably British, so when she came back past me, I stopped her.

She confirmed that she was British, and so I asked her how she came to be preparing a racking in a winery in California. She told me she had completed a degree course in food technology in Loughborough, England, and then she had come to America do a postgraduate degree at the agriculturally famous University of Davis in California. The subject of the postgraduate course she had completed was "fermentation sciences" – nothing less! She was delighted, she said, to be labouring in a winery.

That little encounter and other occasions when I was listening to winemakers discussing some aspect of the skill and I was understanding very little, even though I was hanging on their every word to try to learn, made me particularly conscious of my fundamental ignorance. I had met Australian winemakers who had done correspondence courses in oenology and I had thought of doing the same, but I simply did not have the time while I was working with FAO. Any idea that I might do such a course after I had left FAO to become a consultant was soon knocked on the head by the numerous assignments all over the world that came my way. I always managed to keep the vintage period free, but for the rest of the year I was juggling the demands on my time and just about managing to make ends meet.

I had never used the sort of equipment that I was buying, such as the Vaslin press, or the large piston pump that I had also bought. That pump was an impressive thing on wheels, all stainless steel pressure dome, brass fittings, and glossy maroon paint. It had a large lever that could change the direction in which it pumped, and it could be made to pump at fast or slow speed. An important feature was that it could pump crushed grapes as well as must or wine, and this was a main reason for the large, diameter pipes – more than eight centimetres (three inches) – that were to be used with it. I had bought it new because none of my oenologist contacts had been able to find a good second-hand one.

The faithful little electric crusher/de-stalker that I had bought in the early days of my tractor-garage winery would be perfectly adequate for the bigger winery, but that was the only piece of equipment of which I had any experience, and with which I felt confident.

I started to become anxious in the run-up to the vintage, for the summer had been exceptionally cold and wet and the grapes were not looking at all good. I was also waiting anxiously for my first offer of a consultancy, for my project would need further investment. I also needed an income while I developed the wine business. In that first year, I was hoping to make wine to sell in demijohns, mainly to local people, but still selling most of the grapes from the vineyard. I decided to make one fermenter full of my three variety red wine. That would produce about 5,000 litres of wine. My plan for the coming years was to reduce gradually the quantity of grapes sold and increase the wine produced. Once I had installed a bottling and labelling line, I would also begin to reduce the wine sold in demijohns and increase the sales in bottle. Even taking into account the considerable cost of bottles, corks, labels, capsules, and the extra labour involved, the added value of bottling the wine would be very significant.

After the cold and wet summer, I was hoping that the weather would at least be good for the vintage itself. However, the wet weather continued, and the condition of the grapes was depressing. In fact, my first vintage in the new winery did not turn out to be the happy occasion I had expected. With the frequent rain, I was worried that bunch rot would set in. In addition, the sugar content of the grapes was still so low that the wine would have an alcohol level of only a little over ten per cent. Even if I was going to sell it to locals in demijohns, I wanted it to be at least eleven per cent. However, I did not dare add the eighty or more kilograms (176 pounds) of sugar I would need to increase the alcohol content. Quite apart from the hassle and guilt of buying it in supermarkets, there had been some scary stories going around. It had been reported that, even if you were not caught actually adding it, a new test on finished wine could determine whether any of its alcohol was derived from sugars that had not originated in grapes.

By now, however, I was on friendly terms with most of the oenologists in the Rome area, and one of them was working as the main technician in the new plant at Anagni, mentioned earlier, that had been set up to produce Rectified Concentrated Grape Must (RCGM). I called him to find out whether he could sell me some.

"Well, it's a bit more complicated than that," he replied. "Have you got your bottling register and your chaptalization register yet?"

"No, I haven't even received the formal approval for the winery yet. I'm going to use it in the next few days to make about fifty hectolitres of wine to sell in demijohns. I don't plan to go through all the paperwork and get a bottling line until next year."

"Before you use RCGM, you have to send a telegram to the *Uffico Repressione Frodi* at least forty-eight hours before the operation advising them how much you are going to add, to what tank of wine, on what day, and what time. They may want to send someone to check what you do. If you don't even have a bottling register yet, you don't officially exist with them, not to mention the chaptalization register you'll need to keep a precise record of those operations. Once you've got all the paperwork in order, you'll even be able to get some of the cost back from the European Union. They subsidize the use of RCGM."

"Yes, yes, that's all very well, but there is no way I can get my paperwork in order before the vintage in the next few days. The grapes aren't properly ripe and with this terrible weather it doesn't look as though they're going to ripen much more. What can I do?" I pleaded.

He must have heard the desperation in my voice. "Listen," he said. "I leave the plant at about six in the evening. The person who looks after it at night, the watchman, is called Giorgio. Come to the plant after dark tomorrow evening, at eight o'clock. I'll warn him you're coming. Drive your car round to the back of those large tanks on the right, to the front of you when you enter the main gate. Giorgio will be in the small office there. Let me see . . . to raise the alcohol level of one hectolitre of wine by one per cent, you need about 2.25 kilos of RCGM. So you'll need about 110 kilos of it. Buy a couple of fifty-litre stainless-steel drums to put it in. Bring cash to pay for it."

"Just a minute," I said. "How am I going to get 110 kilos of the stuff into two fifty-litre drums?"

"Oh my God, and I thought you were intelligent," he said, laughing. "You don't imagine that a litre of RCGM weighs a kilo, like water, do you? It's about seventy per cent sugar, and a litre of it weighs more than a kilo and a third. The 110 kilos you need will only be about eighty-five litres."

"Oh yes, of course, of course!" I said, feeling chastened for my crass question. I was to find out that winemaking on a scale larger than my tractor-garage operation required much more common sense practicality. It also required recourse to geometric formulae for calculating volumes of tanks and some basic chemistry, things that were only blurred memories from my student days and had to be refreshed.

The following evening I drove into the compound of the RCGM plant in my station wagon at eight exactly. It was very dark behind the larger tanks, but there was a light in the window of a small building. I knocked on the door and a workman opened it.

He confirmed that he was Giorgio and that he had been warned to expect me. He took my empty drums to weigh them. When he came back he was also carrying a piece of plastic tubing with a tap fitted into one end. We went over to an enormous tank; it must have had a capacity of 20,000 litres or more. He slipped the open end of the tube over a spigot on the tank, opened the tap and the transparent syrup flowed into the first drum.

"Where are you taking this?" Giorgio asked casually.

"Castel Sabino, about sixty-five kilometres (forty miles) from here."

"You know I can't give you an accompanying docket, don't you? If the Carabinieri, or the road police, or the *Guardia di Finanza* (financial police) stop you for a routine check and find two drums of RCGM in your car, it would be serious for us and for you. You should take the back roads, not the main roads. But this is a good time of day because even the police are eating dinner."

We weighed the drums again when they were about three-quarters full and adjusted the quantity of RCGM in them with a jug until the total weight was 110 kilograms. The drums could have taken quite a lot more of the dense syrup. We loaded the drums into the back of the station wagon. It had a horizontal curtain to cover the load area, and I made especially sure that the drums could not be seen. I paid Giorgio in cash, thanked him, and drove away.

I was very uneasy as I wound my way along the twisting cross-country roads leading to Castel Sabino. I rehearsed in my mind what I would say if I were stopped by the road police, financial police, or Carabinieri. These are the three of Italy's *forze dell'ordine* (forces for order) that are the most likely to stop one on the road, but Italy abounds in police forces of every sort that can impact on citizens. For example, in addition to the three main ones just mentioned, there are police units for ports, railways, and prisons, and every town and village has its own municipal police. New provincial police forces have been created as I write this, and nor must one forget that even the forest service goes around armed and can apprehend people.

That night, however, I reached my winery without being stopped, unloaded the drums and covered them with some old plastic sheeting to hide them from any casual inspection. Sometimes I felt that my respect for rules and regulations was totally exaggerated in a country like Italy, but upbringing dies hard. In addition, I had heard too many stories of what *can* happen if you get on the wrong side of the authorities. For example, an English woman, an FAO colleague, was driving from the country into Rome to work very early one morning when she was stopped for a routine check by a Carabinieri patrol. They unhurriedly examined her papers, the car's papers, and the car itself, until she complained that she would be late for work and had an important meeting. They took no notice, and she unwisely made some comment about a police state that had never properly abandoned Fascism. They noticed that all right, and they immediately turned very nasty. They threatened to arrest her on the basis of some law about being offensive to uniformed officials. She had to grovel abjectly before they allowed her to go.

A few days later I had to begin the vintage. The grapes were not ripening any more, and the first signs of bunch rot were beginning to show. The tractor brought the loads of grapes to the winery. We crushed them in the covered porch area outside the main doors, added the small dose of potassium metabisulphite and pumped the skins and must into the fermenter. It took most of the day to fill it to a level that left enough head space to cope with any foaming. Very early the next morning I added the yeasts and pumped over the mass in the fermenter to mix them in.

Pumping over is done by connecting a pipe between the stopcock at the bottom of the fermenter and the pump, and by tying a delivery pipe from the other side of the pump into the open hatch at the top of the tank. When the pump is switched on, it sucks from the bottom of the tank and delivers a continuous gush of must or wine into the top of the tank. Once fermentation begins, the carbon dioxide soon forces the skins to the surface to form that cap which, in my tractor-garage winery with its wide-mouthed small tanks, I broke up and submerged with a piece of wood at least twice a day. I could no longer use that technique in such a big tank, and one that had only a manhole-sized hatch at the top rather than being fully open, as were traditional fermenting vats. I would have to go up a ladder on to the top of the tank and sit there playing the cascade of fermenting wine from the delivery pipe over the cap of skins to wet it and break it up.

The morning after I had added the yeasts I pressed my ear against the side of the tank and heard a faint noise, like something frying very gently in a pan. The fermentation seemed to be beginning. I climbed quickly up to the top of the tank and stuck my nose into the hatch. Sure enough, there was a hint of the unique smell of fermenting wine. Never, during all of my years as a winemaker, did I fail to be astonished by how a still mass of thousands of litres of must or crush in a tank could be brought to life by the tiny yeasts multiplying and working to turn the sugar into alcohol and producing heat and carbon dioxide at the same time.

By the early evening, the fermentation was truly under way. When you put your head over the open hatch of a large tank in full fermentation, the concentration of carbon dioxide pouring out literally takes your breath away. You then understand how people have died of asphyxiation in wineries without proper ventilation. When white must is being fermented without skins, you can see the surface, which is not possible with red wine because the cap hides it. Look down into a large tank of fermenting white must and you will see a seething, foaming cauldron. And you will hear a loud and continuous sizzling noise as the bubbles of carbon dioxide rush to the surface. It is hard to credit such violent activity in a large body of liquid to the work of innumerable micro-organisms.

It was exciting to have my first large-scale operation under way, but I was truly flying by the seat of my pants and was uneasy about how things would go. Perhaps for this reason I did not sleep well, and at about 1.30 in the morning, I decided to go down to the winery to check that everything was in order. I pulled on some clothes and trotted down the steps from the house. The first thing that struck me as I entered the winery was the very strong smell of fermenting wine. I snapped on the lights and was met by the sight of foam and wine pouring down the outside of the fermenter, on to the winery floor and away down the central drainage channel. The sight shocked me. In my inexperience, I had obviously not left enough head space in the fermenter. I needed to get some of the fermenting wine out of it, and very quickly.

I scrambled up the ladder and on to the top of the fermenter. There was wine and foam pouring down its inclined surface. My clothes were soon wet and purple as I untied the end of the pump's delivery pipe from its position on top of the hatch and scrambled down the ladder with it. I rushed to the nearest of the other tanks and fitted the connecting flange to the flange on the tank's stopcock. I frantically screwed tight the wing nut on the clamp that holds the two flanges together.

I rushed back to the fermenter and opened the stopcock that would send wine to the pump, and then back to the pump to switch it on. The faster I stopped this flood of wine going down the drain the better. I flicked the switch on the pump through its first position and into the second, the one for high speed pumping. Nothing seemed to happen for a couple of seconds, and then there was a loud explosion. Suddenly I found myself being hit by a blinding stream of fermenting must and grape skins that was being projected at high-pressure from a split in one of the pipes leading from the pump to the empty tank.

It took me a second or two to pull myself together, remove myself from the purple spray, wipe my eyes clear, and turn off the pump. It took me a few seconds more to remember something that I had read in the pump's instruction book a few days before: when pumping at slow speed, a safety device would stop the pump if its outlet was blocked, but when it was pumping at high speed, this safety device did not operate. I looked across to the tank into which I was trying to pump the fermenting wine, and sure enough, the stopcock was in the closed position. I went across to the tank calmly. There was no longer any hurry because the wine had stopped flowing out of the top of the fermenter. Most of the excess was on me and all over the newly painted walls and ceiling. I fixed another pipe between the pump and the empty tank, opened the stopcock and turned the pump on again. I put it into the slow position for several seconds, and when I had seen that all was well, moved it to the fast position.

Many litres of must and skins came out of that split pipe in a matter of seconds. My pristine winery of which I was so proud was a mess. There were purple splash marks and grape skins everywhere. There were skins stuck to the ceiling, five metres (sixteen feet) above, in places I would have thought quite beyond the reach of the spray. It took me until almost four in the morning with hosepipe, brush, ladder, and broom to clean up.

In retrospect, it was in no way a serious incident, but at the time it upset me greatly. Added to the poor ripening season, the wet weather, and the fact that I had no work, it brought my spirits to a low ebb. Fortunately, the work situation was resolved within days after the vintage when Unicef asked me to undertake an assignment for them, the first of many. Nevertheless, I remained angry with myself for being so stupid in the winery, but it had taught me a lesson: I needed to be deliberate in my actions in the winery. Certainly many operations would require speed and deft hands, but precipitate haste had no place. And for my remaining years with that pump, I never again forgot to turn it on at slow speed first, and check that all was well before going to the fast position.

22

Some Ins and Outs of Winemaking

Serious winemaking proved to be the most challenging activity I had ever undertaken. An inherent problem is that you can only do it once a year, unless you are a high-level consulting winemaker and are contracted to work in the southern hemisphere around March–April and in the northern around September–October. Indeed, that has been happening in recent years, for example, with Australian winemakers coming to France for the vintage. But if you are a learner who comes to the activity in mid-life, as I did, one vintage a year does not allow you to accumulate a great body of experience. I soon discovered that I needed to keep copious notes each year to remind myself of the conditions of the vintage and of what I had done. It did occur to me that perhaps my memory was not as good as it might be, perhaps because of all those neurons in my brain being knocked off by drinking too much of my own produce, but keeping notes was easier than not drinking wine.

The variations in conditions for the vintage from one year to the next were remarkable, beginning with the air temperature. When it was warm, say over 23–24°C (75°F) during the day, the fermentation always began very easily. But when it was cold, as happened on occasion, especially when the vintage was late, I had to take measures to warm the must, and also to keep the winery as warm as possible. This was especially so for white wine fermented without skin contact, whereas red wines being fermented with the skins begin fermenting much more easily, due to the presence of yeasts on the skins. My primitive way of warming a tank of must was to put a pair of fan heaters under it and to wrap a large sheet of insulating material around the legs of the tank to close off the space.

However, in the case of the white wine, a much bigger problem that occurred every year was to keep it cool once it had started to ferment. It is well established that the temperature during fermentation of a white wine is of vital importance for the fragrance and freshness of the end product. The temperature of a fermenting white wine in a big winery is normally kept at about 18–20°C, (68°F) though some producers aim for even lower temperatures. Well-financed wineries have refrigerated tanks or cooling systems through which the wine is constantly pumped. My operation could not run to such investment, so I had to look for alternative means of cooling the Pinot Bianco while it fermented.

Thinking back to that first Pinot Bianco I had made in demijohns, I realized that one of the reasons it had worked out so well was that it had been fermented in tiny quantities. This allowed the heat that was being generated by the fermentation to be easily dissipated. Therefore, as a first step to cooling the fermenting white wine in the new winery, I bought a 3,000-litre stainless steel tank. It was as tall as the 5,000-litre ones I already had, but it was smaller in diameter. This would mean that the core at the centre of the mass of fermenting must would be nearer to the walls of the tank and more affected by their temperature. If I ran cold water down the outside of the tank, that might be enough to keep the fermenting must inside it cool. The water in the deep borehole I had sunk when I bought the property came out of the ground at 14°C (57°F). The trick would be to run a thin film of this water down the outside of the tank, also in the hope that it would begin to evaporate, which would add to the cooling effect.

By chance, a friend had given me an American device for watering gardens. It was a piece of porous canvas hose about three centimetres (1.25 inches) in cross section when it was expanded by water pressure inside it. With the must of the Pinot Bianco about to ferment in the tank, and its temperature just under 20°C, I laid this porous hose carefully around the upper rim of the tank, as close to the outer edge as possible, and connected it to an ordinary piece of plastic hose. When I turned on the tap to see whether my idea would work in practice, the porous hose swelled and the water began to course down the outside of the tank in an even film that covered it perfectly. I was delighted.

I called Ferruccio, who was in the vineyard with the grape pickers, to come and have a look.

"Look at this, Ferru," I said. "The water from the well is cold . . . fourteen degrees. I'm hoping this will keep the temperature of the wine at very close to eighteen degrees (64°F). White wines mustn't get hot while they're fermenting."

Ferruccio looked at the water flowing off the sides of the tank, across the floor, and down the drain. "You mean you're going to leave that flowing all the time?"

"Of course. I shall have to check on the temperature every few hours, even at night, and maybe close the tap if the temperature drops too low, but my main worry is to see whether this stops the wine from getting too hot."

"That'll mean leaving the pump in the well on all the time, for several days and nights. You'll have an enormous electricity bill."

"I'm going to have an enormous electricity bill anyway, what with the crusher, the press, and the pump. I don't care. I'm trying to make high quality white wine."

He looked at the flowing water again and shook his head. "When I see that water running down the drain, I remember all the water I used to have to cart up to my house in a wheelbarrow before the main arrived. Doesn't seem right to waste it like that."

"I thought you only cared about wine," I teased. "You get upset when we lose any red wine on the floor during a racking. You always shout, 'Look out! That's God's blood!' Now you're making a fuss about water as well."

Ferruccio only smiled and shrugged. He had again been without much of his sparkle in recent times. Before that he would have come out with some appropriate and funny riposte.

My primitive cooling system worked perfectly. I checked the temperature of the fermenting Pinot every few hours, sometimes reducing or increasing the flow of water, and it stayed very close to 18°C. For reasons I never understood, but no doubt related to complex matters of surface tension, the uniform film of water running down the outside of the tank would breakdown after a few hours and the flow would start to come down in rivulets, leaving dry spaces on the sides of the tank. I found that spreading the rivulets of water across the tank's surface with a broom restored the film again for several hours.

Once I knew that my cooling system worked, I began in the following years to experiment with the amount of water I needed to use, for despite trying to be funny with Ferruccio about it, I did not like to waste such a valuable resource or use the pump in the borehole unnecessarily. During one of those experiments, the temperature got away from me and rose to just over 21°C (70°F) for most of a morning before I got it under control again. To me, the finished wine seemed the same as usual. However, the following autumn there was a wine fair in Rome in which I participated. In the next stand was a wine producer from Alto Adige, the

German-speaking region in the north of Italy that borders on Austria. It is also known as South Tyrol. It became part of Italy as reparations paid by Austria after World War I. A mere fifteen per cent of the terrain in this mountain fortress can be cultivated, and only then as a result of the centuries of labour devoted to landscaping and terracing. Some of Italy's best white wines are produced in this idyllic area. Its vineyards and orchards – and everything else too – are kept in meticulous order.

The man from Alto Adige in the next stand at the wine fair was one of the top producers. He was an acknowledged leader in the field, and his wines were renowned for their quality. He wandered over for a chat a few hours after the fair opened. He was a fair-haired man in his forties, friendly and easy to talk to.

"People have been telling me that you're producing a Pinot Bianco in the Sabine Hills. Could I taste it?"

That a man of such importance on the wine scene should show interest in my comparatively amateur efforts took me completely aback.

"Of course! Of course!" I stammered.

I hurriedly fetched a glass and poured some of my Pinot into it for him. He looked at it carefully, tilting it and holding it to the light, swilled it in the glass, sniffed it thoughtfully, and then tasted it.

"It's very good," he said. "I wouldn't have expected a wine like this from Central Italy. Your vineyard must be at quite high altitude. It takes quite big differences between day and night temperatures, and a long ripening season, to produce the sort of aromas you have in this."

I confirmed that Castel Sabino was high and told him about the vineyard. He swilled and sniffed again.

"What temperature did you ferment it at?" he asked.

"Between eighteen and twenty degrees," I said.

"Ummm . . . yes. But I think the temperature went out of control for a while. I think it went to twenty-one, or perhaps even to twenty-two degrees, for a few hours."

I was astounded. "How do you know that?" I asked. "You're absolutely right. Please tell me how you can tell?"

He smiled good-naturedly. "It's just something about the bouquet. But anyway, my compliments. You're on the right track."

He wandered back to his stand. I was left dumfounded that such subtle expertise could exist. Would I ever come near to it? Of course, I never did.

With red wines, it is not as usual to control the temperature during fermentation. The producers that do so are attempting to produce richer aromas. The only real problem can be if the temperature goes above 35°C (95°F) when the heat will stop the yeasts from working and block the fermentation. That only happens in areas of much hotter climate than Castel Sabino, where my fermenting red wines never became hotter than 28°C (82°F). However, temperature plays an important part in another aspect of making red wine, the malolactic fermentation. Also called the secondary fermentation, this turns the naturally occurring malic acid in the wine into lactic acid. Malic acid is harsh on the taste buds, while lactic acid is softer. So a wine that has undergone the malolactic fermentation will have a smoother taste, often described as buttery.

It is usual to try to get the malolactic fermentation to start immediately after the primary fermentation has finished, when the new wine has just been racked off and the skins pressed. Whereas it is yeasts that bring about the primary fermentation, with sugar being turned into alcohol, it is bacteria that bring about the secondary one. These bacteria of the malolactic fermentation function best when the wine is warm. In fact, if the wine becomes too cold, and too soon, after the primary fermentation, the malolactic one will probably not start until the following spring when the wine warms up. So I always did everything I could to keep the new red wine warm, but I had no heating in the winery. In the cool conditions at Castel Sabino, it was quite difficult to get the secondary fermentation to start, also because my wines were initially very high in acidity, which inhibits the bacteria.

Then, in one of the early years, I unwittingly bottled a red wine that had not undergone the malolactic fermentation, even though it had gone through one summer and two springs in a tank. The wine then did its secondary fermentation in the bottle, producing carbon dioxide. This appeared as a ring of tiny bubbles that beaded the upper and outside edge of the wine when poured into a glass. It was also slightly *spritzig,* or prickly on the tongue.

A white wine that does its secondary fermentation in the bottle can gain a slight sparkle that makes it very attractive, but it is certainly not desirable in most red wines. I wanted to avoid it happening again. In some countries, such as Australia, it was routine practice to inoculate new red wine with the bacteria responsible for the malolactic fermentation, and the bacteria were freely available there. In Italy, adding these bacteria to wine was forbidden.

I had no guilty feelings about adding the bacteria to new red wine. I could not see that adding bacteria to wine to get a fermentation started was any different from adding yeasts to wine to do the same. Nor did I believe the practice could be harmful to anyone because the bacteria occur naturally in wine anyway. I would just be adding some extra quantities to try to get the process started. I therefore asked an Australian friend to bring me some packets of the dried bacteria when he next came to Italy.

The procedure to use them was quite cumbersome and went on over several days. I had to put them into a small quantity of the new wine and warm it. Every few hours I had to bulk up the quantity by adding more warm wine, until I finally had quite a large amount to add to the tank. The process worked well but I was unable to get the bacteria from Australia every year. Curiously, though, I never had any further problems with malolactic fermentations. One of my oenologist friends suggested that perhaps my first use of the dried bacteria had left a good population of them in the winery.

Another early problem, the excessive foaming of fermenting wine, which led to that burst pipe that sullied my new winery, also disappeared. I suspect that was because I started using a different type of dried yeasts. They seemed to ferment very efficiently without producing gigantic bubbles that built up into a very deep layer before they burst. However, no oenologist I knew could confirm that it was the yeasts that had made the difference.

A very real practical problem in a winery is preventing spoilage on the surface and oxidation of a wine in a tank that is not brim full, or on ullage. And of course, it is never possible to have all of one's tanks full all the time. This was an immediate problem the first year I made wine in the new winery. When the wine was still very new, it still contained quite a lot of carbon dioxide from the fermentation. I reasoned that much of this would be released while the free-run wine was being pumped from the fermenter to the storage tank. It would rise above the wine and form a layer that would protect it from air. But what would I do later when I had to rack the wine from one tank to another and there was virtually no carbon dioxide left in it?

The paraffin discs impregnated with mustard used for demijohns, as mentioned earlier, also existed in a much larger form for barrels and tanks. However, I was not satisfied they would provide the level of protection I wanted over such a big surface. Furthermore, they lose their effectiveness over time and that would mean remembering to renew them regularly. The only real solution was to fill the headspace over the wine with an inert gas. Large wineries in the main use nitrogen for this purpose, and have a system of pipes and valves to keep the tanks topped up with the gas. They may also inject nitrogen into the wine – especially into white wine – in the tube leading to the bottling plant to keep it protected from air. Ultimately, I would need a similar system, but my development of the winery had to be spread over several years, whereas I needed an interim solution that first year for the rackings when there would be no carbon dioxide left in the wine.

It occurred to me that I might be able to manage carbon dioxide in a makeshift way, without valves and the like. The gas is considerably heavier than air: if I had a cylinder of carbon dioxide and connected a long plastic tube to the valve on it, it should be possible to sit on top of a partially empty tank, lower the end of the tube to just above the surface of the wine, and slowly let in carbon dioxide. I imagined that it would settle on the wine, displacing the air upwards and out of the tank until the whole of the head space was filled by the carbon dioxide. I would have to be careful to keep it flowing slowly, for I supposed that if it went in too fast, it would create turbulence and mix with the air, rather than displacing it upwards steadily and evenly.

I asked Andrea Guidoni whether he thought this primitive approach would work. He said that he personally had never tried it, but he seemed to remember having read about it somewhere as a technique that could be used in small wineries. He mentioned that the wine would absorb some of the carbon dioxide, especially during winter when the wine was cold, but that did not worry me unduly. I thought that the gas could be released by a pumping over of the wine, and if some remained up to the moment of bottling, it would come out as the wine cascaded into the bottles or demijohns. In that case, it would also have the positive effect of keeping air away from the wine as the level rose in the bottle.

About a month after the pressing of the red wine in the new winery, the time came for the first racking. When the wine was in the new tank, there was a head space above it of almost half a metre. I climbed the ladder to the top of the tank with the end of the tube that was connected to the large cylinder of carbon dioxide I had bought. Sitting on the sloping roof of the tank and looking into the hatch, I lowered the end of the tube until it was almost touching the wine.

Ferruccio was standing by the cylinder.

"Okay, Ferru," I called down to him. "Open the valve a little."

The gas came hissing out of the tube and agitated the surface of the wine.

"Close it down a bit," I called.

I saw Ferruccio's hand grasp the valve and twist it anti-clockwise instead of clockwise, opening it further. The hiss rose and the gas churned the surface of the wine.

"The other way! The other way!" I shouted.

There was really no need to shout, but I was anxious that my primitive technique might not work, and nor did I want to waste the gas because I had to make a special journey to buy it.

"*Porco Dio!*" Ferruccio muttered, and closed the valve completely. It took several minutes before he got the flow as I imagined it should be, barely ruffling the surface of the wine. I moved the end of the tube slowly around over that dark disc of wine in the tank. A pity that carbon dioxide is colourless and odourless, I thought, for it would have been helpful to see how the gas was spreading and building up in the tank.

After about ten minutes, I pulled a cigarette lighter I had bought for the purpose out of my pocket, lit it, and lowered it slowly into the tank. It continued to burn as I moved it downwards until, about thirty centimetres above the wine, the flame weakened and died. I did not know the proportions of a mixture of air and carbon dioxide in which a flame will still burn, but I guessed there could not be much air left in that layer above the wine. Nor did I know how much of the carbon dioxide would be absorbed by the wine, but I could not take the risk of having it all absorbed and allowing the air to come in contact with the surface of the wine. So I continued to let the carbon dioxide into the tank until the lighter went out as soon as I moved it into the neck of the open hatch at the top of the tank. My primitive system seemed to have worked perfectly. I closed the hatch tightly and came down the ladder.

I was ready to rib Ferruccio about not knowing how to open a valve that opened in the same direction as a water tap, but he was leaning against the wall of the winery, looking pale and exhausted.

"C'mon Ferru. I'll take you home in the car. You're not looking too good."

The next morning Francesca called me very early to say that her father had vomited large quantities of blood during the night and had been taken to hospital by ambulance. The doctors had said that he had had a haemorrhage into the stomach from the varicose veins in the oesophagus that had been caused by the damage to his liver. After a few days, he came out of hospital with the strictest orders never to touch alcohol again. I am not aware that he did, but the damage had already been done.

I continued with my primitive method of protecting wine on ullage for a couple of years and never had any problems, but when I increased the number of tanks in the winery, I decided that I would invest in a proper system of selector taps and valves to be able to control better the carbon dioxide in the tanks. The cylinder would be connected by a tube to selector taps on a plate screwed to the wall above it. The selector taps would allow the flow of gas to be opened or closed to any particular tank. Plastic tubes would run from these taps to special valves on top of each tank. These would open and let in more carbon dioxide whenever the pressure in the tank dropped, for example when the wine in the tank was absorbing it.

I had seen publicity in agricultural magazines for stainless-steel equipment made by a company called Beninox. Purchasing the valves and selector taps from them provided an interesting insight into the small industries in the north of Italy.

I had to go to Lucca at the beginning of the following week for a two-day consultancy assignment in a training centre for people from developing countries. It would not be far to go further north to visit Beninox, so I called them to ask whether I could drop in on the Wednesday morning to buy some items for my winery.

"Of course," said Signor Benini, the owner of the business. "We'll be pleased to see you. Come around eleven and stay for lunch, if that fits in with your plans."

It did, so just after eleven on that Wednesday, I drove into the yard in front of the Beninox factory. It was a scruffy, warehouse-like building in an unattractive industrial area of Pavia. The open space inside was occupied by a handful of workers who were cutting, shaping, and welding things from sheets and tubes of stainless steel. There were more sheets and tubes stored along the walls. In one corner there was a small office partitioned off by glass. There was a man inside, in shirtsleeves, watching a fax churn out a message. I walked towards the door and he waved me to come in.

"You must be Signor Fraser," he said over his shoulder. "Please excuse me a minute. I want to make sure that the rest of this fax comes in all right."

The fax finally stopped after it had spewed out many, many pages. He picked up the sheaf of paper and turned to shake my hand. He was a fit-looking, greying man in his early fifties, with a decisive air about him.

"Sorry, but the fax has been playing up recently. This is an important order from Bolivia for dairy equipment."

He asked me about my winery, the number of tanks I had, and the design of their tops.

"Good. Let's go into the store and select what you need. Come with me."

I followed him into another room that, like his office, was separated from the main area of the factory. The room contained a huge, horizontal, drum-shaped device about three metres (ten feet) long. As I got nearer to it, I saw that it was a series of hanging shelves divided into bins, and that the bins were filled with all manner of stainless-steel fittings. They were quite beautiful, almost like works of art. Some had a brushed satin finish and others were shiny.

Benini pressed a button at the end of the device and an electric motor slowly rotated the drum to bring the contents of other bins into view for him to pick out the valves, connectors and adaptors I needed. At one point, he found that one adaptor needed to be modified.

"Alberto," he called through the doorway. "Can you come here for a moment?"

Alberto appeared in an instant, a wiry man in a workman's blue overalls.

"Signor Fraser needs a flange facing the other way to this one," Benini said, holding out the item. "Could you cut this one off and weld another on at ninety degrees."

Alberto disappeared and came back a few minutes later with the modified piece. It had been beautifully welded, with those regular patterns in the beading that only the most skilled welders can produce.

Just before midday, Benini look at his watch.

"Time for lunch." he said. "We eat at twelve here. I hope it's not too early for you. You've probably picked up the decadent habits of that lot around Rome. Long, late lunches and no work in the afternoons!"

"No such luck," I replied, following him to his office, where he put on his suit jacket. We went out of the building and at that moment Alberto drew up beside us at the wheel of a top-of-the-range BMW. He had shed his overalls and was also wearing a smart suit. We drove off to a simple nearby restaurant, had a quick and light lunch, and were back at the factory on the dot of one o'clock. We finished putting together the items I needed and I paid for them. Benini and his brother-in-law, Alberto, bid me a very cordial farewell, and I was soon on my way south. I reflected about how different the various parts of Italy were, and I realized that I had just seen, at first hand, the backbone of Italy's economy: quite small and often family concerns, making top-quality products and exporting them worldwide.

When I got back to the winery I lost no time in installing the valves on the tanks. I ran plastic hosepipe from them, close to the ceiling and then down to the panel of selector taps I had screwed to the wall next to where I kept the gas cylinder. I was happy to have moved ahead from the primitive way I had been using carbon dioxide until then.

The most intricate operation I carried out in my winery was making white wine from red grapes. It first came about because I was disappointed in the results I was extracting from the Sangiovese grapes. They were still not giving the sugar levels I wanted and were too acidic. One day, over lunch with Andrea Guidoni, I was commenting on the situation when he said, "Why don't you try making white wine out of some of them? White wine with eleven per cent or so of alcohol is acceptable, and the high acidity is, too."

I had often wondered how white wines were made from red grapes, Champagne included. Even if I knew that the juice of many red varieties was generally white, I found it difficult to believe that it was not given some pink tinge from the skins, especially if the grapes were fully ripe.

"How would I make white wine from my red Sangiovese?" I asked.

"It's quite simple. You press the grapes fresh, like for making white wine. The must will probably be pink. You add a higher dose of sulphur dioxide to the must than you would normally, enough to stop it from fermenting for at least twelve hours. Then you add decolouring carbon and mix the whole lot together. You then add some tannin, and then some gelatine that you've dissolved in water first. A few hours later the gelatine will have settled to the bottom of the tank, taking all of the carbon with it. The must that's left above will be completely clear. Just pump it off, add yeasts, and let it ferment. Easy!"

I tried the process at the next vintage, with a list provided by Andrea of the precise doses of the various things to add to the Sangiovese must. The three 600-litre fibreglass tanks I had used in the tractor-garage winery were perfect for the task, for they were semi-transparent, and I could see what was happening inside them. And after I had added the carbon, dissolved first in a small quantity of the pink must, what I saw was a rather disgusting black mess. If anyone from the village had dropped in at that point, they would have been horrified. I added the tannin and gelatine. Within half an hour, the top part of the must in the tank had begun to clear. I ladled a little of it into a glass and was amazed to see that it was completely white. Overnight, the black gunge settled into the bottom few centimetres of the tank and I was able to pump off the clear must above it and ferment it in the usual way. The technique certainly worked.

An English Master of Wine who visited me tasted the resulting wine and praised its aroma and freshness. He suggested I should turn all my Sangiovese into white wine, but my personal ambition to produce good red wines, and the practicalities of decolouring large quantities of must put me off such an idea. I decided to continue with only relatively small amounts each year.

I was never too happy about the amount of sulphur dioxide I used to prevent the must from fermenting during the decolouring process. My general policy was to use as little of it as possible in all of my winemaking, and I seldom reached more than half of the legally permitted levels of it in my finished wines. So I tried gradually reducing the dose of potassium metabisulphite when I was removing the colour from pink must to make white wine. Of course, the inevitable happened: I came down to the winery one morning expecting to pump off the clear must and found the first of the tanks I had filled the previous day as black as the previous evening. The fermentation had begun and brought all the gunge back up. I was only able to save the tank of wine by adding an even bigger dose of sulphur dioxide to block the fermentation. Then, as soon as most of the gunge was near the bottom again, I quickly pumped off the clear must before the mass started to ferment a second time.

The worst job in the winery was cleaning out tanks after rackings in the spring. The winter cold had always precipitated a lot of tartaric acid. Much of it fell loosely to the bottom of the tank, but a lot also stuck firmly to the inside walls of the tank. It formed a hard layer with the consistency of coarse sandpaper. Most large wineries remove it by spraying hot solutions of highly alkaline substances, such as caustic soda, through the hatch on top of the tank. I tried this, but the water heater in the small office area of the winery did not provide enough hot water to deal with one of the 5,000-litre tanks. There was no room for a larger heater. Furthermore, there were always areas high up on the tank sides, and on the roof if the tank had been completely full, that I could not reach properly with the spray. I was obsessive about getting the tanks completely clean, always concerned about leaving bacteria lurking in any residues and having them cause problems in the next batch of wine.

My insistence on cleanliness was probably overdone. I know Ferruccio thought it was, especially when I got into the tanks to remove tartaric acid crystals by hand. I would don waders and tell him to help me get in. With my head and shoulders through the hatch, he would lift my legs from the floor and bundle me unceremoniously the rest of the way inside, passing after me a ladder, brushes, scrapers, buckets, hosepipe and other things I was going to need. When I finally came out, as much as an hour or more later, he would look at me with a quizzical expression. It was far more eloquent than words in expressing his opinion that so much time and effort spent cleaning a wine tank was quite unnecessary, and totally foolish. My defence was always to deliver a little homily about micro-organisms and how much damage they could do to wine. He would nod in apparent agreement, but that quizzical expression and slight smirk never left his face. As with the moon and when to cut chestnut poles, we just left it as a point of difference.

I was finally so tired of the whole tank-cleaning operation that I bought a steam cleaner. It made the operation much easier and faster, but from the open hatch at the top of the tank, I still could not reach some of the higher areas properly with the jet, especially the roof, because of the awkward angle. I still needed to get physically into the tanks.

The first time I used the steam cleaner inside a tank, I donned my waders and an oilskin coat and hat, and Ferruccio bundled me in as usual. He passed me the steam gun and I set about blasting the areas of the roof that I had not been able to reach. The tartaric acid crystals came cascading down on me, mixed with the water droplets and steam that filled the inside of the tank. It was a most uncomfortable place to be. The rim of the oilskin hat prevented me from looking up at the roof properly and I had to take it off. The water then rained down my neck.

When Ferruccio helped me out, I must have been a sorry sight, with my hair plastered down and full of dark tartaric acid crystals, and with my glasses steamed up. I was also muttering a few of his favourite obscenities. This time, the quizzical expression on his face was replaced by open laughter.

"Signor Colin," he said, "I've heard about those counts and dukes and other nobles that make those expensive wines. Do they come out of their tanks looking like you do now?"

"Don't be silly, Ferru! They've got people they send into the tanks, not like you. You just stand around laughing. But I can't send you in because you wouldn't fit through the hatch with that gut of yours, and even if you did, you wouldn't clean the tank as I want it done."

"I'm happy you think that," he said, "because I wouldn't go into the tanks like you do for all the gold in the world. I'd be frightened in a closed-in place like that".

His face showed that, indeed, he feared confined spaces, something he had never told me before.

"Don't worry," I said, "I'll go on doing it, but just remind me every time you help me into a tank that producing wine is supposed to be an occupation for noblemen. I won't feel the water going down my neck so much, or be so blinded by the steam, if I remember it's a nobleman's job I'm doing".

There was one particular piece of winemaking legislation that caused me more problems than any other. Anyone who produces more than fifty hectolitres of wine must take their *vinaccie* (pressings) to a distillery. They are paid for them according to the alcohol they still contain, but the sum is minimal. The purpose of this legislation is, of course, to prevent people illegally distilling spirits, but it does not succeed. Indeed, a man I knew in Castel Sabino who bought grapes from me asked me once whether I would give him some of my pressings. He told me that he had a small still to produce *grappa*. I agreed and he came to collect them. He did the same every year for several years, and the *grappa* he produced was quite good. The only surprising thing about this arrangement was that the man was an important inspector in the *Guardia di Finanza* (financial police). I heard from several sources that he was brutal in his interrogation when he dropped in unannounced on some small business that was unfortunate enough to have come under financial scrutiny. He was like a bloodhound in tracking down every detail in the books and in the numerous bits of paperwork that the Italian State has established to try to prevent people evading taxes. Of course, the State has not succeeded in this objective, any more than it has stopped the very staff it employs to hunt down tax evaders from distilling *grappa* illegally.

The problem that I had with my pressings, once their quantity became too great for my local and illegal distiller, was that the nearest official distillery where I could take them was almost a two-hour drive away. For several years I hired

Bertini and his truck, and the cost was far more than I was paid by the distillery. Another aspect of the problem was that the pressings needed to be as fresh as possible to get the best price for them, but the pressing of the fresh-picked and unfermented Pinot Bianco was about three or four weeks earlier than the pressing of the fermented red varieties. I would load the Pinot pressings into my farm trailer, pack them down, and cover them tightly with a large plastic sheet in the hope that they would ferment properly. When the red pressings were ready, we loaded everything into the truck and set off for the distillery.

The distillery was enormous. The distilling area and the storage tanks for the alcohol it produced were in several large buildings, and around them were open-fronted sheds like aircraft hangars. In these were great piles of grape pressings many metres high. The piles were in the form of a wedge so that a crawler tractor could trundle up and down the sloping side of the pile to compact the pressings and keep air out.

Its manager was a kind man, but he always complained that my white pressings had not fermented properly. They had a high content of vinegar rather then alcohol. This always surprised me because I thought I had done more to keep the air out of them than he was doing with his enormous piles of pressings. Anyway, after completing what seemed like a never-ending amount of paperwork, I would receive a footling amount for my efforts to stay within the law, and I was always considerably out-of-pocket.

After about five years of this nonsense, the owner took pity on me. By then our annual meetings had become quite friendly, and I had toured his tanks with him and tasted many of his excellent *grappe*.

"Bringing your *vinaccie* all the way from Castel Sabino must be expensive and a nuisance for you," he said as we stood in front of a tank, glass of *grappa* in hand, during one of these tours.

"Yes, and it's more than that," I said. "It's often very difficult organizing the whole operation with the truck and arranging the free time for myself. After the vintage, I'm usually being called urgently for some consultancy somewhere, and I have to stall until I've been able to come here with the pressings. Being a wine-producer and also a consultant often creates time conflicts."

"Well, next year, just come down here with your winery stock register," he said. "We'll calculate what weight of *vinaccie* you should have brought in and do the paperwork as if you actually had. You'll have to sign a receipt as if you had been paid in cash. Just dump your pressings somewhere on you property, but where they're not too obvious."

I was so delighted I could have hugged the man. Some people think that Italians are only willing to bend the rules in their own favour, but I can vouch for their generosity in bending them for others too. I have been so favoured more times than I can remember. This particular favour at the distillery meant that I never took any more pressings there, but I had my annual chat with the owner while his office staff organized the paperwork, and we tasted a *grappa* or two. Every year, I dumped my pressings over the retaining wall of the drive down to the winery entrance. My only concern for the few weeks that followed was that some inspector might turn up and notice the vinous smell wafting up. But a couple of rain showers usually got rid of the smell, and by spring the pressings had rotted down and were almost invisible among the weeds growing there.

The solution to my problem with my wine pressings reminded me of something said to me by a lawyer when I first went to live in Italy. I was asking him about what tax return I should make as a foreigner. I spoke no Italian at the time, but the lawyer spoke good English. His summing up was: "In Italy the tax laws are very complicated, but anything can be arranged."

However, that was some forty years ago, and it certainly no longer applies, for Italy has modernized and tightened up enormously. Its membership of the EU has allowed its Governments, frequently incapacitated by party politics and factionalism, to push through unpopular reforms on the basis that they were essential to meet requirements set by Brussels, or Maastricht, or wherever else European Union agreements have been signed.

23

Of Names, Labels, Corks, and Bottles

With the winery built and with second-hand bottling and labelling equipment on the way, the time had come to give serious thought to the names for the wines. The Pinot Bianco was already of a quality that merited sale in bottle, and the red wines were improving year by year as we got the pruning better adjusted to the conditions at Castel Sabino. I was reaching twelve per cent or more of alcohol in most years with less and less use of Rectified Concentrated Grape Must. The concentration of the wines was also improving as the yields of the Sangiovese were reduced. The saying about red wines being made in the vineyard and white wines made in the winery was proving true, for it had become evident in my case that the quality and ripeness of the grapes was the key to making good red wines. In contrast, the quality of the Pinot Bianco depended more on scrupulous attention to details such as the temperature of fermentation, protecting it from air at all stages, and careful filtering.

My experiments with making a rosé wine from the Montepulciano d'Abruzzo grapes had turned out very well. I was pumping off the must after 24–36 hours of maceration with the skins, when its colour was a strong pink. Later, and in the rosé's final form, I included some Sangiovese and Cesanese grapes as well. Everyone who tasted the rosé enjoyed it, for it was fresh and fragrant with plenty of fruit flavours.

I wanted a name for each wine that seemed to sound like, or allude to, its characteristics. For example, a serious red wine, rich in bouquet, body and the warmth of alcohol, and demanding of meals with flavours to match it, can hardly have a flippant-sounding name. On the other hand, rosé wines that are associated with less-demanding food flavours, and perhaps with drinking on a hot day over a cold lunch on a shady terrace, can well benefit from a lightweight name. These were the ideas that guided my quest for appropriate names.

My love of birds gave me the idea of using their names. I started thinking about some of the birds that were often present in the vineyard and tried their names out on friends. Given the constant summer presence of the Golden Orioles in the trees at the bottom of the vineyard, the Italian name for that bird, *Rigogolo,* naturally came to mind. To me, its rolling sound seemed redolent of rolling a good wine around in one's mouth and enjoying its aroma as it wafted up behind the nose. Yet at the same time, it was light enough to match a fruity, fresh white wine. It became my top candidate for the Pinot Bianco. After several friends had also found it appropriate, the name was fixed without further ado.

The names for the red and the rosé wines that I planned to bottle went through many phases of selection and rejection, particularly for the red wine. The Jackdaws that nested in the castle walls very often visited my land, and for some time I considered the Italian name for them, *Taccola.* However, it never sounded quite right to me for a full-bodied red wine. There was also the problem that Italians in general seem to think that all large, black birds of the *Corvus* family are crows. Crows do not enjoy a particularly benevolent image anywhere, I thought. Thus, even if the large and well-known Sicilian wine enterprise the Duca di Salaparuta estate markets many of its wines under the name *Corvo,* I decided to reject anything to do with the Crow family.

Then one day, I suddenly remembered a particular morning of early summer, just a few years after I had bought the property. I had gone into the vineyard to wander around and see how the vines were progressing, but the day was so spectacular that I had stopped in my slow walk along the rows. I just wanted to stand still in the vineyard among the joyful exuberance of young vegetation, absorbing the beauty of that limpid day and of my surroundings. There was a gentle breeze on my face to counter the already warm rays of the sun. Everything seemed perfection and peace. I looked up and into the distance above the lake down the valley, and there I saw a large bird soaring in the crystal sky. It was too high and too far to identify, but it suddenly stopped its graceful circling, and with a few powerful strokes of its wings, set off on a glide in my direction. As it passed, very high and almost overhead, its silhouette was unmistakable. Its forked tail and powerful flight could only belong to a Red Kite. It planed away northwards, circled again for a while, and then with a few more of its powerful wing beats, melted into the distant blue.

I had never seen another Red Kite in the area since that morning, but if the Italian name for that bird sounded right, perhaps it could be the name of my red wine. I looked up Red Kite in Italian and found that a Kite was called *Nibbio*, and that the Red species was called *Nibbio reale* (Royal Kite). I did not need the pretensions of the word "royal", but I thought that Nibbio alone sounded good for a full-bodied red wine. Furthermore, birds of prey seem to enjoy a good image everywhere. Their power, swift grace, and bright-eyed haughtiness, make raptors the aristocrats among birds. To name a wine after one should be all right. My informal market pre-test with friends confirmed the choice.

The many Goldfinches on the property gave me the name for the rosé. Their cheerful twittering as they danced in flight from one place to another accompanied many summer lunches in the shade of the porch with friends downing liberal quantities of my rosé. The Italian name for the Goldfinch is *Cardellino*. The suffix "*ino*" is a diminutive in Italian, and it seemed to suit an unpretentious rosé wine, as well as having a cheerful sound about it.

It was while I was ruminating about bird ideas that the generic name for the wines emerged. The crest of my branch of the Fraser clan is a Phoenix, the mythical and gorgeous bird that, according to legend, is the only one of its kind and lives for 500–600 years in the Arabian Desert. It then burns itself on a funeral pyre ignited by the sun, fanning the flames with its own wings, before rising from its ashes with renewed youth to live another cycle.

The notion that my property, which had been abandoned long before I bought it, was now rejuvenated and productive again had an obvious connotation with the rebirth of the Phoenix. Furthermore, the Phoenix crest is visually striking and I thought it would look good on labels and wine cartons. However, the name *Fenice* (the Italian for Phoenix) used alone did not seem quite right. Further thought led to the idea of adding some allusion to the physical characteristics of the property itself and its position quite high above the village. In fact the traditional local name for the area in which my property was situated was *Colle Fiorito* (Flowery Hill). It was not far from that to my choice of *Poggio Fenice*, (Phoenix Knoll or Hillock).

I registered these as trade names, a lengthy and quite expensive operation. Despite this, however, friends told me several years later that they had seen other wines named Nibbio and Rigogolo. This of course could be a cause for litigation, but life is short, and litigation is very complex in Italy. I preferred to look upon imitation as a compliment on my choices.

The design of the labels was another lengthy procedure. In fact it spread over about three years before they were in final form, with numerous visits to the typographer to introduce small changes. Various friends with artistic talents helped out during the process. I finally finished with a red Phoenix set in a gold medallion at the top of the label. Below it were the words POGGIO FENICE. Below them, in the centre of label, was a stylised drawing of the house and vineyard, and below that was the name of the wine, for example RIGOGOLO. In the lower part of the label was the legally required information describing it as a *vino da tavola* (table wine), stating where it was produced, by whom, and in what year, with the number of the bottling register, alcohol content, content of the bottle, and so on. All of this was framed by a vine cane, complete with leaves and grape clusters, set about a centimetre (half an inch) in from the edges of the label.

The denomination of *vino da tavola* had mixed connotations. On the one hand, it was the lowest category of wine, but on the other, many of Italy's very famous wines were in the same category. This was because obtaining the classification of *Denominazione di Origine Controllata* required a minimum quantity of production that was usually far more than a single producer could turn out. The *vino da tovola* denomination did not upset me too much, for many of Italy's most innovative wine producers, the ones who were at the forefront of the quality revolution in Italian wines in recent decades, were in the same boat.

The label had an admonition to the eventual consumer of the wine, and it also had to be there by law. It was printed vertically between the vine frame and the edge of the label, and it read *Non disperdere il vetro nell'ambiente* (Do not discard the bottle in the environment). Italian homes are spotlessly clean, and Italians are scrupulous about personal hygiene, but their lack of respect for the countryside defies belief. People throw cigarette packages and other wrappings out of their car windows, leave their plastic picnic litter in beauty spots, and fill gullies and ravines below the roads with thrown-out mattresses, refrigerators, stoves, and everything else imaginable. The hope that the messages about bottles on the label would make some difference was laughable, but in Latin societies there is the idea that because "It's been said, it's been done". In other words, the law has been passed, and that is the end of the matter. The need to follow up and actually apply it gets lost to sight.

Bottling in the winery required a filter, in addition to equipment for filling, corking, and labelling. White wine cannot be bottled without first filtering it. Unlike red wine, it almost never clears fully, even when treated with clarifying agents. There are many of such agents, ranging through organic compounds like gelatine or albumin to various sorts of mineral clays, like kaolin and bentonite. The organic compounds combine chemically with substances suspended in the wine and precipitate to the bottom of the tank, while the mineral clays have a physical action in achieving the same effect.

Andrea Guidoni found me a second-hand filter. It was the type that uses cellulose sheets that are forty centimetres (sixteen inches) square and look like cardboard. I had seen such filters parked in a corner of wineries, but I had not the slightest idea of how they functioned, so I had to find my way around mine when it was delivered. Luckily, Andrea Guidoni came to the winery one Saturday and introduced me to its intricacies.

It was built of stainless steel and, basically, it consisted of a longitudinal frame of two tubes with a fixed plate at one end and at the other end, a plate that could be moved towards the fixed plate by turning a screw on a threaded shaft. It had inlet and outlet pipes with stopcocks, and on the outlet pipe there was a sight glass so that one could see how the filtered wine looked as it came out of the filter, and a small tap for taking a sample to examine and taste. The lower part of the device was a tray to catch wine dripping from the filter pack above. The whole was mounted on wheels so that it could be trundled around the winery.

My particular filter came with twenty, black plates made of thick, heavy-duty plastic material. These were the supporting plates for twenty cellulose filter sheets that were to be sandwiched between them. The plates had a protruding ear at the top of each side so that they could be suspended vertically from the tubular frame of the filter, like folders in a filing cabinet. The top corners of each supporting plate also had a round hole – six or seven centimetres (2.5 inches) in diameter – moulded into it, and set into that there was a rubber seal. Inside just one of these two round holes on each plate, there was small port through which wine could enter or exit from the surface of the plate. The plates had to be hung on the frame so that their small entry or exit port alternated between the left side and the right side of the pack, the side of the inlet pipe or of the outlet pipe. The wine could spread easily and evenly over the two faces of the plates through a pattern of small channels moulded into them.

When the filter was set up with its supporting plates and filter sheets in place, the whole pack was squeezed tight by forcing on the long handles provided to turn the screw that moved the stainless-steel plate along its shaft. The round holes on the plates then came together to form a pipe at the top of each side of the filter pack; one pipe was on the inlet side where alternate plates had been mounted with their ports, and the other pipe was on the outlet side, where the outlet ports were located on alternate plates. The pack needed to be compressed very tightly to avoid wine squirting out from the rubber seals on the plates.

The wine was pumped into the filter at quite high pressure through the inlet pipe formed by the supporting plates. It entered alternate plates through their ports, spread across the surface of each plate, passed through the filter sheet and onto the plate on the other side, and exited through the port leading into the outlet pipe along the other side of the pack. In practice, each of my twenty filter sheets would work as a separate filter, whereas in my total ignorance, I had always imagined that all of the wine went though all of the sheets. So, the flow was in parallel rather than in series.

The sheets for such filters come in varying degrees of porosity, the coarser ones for removing the worst of the cloudiness, down to ones so fine that they can even take bacteria out of the wine just before bottling. At the same time, they make a white wine as clear and bright as crystal. But too much filtering can detract from a wine's qualities; in fact, I never filtered my red wines. In addition, the filter sheets were quite expensive, and this was a further inducement to filter wine as little as possible.

The filter was ingenious, but setting it up and using it called for a lot of care, especially in mounting the supporting plates so that their inlet and outlet ports alternated and getting the filter sheets facing the right way. I had a number of tense and frustrating experiences with filtering. The problem was the decision about which porosity of filter sheets to choose for a first cleaning up of the white wine before its final filtering and bottling, for which the finest sheets are always used.

As the wine passes through the filter sheets, they slowly become clogged by the particles they are trapping, and the flow of wine gradually decreases. The pressure of the bypass valve on the pump feeding the filter can be increased as necessary, up to about three atmospheres, to compensate for this. However, if one is using filter sheets that are too fine for the amount of solid matter suspended in a batch of wine, they will clog up completely before all of the wine has been filtered. Opening the filter to insert new sheets exposes a lot of the wine to air, which is precisely what you are trying to avoid, especially with a white wine. Worriedly trying to gauge the amount of wine left in the tank against the trickle still coming out of an almost blocked filter, and wondering whether you are going to succeed in getting it all through, was not a relaxing pastime for an obsessive winemaker like me.

If it was the final filtering as the wine was being bottled, and if I had not got the wine clean enough previously for all of it to go through the finest filter sheets, the situation was even more serious. If the sheets blocked and I had to open the filter to put in new ones, the wine affected by air would be different to the rest, and those bottles would be different to the rest of the batch. I was trying very hard indeed to avoid such variations.

Ferruccio would look at me on those occasions and have the wit to keep his mouth shut. I do not know whether he ever grasped why opening the filter and putting in new cartons left me so bad tempered, but he certainly realized that the atmosphere in the winery was merrier when the last of the wine came through the filter while it was still running reasonably well.

On other occasions when things in the winery went wrong, but were not going to have a direct effect on the quality of the wine, Ferruccio, poked quiet fun at me if I got upset. This was particularly so with the labelling machine, which although it was second-hand, had been professionally overhauled before it was delivered to me. It was a clever piece of engineering, but it was also highly temperamental. It took me a long time to master it.

The glue that came as a paste in large tubs had to be diluted with water to just the right consistency: too solid and it did not flow properly to the rubber roller that applied it to the flat forks that, in turn, applied it to the back of the labels; too liquid and it got past the roller and ran down the forks and all over the place, creating just the sort of mess I abhor, and one that took hours to clean up.

The labels had to be placed very carefully into their spring-loaded holder, in just the right initial quantity. And even when I thought I had got it right, the machine would suddenly start spewing labels everywhere, or sticking two or three labels askew on each bottle.

"Stop! Stop!" I would shout furiously, and one of our team would rush to the switch on the wall to turn off the machine. I was irate because I always had a calculated number of labels printed for any particular batch of wine, and the few extras included for this sort of foul up were limited.

My verbal abuse of the machine in a mixture of Italian and English as I tried to correct the problem always amused Ferruccio. If I looked up and caught his eye, I would see the old twinkle there. The next moment he would be laughing at me and making some comment about taking the machine to a wedding because it was perfect for throwing confetti, or about how he would like to learn some of those elegant-sounding English expressions I was using.

I had to decide what type of bottle to use for the wines. The first Rigogolo I ever bottled in the winery went into those tall, tapered bottles traditionally used for white wines, especially in Germany and Alsace. They were appropriate for my Pinot Bianco. Everything had gone rather well that first Saturday we bottled Rigogolo, and we had more than six thousand bottles of it stacked along the wall of the grotto by mid-afternoon. They were about six deep and they ran for many metres. They made a splendid sight. In fact, the next day, a Canadian friend and his wife, both wine enthusiasts, visited me and we went into the grotto. When the wife saw so many bottles stacked together against the wall, she went silent and contemplated them for several seconds. Then she said, thoughtfully, "You know, Colin, that sight gives me a feeling of security".

I remembered that notion of security the following weekend when we were preparing to label some of the bottles. Ferruccio had gone into the grotto to start bringing bottles out while I was preparing the labelling machine. I suddenly heard a tinkling sound that seemed to go on and on . . . forever and ever. Above the tinkling, I heard Ferruccio shout one of his usual expletives. I rushed into the grotto. There were bottles rolling about all over the floor, while Ferruccio was frantically trying the stem the cascade of them tumbling from the top of the heap. He was bent forward, groping arms outstretched, and dodging from foot to foot like a soccer goalkeeper, but every time he stopped a bottle, more seemed to roll off the heap. They did finally stop, more or less on their own, putting an end to the diabolical tinkling. Ferruccio and I stood in the sudden silence. I looked at him accusingly.

"I only moved one bottle, Signor Colin, and they all started rolling everywhere," he said.

Surprisingly, there seemed to be very little wine on the floor, and in fact, once we had restored order, we found that only three bottles had broken of the many hundreds that had tumbled and rolled. Obviously, we had not fixed the stack properly, but apart from that, those fluted hock bottles are too conical to form a stable stack, unlike the straight-sided Bordeaux-type bottles. Later, as we became better organized, we stored bottles in wire-sided cages on pallets and moved them around with a manual pallet trolley. I also decided to use only Bordeaux-type bottles, brown for the Nibbio, green for the Rigogolo, and white for the Cardellino. An additional reason for dropping the hock-type of bottle for white wine was that they are a little taller than the Bordeaux type, which by tradition I had to use for the red, and that would have meant having different sizes of carton.

It was about in this period in the 1980s that heavy bottles were introduced widely into the wine scene. They may have the same shape as a normal bottle, or may have a subtly different and more elegant form, but they usually weigh about half as much again as standard bottles, and sometimes even twice as much. They are, naturally, more expensive. The theory is that the heavier bottle imparts a sense of extra quality to the wine inside it. Perhaps it does in some cases, but I tested a few friends by putting a heavy bottle and a normal one, both of the same size, from other wineries in front of them. I asked them to tell me what impressions the two bottles gave them. They invariably picked them up to look at the labels more closely and turned them around in their hands, but very few even mentioned that one bottle was heavier than the other.

I realized that my very limited, little market test was a long way from being a proper survey, but it was good enough for me. Despite several suggestions that I should use heavy bottles, I always refused. It seemed to me to be a total waste of glass, not to mention adding useless weight for transport. Furthermore, cases of twelve normal bottles were quite heavy enough for someone to hump around. For me, therefore, the heavy bottle is a piece of useless marketing that has a negative impact on the environment, on people's pockets, and on their spinal columns. What is more, I very recently heard that some wineries are now selling their heavy bottles in six-bottle cartons instead of in the traditional twelve-bottle size. This, presumably, is to spare people's backs, but it means you have to walk twice the distance to carry and load the same number of bottles, and that more paper pulp goes into making the cartons. I do not know why someone does not produce bottles of normal weight, but in more elegant forms and styles than the traditional ones. I suppose, however, that there must be firm evidence to show that people can be subconsciously influenced about the quality of the wine by a heavy bottle, and that once they have hefted it to look at its label, they will be more willing to buy it and pay more for it.

I was, in fact, very pleased with the appearance of my bottles once they were labelled, capsuled, and ready for sale. I always preferred opening them for home consumption, rather than still-unlabelled bottles of the same wine. I knew that it was a small extravagance, but it gave me great pleasure to have a professionally presented bottle of my own wine on the table. My son Stuart, who later became a management consultant, had early tendencies in that direction. He would inevitably make some comment about the waste of a label and capsule and exhort me to open plain bottles. I took no notice. That elegant bottle on my table and its contents were the expression of years of plans, dreams, hopes, commitment, and work. Even my son was not going to deprive me of enjoying it.

Corks are a pernicious problem for wine producers. In the first place, they are expensive, and even if you buy top-quality corks, there is still no guarantee that some of them will not be infected by the fungus that develops in contact with the wine in the bottle. The result is that mouldy smell and flavour of a corked wine. On one occasion when I went to the Vinitaly wine fair in Verona, I dropped in on the stand showing Australian wines. One of that country's top producers, and a famous name, had brought twelve cases of his Chardonnay. When I got to the stand, the people there were tearing their hair out: they had opened twenty bottles of the Chardonnay and found that fifteen of them were corked.

I bought corks that were in the medium-high price range and hoped that not too many of my customers would need to complain about my wines being corked. Not too many did, and I never had to tear my hair out, but the problem was always present, even if in a minor key. The plastic corks and screw caps that have come on the scene in recent years are a potential godsend to the wine industry. But who knows how long it will take for wine drinkers in general to overcome their prejudices and accept them in quality wines, as they now have for even expensive white wines in Switzerland. When and if they do, God help the thousands of people who make a living out of the cork oaks in places like Portugal and Sardinia.

Naturally, Ferrucio and I alone could not handle all of the equipment in the winery. In fact, it was really only the winter rackings that we did without the help of others. During the vintage itself, Ferruccio was always with the pickers in the vineyard. The tractor driver would bring in load after load of grapes and help me to put them through the crusher. For several years, Giovanni Targa, one of the brothers of Felice who had cut off the tips of his fingers in a hammer mill, helped out as the tractor driver. He was a quiet, slow-spoken man with a good sense of humour. During the vintage, when he was bringing the grapes to the winery, he had a permanent routine: once a load of grapes had been crushed, and before going off to collect another, he would pick up a glass, wander over to a tank of the previous year's wine, draw off an abundant quantity, and gulp it down in a single draught. My stock comment to him each time was that he was drinking my wine faster than I could make it. He would reply that if I was looking for a drinking-versus-making competition, he was ready to prove he could win.

I often had a voluntary helper in the winery during the vintage, a neighbour called Enrico. He was a retired driver of Rome trams, a large, paunchy, bald, red-faced, and very temperamental man. When he became angry, which he often did, you could hear him a mile away, but even when he was placid, his voice boomed. Despite the volume, he was not always easy to understand, for he was somewhat toothless. It was especially difficult in the winery where the acoustics were bad.

I was very grateful indeed for his help, year after year, but at the same time he often drove me scatty. During the vintage, in addition to the physical work of the crushing or the loading of the press and the unloading of the pressings, there were always calculations to be done, decisions to be taken, and things to be recorded. In addition, a day in the winery during vintage could easily last sixteen hours or more. I would be in the middle of some calculations and considering some decision when invariably Enrico would yell to me from the other end of the winery.

"Coli!" would come the roar. Words that end in consonants, like my name, are difficult for many Italians because nearly all of their words end in vowels.

I would have to stop what I was doing and ask him what he wanted. He would start some long discourse that boomed unintelligibly around the high ceilings. Out of courtesy, I would have to go nearer to him to understand what he was saying. He was so prickly, despite his generous help, that I did not want to offend him. It took me a couple of years to explain to him that I was often involved in some calculation and that I would appreciate it if he would come over to me rather than bawling "Coli!" from the distance. He did come nearer after that, but he interrupted whatever I was doing just the same. But what more can you say to a man who would never accept any payment from me for the many hours he worked with me in the winery, just a demijohn of wine at the end of vintage?

For bottling and labelling we were always a group of four or five people to feed the machinery and take away the filled or labelled bottles. The helpers were people who worked in the vineyard as well. Each had to have an annual medical examination before they could legally work in the winery, as I had been forewarned by Baroni of the Office for the Repression of Fraud. Most of the group were women, and a day of work in the winery was usually a happy occasion, at least if I did not get cross about something that went wrong. Even then, there would be half-smiles all round, with Ferruccio setting the tone.

Sadly, that normally cheery tone of Ferruccio's took a cruel knock in 1988. One morning in the summer, when I was in the kitchen of Ferruccio's house to discuss something about the vineyard, Giuliana offered to make me a coffee. Before Ferruccio's problems with his liver, we would have drunk a glass of wine together, but things had changed, and he seemed to be managing rather well without drinking alcohol. Giuliana started to prepare the coffee pot, but she stopped without putting it on the stove and ambled out through the front door into the sunny morning outside.

"Did you see that, Signor Colin?" Ferruccio asked. "She started to make the coffee and then stopped. *È una croce con le donne.* (I don't know what's the matter with her.) She's been very strange in the last few weeks."

"In what way?"

"Like what you just saw. And she doesn't talk much."

He got up and went to the door.

"Giuliana!" he bawled. There was no reply.

He stumped outside and bawled her name again. I followed into the sunshine and stood beside him. There was no sign of Giuliana. We walked around the corner of the house and found her standing in a patch of waist-high sunflowers that she had planted in the spring. Ferruccio called her name again, but she paid no attention; she just continued looking down at the flower heads and running a hand absent-mindedly over them.

"*Porca Madonna!* Giuliana! Come here!"

She looked up, turned and walked slowly towards us. She came past us, as if in a trance, and went back into the house. Ferruccio followed her without a word.

"What's the matter?" he asked her.

"I've got a headache," she said quietly. "I'm going to lie down."

Francesca and Maria Lisa told me later that they had taken her some food at lunchtime but that she had refused to eat. In the evening, their father had tried to wake her, but had been unable to do so. They called the doctor and she was whisked off to hospital. The next morning it was discovered she had a brain tumour. She was transferred to a larger hospital in Rome for surgery, but she died without recovering consciousness after the operation.

Ferruccio never showed much emotion about losing Giuliana, unlike Francesca and Maria Lisa, who grieved more openly. It was quite clear, however, that he missed her greatly. Francesca took over the running of the house, so his practical needs were looked after. However, he was lacklustre without her and, without doubt, he missed a patient butt for his humour.

24

Last Lap

With the wine in bottles and all of the incredible number of bureaucratic requirements taken care of, I could at last start marketing my three wines. I had capsules and corks with Poggio Fenice and the Phoenix printed on them, cartons for twelve and three bottles, and all in all, the appearance of the products was in good order. Of course, I was not going to bottle all of the wine from the beginning, for I had quite flourishing sales of wine in demijohns to local people. However, it was much less profitable than selling in bottles, so my intention was to work steadily towards bottling all of my production, once I had generated enough market.

Many friends became customers for my wines from the beginning, but even if some of them bought good quantities, I believed that local and Rome restaurants would be the major market. One of the Rome restaurants that I occasionally frequented, and which had quite a good wine list, was the first to buy my wine, four cases of Rigogolo. About a week after I had delivered them, I went back for a meal. As I sat down, I saw a bottle of Rigogolo on the table of a couple eating nearby. I was absolutely delighted. It was the first time I had seen an unknown restaurant client drinking my wine. I tried to contain myself but, of course, I could not, so I got up and approached the couple.

"Good evening. Forgive me for bothering you, but are you enjoying that wine?"

The man smiled, probably relieved that I had not asked him something more difficult.

"Yes, it's good. Aromatic. Fresh. I can recommend it if you're going to eat fish, like we are."

I was even more delighted.

"No, no. Thank you. I wasn't asking your advice about whether to order it. You see, I made it. That's my name on the label. You're the first people in a restaurant I've seen drinking my wine."

The man picked the bottle up and looked carefully at the label.

"I see," he said, evidently unimpressed. He was probably thinking the Italian equivalent of "silly twit"!

"Well, thank you. I'm glad you're enjoying it," I said lamely and went back to my table. The man and his partner must certainly have thought me strange at least but, of course, they had no way of knowing how much seeing that bottle of Rigogolo on their table meant to me, after so many doubts and so much effort.

It proved more difficult than I had expected to convince restaurants in the Castel Sabino area to stock my wine. I had imagined that clients of those restaurants would often ask for a local wine, and visitors from outside of the area often did so. But the core clientele of those restaurants were local people, and in rural areas, very few people drink anything other than open wine. I was again up against the idea, so common among rural people in wine producing countries, that bottled wines are doped up with chemicals and may not be made from grapes at all. In other words, wine in bottles is not to be trusted; it is not *fatto d'uva* and *genuino,* as they describe the infernal gut-rot they usually drink.

Slowly, however, I began to win more sales from local restaurants, mainly from the higher class ones in Rieti, where the clients included tourists and people from outside the province, particularly from Rome. Curiously, almost none of the restaurant owners ever telephoned me to ask for another consignment, but when I called them they usually sounded pleased and placed an order. For a long time I wondered why this was so. Then one day I asked the owner of one of the best restaurants in Rieti, a man with whom I had become friendly, why he never called me to order wine when he was running out. He told me that he was inundated by visiting wine salesmen from mainly big producers; he was simply not accustomed to ringing up producers directly and asking them to deliver wine. I realized then that I would have to continue to take the initiative and call my customers when I thought their stock of my wines must be close to running out.

Getting paid for the wine was a much bigger problem than selling it. Very few restaurants ever wrote out a cheque when the wine was delivered. That I could understand, but what I found annoying was when a restaurant had sold all of one delivery, took a second one, and then told me to come back in two weeks, or a month or whatever, to get paid for the first. It happened quite often, and I was irritated by it because of the high margins restaurants charge on wine. Furthermore, they had already pocketed the revenue from the first delivery they had sold.

I chided quite a few restaurant owners about the margins they charged on all of their wines. A bottle that I sold to them for 6,000 lire was invariably on their wine list for 14,000 or 15,000 lire. They told me that all restaurants charged well over double their costs for wine.

"Well," I said to one restaurant owner, "there's too much wine swilling around in Italy. If you charged less for it, you'd sell more and help do something about the European wine lake".

He grinned rather malevolently at me.

"I know what I'll do," he said, "I'll charge a much smaller mark-up on your wines, and we'll see if I sell more of them".

That brought me up short, for I realized at once that if my wines were on his list at a lower price than most of the others, potential customers would think my wines were inferior and not buy them. I could only laugh and back off, telling him that I did not want to see my wines look inferior on his list when they were as good, if not better, than many of the others.

I organized open days for wine tasting and buying at the property, usually in the late spring when the new Rigogolo had just been bottled. Many friends and customers would come and bring other friends. I would have cold snacks available and most of them would sit around in the garden for much of the day, talking, visiting the winery, and drinking wine. When they left in the early evening, they would load many cases of wine they had bought into their cars and drive happily away.

On one such occasion a young lady from Latin America, a friend of a friend, came up to me as she was leaving. In charmingly accented and idiosyncratic English, she said, with a big smile, "Thank you so much for a lovely day. Your wines are very good and I am pissed delicious".

She may have been slightly tipsy, but even after days like that, the quantity of wine drunk was really insignificant compared to the amount I sold.

I took my wines to as many wine fairs as I could. Many were linked to the feast day celebrations in small towns in the province. They were amusing occasions and I sold a lot of wine. At these fairs, too, I was always surprised by how little wine was drunk during tasting compared to what I sold. Fifteen or twenty bottles drunk during tasting could sell well over a thousand.

Wine fairs in Rome were not occasions for selling, only for tasting and public relations. At one of those fairs, a young man suddenly appeared on my stand. He was rather small, with fair hair and a clipped moustache, and he was very dapper in his well-cut suit, white shirt, and dark tie. He introduced himself as Aldo Giovanelli, and told me he was the sommelier in a certain Rome hotel. I knew it to be a small and very exclusive hotel with an elegant and luxurious restaurant. He looked perfect for the part of working in that establishment, and I expected he might be rather snotty as a result. On the contrary, however, he turned out to be natural and friendly.

"I've been hearing quite a lot about the wines you're producing in the Sabine Hills. I'm curious because that area has always been known for olive oil rather than wine. Can I taste some?"

He tasted all three wines carefully and commented graciously on them all. I was hoping he might place a big order for his hotel then and there, but instead he said he would be in touch and disappeared as unexpectedly as he had arrived.

I thought no more about him, but about two months later he telephoned.

"Listen," he said, "I didn't mention it when we talked at the wine fair, but I'm one of the people working on the *Gambero Rosso* (Red Prawn) wine guide. Can we fix a day for me to visit your place, look around, and taste the wines again? My colleagues and I think we'd like to include them in the guide, but we want to know more about your place and how you make the wines."

I fixed a date immediately, a Saturday morning in ten days time. This was much more important than an order from that posh hotel where he worked, for *Gambero Rosso* was – and is – a very important information presence in the food and wine field in Italy. Today, in addition to its publications, it even has a food and wine satellite TV channel.

It all began rather inauspiciously in 1986 as a monthly food and wine supplement in Italy's extreme Left newspaper, *Il Manifesto*. The supplement was called *Gambero Rosso – il mensile per consumatori curiosi e golosi* (Red Prawn – the monthly for curious and greedy consumers). Its publication ignited a fierce debate about whether the Left should put out such frivolous, anti-intellectual material. But the monthly supplement continued despite the critics.

The next year, the *Gambero Rosso* publishing house was set up, and its first guide to Italian wines, *Vini d'Italia,* was brought out. It was a joint publishing venture with a linked group called *Arcigola*. In the following years, it consolidated its success and was published in several languages. *Arcigola* later became the association *Slow Food*, which has now spread to many countries. It sets out to promote and conserve the traditions and consumption of local foods, and the culture and production methods linked to them, in the face of the aggressive expansion by the global food industries, which is leading to the standardization of foods and culture.

The annual *Vini d'Italia* guide from *Gambero Rosso* was an immediate success; it was already the bible when Aldo Giovanelli first approached me. To have my wines in that selective and authoritative guide would be an achievement beyond all my dreams.

Aldo Giovanelli turned up punctually, almost as smart in well-pressed slacks and open-neck shirt as he had been in his suit at the wine fair. We wandered around the vineyard and winery together while he questioned me intently, though he was always affable and friendly. We returned to the house where I had cooled a bottle each of Rigogolo and Cardellino and opened a bottle of Nibbio to breathe. He tasted them and was again complimentary.

We discussed at some length the pros and cons of aging my Nibbio in wood. I told him about a wine-grower near Bologna, called Enrico Vallania, with whom I had become friendly. I had visited him several times, including for lengthy family lunches. This had all come about because I had drunk a bottle of Vallania's Cabernet Sauvignon in a Bologna restaurant. I was so impressed that I asked if the restaurant had his telephone number. They did, so I called to make an appointment and visited him for the first time the next day. He was a genial man in his sixties, a doctor who had taken over his family land when his father died and retired early to dedicate himself to wine production.

He was one of the very first people in Italy to plant Cabernet Sauvignon and Chardonnay grapes, which at the time was against the regulations, just like my Pinot Bianco. He was making top-quality wines, red and white, in an area near Bologna where no one had ever done anything like that before.

I told Aldo Giovanelli what Enrico Vallania had told me about ageing red wines in wood: that when he took over the place from his father, the first thing he did was burn all the wooden barrels. They were only sources of mould, bacteria and other enemies of wine. He made all his wines only in stainless-steel tanks.

"I know Vallania's wines," said Aldo Giovanelli. "They're excellent. By the way, I think you and he have something in common. You both began producing wine in areas that were not known for it, only became involved quite late in life, and have done very well."

"I'm nothing like at his level, but you may be right. That could explain why he has been so kind and helpful to me, something of a godfather figure for winemaking. Anyway, if he can produce his excellent red wines without ageing them in oak barrels, I'm going to try to do the same. Or perhaps I should do what I've seen some wine-growers in Australia do . . . throw some sawn oak planks into a stainless-steel tank of red wine and leave them there for a few months."

Aldo Giovanelli laughed. He had not heard of the practice and found the Australian down-to-earth approach amusing. We ended up agreeing that it was well worth trying to emulate Vallania, despite the growing tendency to think that all good red wines must be aged in oak barrels. The very high cost of new oak *barriques,* which have to be renewed every few years when they are no longer transferring oak tannins to the wine, and the extra work involved in using them, could not be justified for me, at least at that stage.

Aldo Giovanelli left with two bottles each of my three wines for a tasting with his colleagues. I awaited the publication of the *Gambero Rosso* wine guide on tenterhooks to see whether they had included my wines, and if so, how they judged them. When it finally came out, a few months later, I found that it did me well. The wines included in the guide are graded by a system of wine glasses next to their name: no glass for wines in the range of 60–70 points out of 100, one glass for 71–80 points, two glasses for 81–90 points, and three glasses for 91–100 points. I had been awarded one glass each for my wines and an asterisk that denoted special value for money. Only 102 wines of the 3,000 or so in the guide, from 735 producers, had earned the top award of three glasses. Furthermore, many much larger and more important producers, some with famous names in the wine sector, had done no better, or even had lower ratings, than I had. So I was happy with my single glass.

The text describing my operation said that I had "wagered and won, producing good wine in an area like the Sabine Hills, famous for very good extra virgin olive oil and for terrible wines". After a description of the "delightful'" property and the vines I had planted, including "by happy intuition, Pinot Bianco," the text described Rigogolo as "truly interesting, with a complex bouquet and a flavour which is soft and lively at the same time, an unexpected white wine from the area".

The guide continued to include my wines in the following years, with one glass each time for all three wines. There were more favourable descriptions of the Rigogolo, for example that is was "vinified with great care" and was "fresh, with a rich baggage of primary aromas, elegant, and truly pleasing". The Nibbio earned praise for its "ample bouquet with aromas of spice, red fruit and coffee . . . and good structure, persistence, and elegance". The Cardellino was described as "very pleasant . . . a fragrant and lively wine with an unmistakable and harmonious aroma of small fruit".

Other guides began to include my wines. One was the Veronelli guide in Italy, another was Burton Anderson's *Wine Atlas of Italy*, and they were also mentioned in Hugh Johnson's *World Atlas of Wines.* More and more people would telephone for an appointment to come and buy wine, or just turn up. There were more restaurants, some of them very well known, buying my wines, and I even received an order from a chain of wine shops in Germany for a "trial shipment" of 5,000 bottles of Nibbio. I declined that request, however, for I could not take the risk of becoming tied to a single, large-scale buyer. Local recognition of my efforts was also growing. The provincial authorities began inviting me to bring my wines to important fairs and events, and presented me with an inscribed plaque for my services to agriculture.

I also had some exposure in Britain through two BBC radio programmes. One of these was for Tom Vernon's *Fat Man on a Bicycle* series. The programme containing his interview with me was repeated so many times on air that friends in England began to complain to me that all they heard when they turned the radio on was "bloody Colin". The second programme was for *On Your Farm*, a long interview about farming in Italy and my wine operation. I hoped that it would bring in some orders from Britain, but it did not; the consignments that did go there were for friends who knew my wines and sold them onto other friends.

Most Italian people still thought that producing good wines in the Sabine Hills was extraordinary, and that I had taken a big chance. However, it was not really so much against the odds, for Italy is indeed blessed with many, many areas that can produce good wines. As the Tuscan who encouraged me to buy the property all those years before had correctly identified, my piece of land was essentially well suited to viticulture. The only really negative factor, as I discovered, was the winemaking isolation in which I found myself in the Sabine Hills. My progress was slowed by the lack of peers in the area with whom to consult and discuss problems. Another negative factor was that my wines had to be promoted more effectively than if they had come from a recognized and DOC area, but overall, things were going well.

Sadly, Ferruccio was unable to share, as I would have wished, in the successful outcomes of so much work and effort together. His health was failing, in fact, it never recovered fully after that occasion when he had looked so exhausted and pale in the winery, and after the haemorrhage into his stomach that night. But he came back to work, and it was about a year later that I went out one morning to talk to him and the others who were pruning in the vineyard.

I found Ferruccio sitting on the ground, again looking exhausted. His abdomen on the side of his liver was enormously extended. It had been evident for quite some time that he was no longer well enough to work properly, but I did not have the heart to ask him to stay at home. He struggled to his feet as I approached, evidently embarrassed at being seen sitting down while the others were working.

I took him by the arm and we walked slowly away from the others to be out of earshot.

"How are you feeling, Ferru?" I asked.

"I'm not well, Signor Colin. I feel tired all the time." He paused, looking down at the ground. "It's a big effort to work. I'm not sure if I can go on." He paused again, and then looked up and into my face. His expression was one of great sadness.

"It might be best if you ask Scrocco if he'll take charge of the vineyard for you," he said slowly. "I'm sorry, but I think it's too much for me now."

I was relieved that it was Ferruccio who had raised the problem and its solution.

"I'm sorry too, Ferru. Really sorry, but if that's what you prefer, I'll ask him. You know, though, that you're welcome to come back whenever you feel well enough to work. Can you manage all right? You've got your disability pension, no?"

He nodded. We walked back to his house in silence.

Over the coming months, he did return for the occasional day, probably to break the boredom of being at home all the time. I would often go and chat to him in the evenings when I could. Sober, he was not the amusing company that he had been when he was liberally imbibing. I suspect that although he never complained, he felt unwell most of the time. I tried to cheer him up by recalling some funny incidents of our joint efforts of the past, and we would laugh together again. Whenever I told him of some new success with the wines, his wan face would light up with pleasure.

Ferrucio continued to decline, and he was in and out of hospital several times before finally dying in 1992. I was away in South America on a consultancy mission at the time and could not attend his funeral. I was very saddened by his death, for he had been a personality in my life, and he had played an enormous role in my project. With all his faults of chauvinistic and authoritarian treatment of his family, I could not complain about anything in his working or personal relationship with me.

I called my son Stuart a couple of weeks later and told him that Ferruccio had died. Iain, by now a doctor and working in Papua New Guinea, was more difficult to contact. Stuart was quite upset with me for not having told him immediately after I had heard of Ferruccio's death. I remembered, then, the numerous occasions after dinner when Stuart had asked me whether he could take my car to drive up to Ferruccio's house for a chat and a glass of wine. He would come back rather late, on foot and "pissed delicious". The next morning, Ferruccio would call me to tell me that my car was at his house because he had advised Stuart that, in his state, it would be safer to walk home. What they talked about, as they downed so much wine together, I never found out, but they had established a good friendship. Stuart was also saddened by his death.

I reflected a lot about Ferruccio after he had gone. Despite his essentially subsistence farming background, he quickly came to understand the need, in a commercial venture, for more advanced techniques in viticulture and winemaking. Most of these were completely new to him, and so I used to explain what we were doing and why. He would listen carefully and help as necessary. He was always willing to work at weekends with me in the winery and was accepting of my maniacal attention to detail. My pernicketiness about winemaking must have exasperated him, and he must often have thought I was as daft as a brush. Nevertheless, he was loyal to the point of never gossiping, even with his friends in the bar, about how we grew grapes or made wine. Some of those traditional people in the bar would have been delighted to criticize the way we did things, but he never gave them the ammunition to do so.

Ferruccio had been a good friend, an ever-amusing companion, and a diligent, hardworking team-mate. We had been through a lot together during the transformation of the abandoned property I had bought some twenty years before. He had always shared my delight when things progressed well, and my concerns when they did not. I particularly remembered our shared pleasure when, for the first time, we had just finished labelling and putting capsules on about three thousand bottles of Rigogolo. He picked up a bottle and examined it carefully. He turned it this way and that and ran a hand lovingly over the label and capsule of what, indeed, was a satisfyingly elegant presentation.

"It looks like a real bottle of wine," he said, nodding approvingly. "Who ever would have thought it when we were tramping up and down in the mud marking where to plant the Pinot vines and you were shouting, 'Get marching, Ferru'? And all those idiots round here who said you were an idiot. We've shown them who the idiots are, haven't we?"

We began to laugh and he made a well-known vulgar gesture that signified, put politely, that all those idiots should take a running jump into the lake.

I had missed Ferruccio from when his health prevented him running the vineyard for me. Marco took over Ferruccio's responsibilities very well and assumed others. He had a car and delivered wine for me to restaurants in the area, collected payments, and the like. He was completely dependable, and I relied on him totally. Nevertheless, without Ferruccio, much of the sparkle and fun had gone. Marco, too, was a friend, but he was an essentially serious man. Without laughter, life is indeed dull.

I continued with Marco for about three years after Ferruccio's health had forced him to give up working with me, but the operation had become somewhat routine. The challenges, the strivings, and the dreams that had enthused me, and driven me, for all those years were missing. More important, however, was that Poggio Fenice had reached another turning point, and I was going to have to take a major decision.

In those years, wines – even of high quality – were selling cheaply in Italy, for it was before the market trend of the last decade or so that has seen the price of good wines rise by double or more. Costs of labour and inputs for the vineyard, and of bottles and corks and the like, were rising constantly, and it gradually became evident that under the prevailing conditions, the wine from my relatively small vineyard could not produce the sort of profit that I could live off. In simple terms, Poggio Fenice was too big to be a hobby, but it was also too small to be a business that could provide a decent livelihood.

One way forward would be to buy in additional grapes, say from the Abruzzo region. The winery was big enough to vinify more, but by now, Poggio Fenice was established as an estate that bottled wines from its own grapes, thereby acquiring a certain cachet. To buy in grapes would debase the prestige and status of the wines.

A second option would be to buy more land and plant more vines. There was a piece of abandoned land of about a hectare and a half next to mine. It would probably not have been enough to make my operation completely viable, but even so, I enquired from its owners whether they would be interested in selling it. Several brothers and sisters owned it, as is common in Italy where inheritance laws divide property equally between all of the children when parents die. It took them more than a year to reach an agreement among themselves about a possible sale. When they did, they asked a building-land price for it, even though it was not an area set aside by the local authorities for development. They wanted much more than I had paid for the whole of my property. So if I wanted to expand the vineyard area, I would have to find a piece of suitable land elsewhere in the neighbourhood, an idea that did not appeal to me much because of the logistical and management problems it would entail.

Of course, an expansion in the vineyard area would require more investment, via loans and probably a mortgage on the property. It would also make many more calls on my time, especially for marketing the extra wine, and the marketing had always been less pleasurable for me than the more creative aspects of wine-growing. Time was an important aspect because, until then, I had been riding two horses: the vines and wines, and my professional work as a consultant, for which I had many calls and which involved a great deal of travel worldwide. Riding these two horses had often been stressful, and I would not be able to give up the consultancy work until the new vineyard was in production and I had more wine to sell.

These considerations ran through my mind for months on end, but with an additional and important element: my life was becoming entwined with that of the Latin American lady who had said, after a day-long tasting, that my wines were "very good" and that she was "pissed delicious". My attention was being diverted towards her marvellous continent, where I had so often worked.

Thinking back over all those years, I felt that, on balance, I had achieved what I set out to do. I had turned an abandoned piece of land and its derelict house into a property that many described as a gem. I had grown grapes, learnt to produce respectable wines, and established their reputation. I had also had the enriching experience of meeting innumerable Italians whose help and support were unstintingly generous and disinterested. Many became real friends. These were the sort of people that help to make Italy so beguiling. Furthermore, it is only their humanity and warmth that make it possible to operate in the Italian environment of legislation run amok. They more than compensate for the plethora of complex rules and regulations that can be such a pitfall for the unprepared.

I finally concluded that a phase of my life was at an end. I had realized a dream. Going into debt to expand what was by now a rather routine operation was not what I wanted. The time had come to move on. So after some twenty years as a wine-grower, I sold the property, lock, stock, and barrel, to a Roman lawyer and his wife, a dynamic lady who runs the vineyard and winery and produces the wines with the same names, plus a new one – also with a bird name – for white wine made from the red Sangiovese grapes. The wines are still under the name and logo of Poggio Fenice, which provoked a crack from my son Stuart to the effect that I had "sold the family crest".

Ten years later, in 2004, I got into conversation with a young waiter in a Rome restaurant who was interested in wine. I chose a wine from the list from that well-known producer from Alto Adige who had sniffed out that my Rigogolo had fermented briefly at more than 20°C (68°F), as related earlier. I told the waiter that I had been wine-grower and recounted the story about the producer of the bottle I had just ordered and my lapse in temperature control during fermentation. The waiter asked me what my wines had been called.

"I know Poggio Fenice wines," he exclaimed after I had told him. He trotted off to the back of the restaurant, and when he returned he was holding a book in one hand and flicking over the pages with the other. I saw from the cover that it was a recent edition of one of Italy's most prestigious wine guides.

"There!" he said triumphantly, placing the open book in front of me on the table. And sure enough, there was the entry for Poggio Fenice. My eyes raced over the words of the introduction and my heart leapt when I read:

"The vineyard was planted by an impassioned Scottish agronomist, Colin Fraser. He fell in love with the place in 1974 . . . tore out what was left of the remaining olives and planted vines that were not all typical of the area. After many years dedicated to improving the vines and wines, he passed on the baton to the present owners in 1994."

It was a nostalgic and moving moment, but it was also a pleasure to know that the Phoenix, risen to new life from its ashes, the Poggio Fenice I had resurrected, was still thriving, with very favourable judgments of its wines in the guide the waiter showed me.

I often miss the property and being a wine producer. But alas, I do not have the years left to start out again. If I had, I would apply what I learned that first time round and make even better wine. So now I content myself with drinking wines made by others, but with the critical appreciation of an insider. As I do so, I remember the challenges, the work, the triumphs, and the fun with Ferruccio and the others in those sublime Sabine Hills.